CW01430357

Palgrave Studies in the History of the Media

Palgrave Studies in the History of the Media

Series Editors: **Professor Bill Bell** (Cardiff University), **Dr Chandrika Kaul** (Department of Modern History, University of St Andrews), **Professor Kenneth Osgood** (McBride Honors Program, Colorado School of Mines), **Dr Alexander S. Wilkinson** (Centre for the History of the Media, University College Dublin)

Palgrave Studies in the History of the Media publishes original, high-quality research into the cultures of communication from the middle ages to the present day. The series explores the variety of subjects and disciplinary approaches that characterize this vibrant field of enquiry. The series will help shape current interpretations not only of the media, in all its forms, but also of the powerful relationship between the media and politics, society, and the economy.

Advisory Board: Professor Carlos Barrera (University of Navarra, Spain), Professor Peter Burke (Emmanuel College, Cambridge), Professor Denis Cryle (Central Queensland University, Australia), Professor David Culbert (Louisiana State University, Baton Rouge), Professor Nicholas Cull (Center on Public Diplomacy, University of Southern California), Professor Tom O'Malley (Centre for Media History, University of Wales, Aberystwyth), Professor Chester Pach (Ohio University)

Martin C. Kerby

Sir Philip Gibbs and English Journalism in War and Peace

palgrave
macmillan

Martin C. Kerby
Humanities & International Studies
University of Southern Queensland
Toowooomba, Queensland, Australia

Palgrave Studies in the History of the Media
ISBN 978-1-137-57300-1   ISBN 978-1-137-57301-8   (eBook)
DOI 10.1057/978-1-137-57301-8

Library of Congress Control Number: 2016931986

Printed on acid-free paper

This Palgrave Macmillan imprint is published by SpringerNature
The registered company is Macmillan Publishers Ltd. London.

Dedicated to my wife, Margaret

Memories of My Grandfather

Philip Gibbs was known in my side of the family as 'Gruffer'. This came from my childhood attempt to say 'grandfather'. I was very proud that both my grandfathers were 'Sirs'. The other one, Charles Martin, was a successful medical scientist. But Philip was much the more famous of the two. Often, when I admitted my surname was Gibbs, people would ask, 'Are you related to *Philip* Gibbs?' And if they were middle-aged ladies they would very likely say they were waiting for his next book to come out. They generally did not have to wait long. Between 1899 and 1963 more than 90 of his books were published, an average of 1 every 8 months. His prolific output included both fiction and non-fiction.

But writing books was of course only one of his occupations. He had also had a successful career as a journalist and was probably the best-known British war correspondent in the First World War. That was before I knew him but was what led to his knighthood and, in due course, the present book.

My earliest recollections of him were from the 1930s when he was about 60 and he and my grandmother Agnes were living at Bildens Farm, Ewhurst, Surrey. Soon afterwards they moved back to Dibdene in nearby Shamley Green, an early Victorian house that Agnes had been doing up for them. The property included a cottage by the village green which was used as a nursery school for many years. My sister Frances was one of their early pupils. Later the cottage was occupied by Philip's sister Helen (a former nun) and her husband, Eric Ibbotson.

Philip was extremely sociable and loved to be surrounded by visitors. One couple whom I remember from the pre-war years at Dibdene was

General Ralph Wenninger, an official at the German Embassy, and his wife. They were regular visitors until war became imminent and the general was recalled to Germany. It is believed he was eventually shot dead by a Dutchman in a street in German-occupied Holland.

Regular entertainment required a significant number of staff. It was almost like the feudal system in that staff were expected to stay for life. This certainly applied to 'Amy' who started as a housemaid at the age of 14 and went on working for our family until she was in her eighties. The head gardener was Mr Batchelor, always known as 'Batchelor', whose wife and daughter also worked for Philip at times.

Agnes died from liver cancer in October 1939. Although she had been ill for some time her death was a tragic blow for Philip. They had been together for over 40 years, having originally had what Philip called a 'marriage of babes', and he relied on her for so many things. Being the practical one, she had always looked after matters such as house maintenance. And she could drive, whereas he could not.

Her death and the outbreak of the Second World War led to a considerable amount of family reorganization. My father, Tony, my mother, Maisie, Frances, and I went to stay with Philip. Our house at Peaslake, a few miles from Shamley Green, was lent to a group of nuns headed by Agnes' sister Beryl Rowland, who wanted to escape the bombing in London. The cellar at Dibdene had been fitted out as a kind of air raid shelter with bunk beds, and the like. I do not think we ever heard any actual bombing there but the warning sirens went off occasionally and we all went down to the cellar, much to the excitement of Frances and me.

In June 1940 the war was going badly for the Allies. France had surrendered and it looked as though an invasion of England was imminent. Following a series of late night discussions at Dibdene it was therefore decided that our family of four should go to Massachusetts to stay with Philip's brother Arthur and his American wife, Jeannette. We must have been rather a burden on them. After a while they put us in a house they owned across the road and charged us rent. But the rent was often unpaid because we had not been allowed to take any money out of England and Tony had not been able to earn as much from lecturing and writing articles as he had hoped. So we were eventually served notice to leave. Tempers flared and Philip decided he would have to come over to America to sort things out.

He managed to placate Arthur, whom he described as an 'ugly-tempered man', before setting off on an exhausting lecture tour of the USA. This

brought in a considerable amount of money because he was a good lecturer and his name was almost as well known in that country as in England.
He generously gave most of his earnings to Tony before he returned to
England having wangled a seat in a bomber through his brother Cosmo
who worked in Whitehall as a government censor. Meanwhile our financial
situation improved dramatically when Tony was given a well-paid job writing films in Hollywood and we went out there to join him.

Things gradually returned to normal after the war ended. We had come
back from America and, having stayed for a while in Cambridge with
my Martin grandparents, we said goodbye to the nuns and went back to
live in our house at Peaslake. Philip had let Dibdene while he had been
in America so he stayed at Shamley Green with an old friend, Dorothy
Webber, who Cosmo felt was 'straining every sinew to become her ladyship number two'. He must have been tempted by the idea because in
1943 he wrote *The Interpreter*, a novel in which the hero had recently lost
his wife and was agonizing over whether it would be disloyal to her if he
married again. But Philip resisted and was soon able to escape to the safety
of his own house where Agnes' nephew Barry Rowland, who worked in
publishing, together with his wife, Joyce, and small son, Richard, often
came to stay. They all called him 'Gungy', from Richard's early attempts
to say 'Uncle'.

Philip's eyesight began to deteriorate seriously but he went on writing
books, hammering out 'cryptograms' on his typewriter that his devoted
secretary was just able to decipher and retype. During this time I went
on a trip to Paris with him and acted as his eyes, holding him particularly
securely when we went up or down stairs, of which there seemed to be a
great many in Paris. While there, we met his old friend Harold Callender,
an American journalist, and his wife, Bessie, a successful sculptor.

On our return he had a cataract operation at the Charing Cross hospital, no doubt getting the best possible treatment available there because
he was the chairman. At any rate the operation was a great success and he
was able to see clearly afterwards.

He continued to live at Dibdene for the rest of his life, looked after
by a succession of housekeepers. Tony visited him every week and I went
there regularly on my motorcycle when I was not at boarding school or
university.

He was a brilliant raconteur and always enjoyed telling the stories of his
life, though I do not remember much being said about his experiences in
the First World War. One of the stories I particularly enjoyed was when

he was lost in New York and went up to a traffic policeman and said in his polite English voice, 'Excuse me but I want to go to the Plaza Hotel.' This led the cop to reply, 'Well, why the hell don't you go there then?'

He loved games, the main ones at Dibdene being billiards, played on a small-sized table in the playroom, and a cut-throat form of croquet called 'madders', played on the well-cut lawn at the side of the house. The winner of the latter game was the one who got 30 points first (2 points being awarded for each hoop gone through and one for hitting the 'stick') but you could acquire many of your opponent's hard-earned points if you hit their ball.

I sometimes walked round the village with him. He knew everyone and was always met by a cheerful 'Hullo, Philip'. He made friends with several of the young mothers who lived in the village, including Eve Branson whose son Richard eventually achieved international fame as the head of the Virgin group of companies. Above all there were the children. He had a marvellous ability to communicate with children and often seemed to attract a little gathering of them, like the Pied Piper.

On one occasion we came across a group of German prisoners of war who had not been returned to Germany immediately after the war. As a poor linguist I was full of admiration for him when he went up to them and chatted to them in fluent German.

He was often short of money and, as might have happened in days long gone, was afraid of being 'thrown into prison' in consequence. This was partly due to his generous nature and his willingness to support other members of the family and partly due to the vagaries of the tax system. The bill for the tax on each of his books' earnings arrived some years after those earnings had been received and spent. The only way to find the money for the tax was to write another book, which in due course led to another tax bill, and so on. And as he got older his ability to generate income from writing books gradually diminished. When I was a young accountancy trainee he once asked me to explain a royalty statement he had received from his publisher. To my lasting shame I just told him it showed he had not earned the advance he had been given. Ever since then I have wondered if I could not have put it more kindly.

Anyhow, he continued writing for the rest of his life, despite suffering from occasional writer's block. I remember visiting him one weekend in the early 1950s when he was desperate for new ideas. I suggested he might write a novel about the American airmen who were being posted back to England as part of the Cold War, and meeting the girls they had left behind after the Second World War. A week or two later I found him furiously typing so I asked him what he was doing. 'I'm writing a novel about an American airman who comes back to England and meets the girl he left behind after the war', he replied, apparently having completely forgotten our previous conversation. The book was published in 1953 as *Called Back*. It was the only one of his books to which I can claim to have made any contribution.

He smoked all his life but as he got older he hit on a clever idea for reducing the cost of this habit. As soon as he got a new packet of 20 cigarettes he would cut them all in half and then smoke them through a holder. That way the packet of 20 would give him 40 'lights'.

Despite a lifetime of smoking he lived until the age of 84 before he finally succumbed to pneumonia in March 1962. The typescript of his last book, a novel entitled *The Law-breakers*, had been delivered to the publishers a few days before his death. It was published posthumously the following year.

Martin Gibbs,
Wimbeldon, 2015

PREFACE

Sir Philip Gibbs (1877–1962) was one of the most famous and widely read English journalists of the first half of the twentieth century. Prior to the outbreak of the First World War he reported on the great crises facing Britain domestically and the technological advances which came to symbolize the age. Industrial unrest, Ireland, the suffragette movement, royal births, deaths and coronations, and the sinking of the Titanic were all topics which Gibbs reported on and interpreted for his countrymen. Advances in technology such as the advent of automobiles and the nascent years of aviation in Britain found their place in his articles alongside broader European events such as the revolution in Portugal in 1910 and the Balkan War in 1912. His articles, books, and correspondence are used to examine his life, subsequently contributing to an understanding of the role of the war correspondent during the tumultuous years from 1914 to 1918. His prodigious journalistic and literary output offers a broad insight into British social and political developments of the period; government/press relations, propaganda, and war reporting during the First World War; the state of interwar Europe; the Second World War; and the Cold War.

Though well regarded prior to 1914, it was his work on the Western Front which was to win him fame and, to a lesser extent, fortune. As one of five official correspondents accredited to the British Army on the Western Front, his articles, which appeared on both sides of the Atlantic, did much to shape civilian attitudes during the First World War and its immediate aftermath. Many critics, however, have dismissed Gibbs' work as propaganda and his acceptance of a knighthood in 1920 as little more than a reward for his participation in a conspiracy of silence.

Given the renewed interest in the role of the war correspondent generated by the continuing conflicts in Afghanistan and Iraq, it is surprising that there has not been a commensurate revival of interest in the war correspondents of the Western Front *as individuals*. There is regular and often quite derivative repetition of the charges against them—that they were willing participants in a cover-up which struck at the heart of the democratic system, or more leniently, they were the dupes of the military who manipulated them to report on the war as a patriotic duty rather than a journalistic one. They become a literary device, useful as a group representation of the lies of governments past and present rather than individuals who were, as Winston Churchill described Douglas Haig, 'unequal to the prodigious scale of events; but no one else was discerned as [their] equal or better'.[1] It is possible that their own post-war silences may have contributed to their lack of recognition as individuals. Martin Farrar found it 'odd' that three of the five who were subsequently knighted chose to 'remain silent' at the end of the war, an action which is suggestive of collusion, perhaps even of guilt.[2]

It is this need to place the correspondents in context, and to understand why they failed, which is at the heart of any assessment of their wartime writings. As the most prolific of them, Gibbs' experience is particularly instructive. It is not a 'calling back of ghosts', however, as Gibbs described one of his autobiographies.[3] We live in an age of mass media and instant news where battlefield analysis can be delivered in 'real time' with the accompanying sights and sounds of war. Though this immediacy gives both the reporter and his 'dispatch' instant credibility, he or she is just as subject to outside pressures as Gibbs and his compatriots. As with any individual in any profession, correspondents are not islands unto themselves, free to deliver an objective truth. They belong to a wide variety of media outlets and are subject to the dictates of officialdom, as well as the pressures of time, space, and deadlines, all exacerbated by their participation in a competitive profession. Yet even beyond that, they are citizens of countries, members of ethnic or racial groups, and adherents to religions,

---

[1] J Terraine (1970) *The Western Front 1914–1918* (London: Arrow Books), pp. 212–13.

[2] M Farrar (1998) *News from the Front: War Correspondents on the Western Front* (Phoenix Mill, Gloucestershire: Sutton Publishing), p. 227.

[3] P Gibbs (1946) *The Pageant of the Years* (London: Heinemann), p. 4.

products of educational institutions, and a wide variety of other social groupings whose influence will vary from individual to individual. These journalists are then, by the very nature of their profession, called upon to report on the most emotional, divisive, and tragic events, often involving their countrymen and women, yet all the while maintaining a veil of objectivity.

Brisbane QLD, Australia   Martin C. Kerby

Fig. 1 Portrait of Henry Gibbs. All illustrations courtesy of Gibbs Family Archives

Fig. 2 Helen Gibbs, circa 1885. All illustrations courtesy of Gibbs Family Archives

Fig. 3   Gibbs (left) waiting for a train at Nova Zagora with Horace Grant (centre) during the Balkan War in 1912. All illustrations courtesy of Gibbs Family Archives

Fig. 4   Philip Gibbs. All illustrations courtesy of Gibbs Family Archives

Fig. 5   Gibbs in uniform sans helmet. All illustrations courtesy of Gibbs Family
Archives

Fig. 6   Gibbs with helmet. All illustrations courtesy of Gibbs Family Archives

Fig. 7 Gibbs at the Western Front, back seat, right-hand side. All illustrations courtesy of Gibbs Family Archives

Fig. 8 Arthur Gibbs. All illustrations courtesy of Gibbs Family Archives

Fig. 9 Agnes Gibbs, circa 1920. All illustrations courtesy of Gibbs Family Archives

Fig. 10 Tony Gibbs, 1926. All illustrations courtesy of Gibbs Family Archives

Fig. 11   'Overponds', 1927. All illustrations courtesy of Gibbs Family Archives

Fig. 12 Gibbs the artist, La Rochelle, 4 September 1928. All illustrations courtesy of Gibbs Family Archives

Fig. 13   Gibbs the artist, Salzburg, 30 September 1928, Hotel Bristol from the bedroom window. All illustrations courtesy of Gibbs Family Archives

Fig. 14   Gibbs at Bildens Farm, circa 1932. All illustrations courtesy of Gibbs Family Archives

Fig. 15 Philip and Agnes Gibbs at Bildens Farm. All illustrations courtesy of Gibbs Family Archives

Fig. 16 Gibbs and his grandson Martin near Paris, April 1947. All illustrations courtesy of Gibbs Family Archives

ACKNOWLEDGEMENTS

I would like to acknowledge the assistance of:

Professor Paul Pickering (Australian National University) and Professor Cameron Hazlehurst (Adjunct Professor, Australian National University), who were instrumental in the completion of the research on which this book is based.

Martin and Frances Gibbs who were extraordinarily generous in providing access to a wealth of material concerning Martin's grandfather and his wider family. The photographs included with this text are courtesy of the Gibbs Family Archives.

My good friends Dr Cavan Barratt and Trond Ruud who were unfailingly generous in providing accommodation in London during a number of visits to conduct research.

CONTENTS

Victorian Childhood: 1877–1895

In the opening line of *The Pageant of the Years*, the longest of his four autobiographies, Philip Gibbs observed that his childhood was spent in 'the England of Dickens'.[1] In later life, as he felt increasingly alienated from social and political developments with which he had little sympathy, it may have offered Gibbs some comfort to boast that he 'belonged to Victorian England'.[2] Yet this identification with an era and its greatest author was more than just a prosaic description of time and place. It was an introduction to his personal manifesto, a statement of allegiance to a world view that valued above all else 'personal responsibility, of duty, and of living for something other than the satisfaction of the immediate needs of the self'.[3] These values, inculcated during his youth and which he saw as defining the Age, would later be stirred but not shaken by his experiences as a correspondent during the First World War and the chaos of the interwar years. Unlike his brother Arthur, whose wartime experiences led him to question the entire moral fabric of society, Gibbs saw in the slaughter on the Western Front the legitimacy of this world view. It is here, in the final decades of the Victorian Age, where the origins of his wartime journalistic output are to be found.

---

[1] P Gibbs (1946) *The Pageant of the Years* (London: Heinemann), p. 1.
[2] P Gibbs (1957) *Life's Adventure* (London: Angus & Robertson), p. 91.
[3] L Seaman (1973) *Victorian England* (London: Methuen and Co), p. 6.

© The Editor(s) (if applicable) and The Author(s) 2016
M.C. Kerby, *Sir Philip Gibbs and English Journalism in War and Peace*,
DOI 10.1057/978-1-137-57301-8_1

Philip Armand Thomas Hamilton Gibbs was born in West Brompton, London, on 1 May 1877 into the 'shabby genteel middle class' which was growing in number, wealth, and influence due to the expansion of manufacturing and trade associated with industrialization. It was also one which, in his view, produced in the Victorian era 'so much quality and character'.[4] He was the fifth of nine children born to Henry James Gibbs (1844–1906), a civil servant at the Board of Education in Whitehall, and Helen Hamilton (1847–1911). The family assumed both the outward signs of middle-class life, such as the idealization of family, the cultural pursuits, and the family entertainments, and the pervasive belief in the values of hard work, sexual morality, and individual responsibility. Gibbs described his father Henry as 'imaginative, well read, passionately interested in humanity, witty and eloquent'.[5] He enjoyed a relatively successful career in the Education Department, rising from a junior to a first-class clerk, and by 1875 he had written the first of a number of booklets about elementary education law in England and Scotland. Given his own uncertain yet successful years as a freelance writer, it is not surprising that Gibbs felt it was a tragedy that his father should have been 'fettered to the soul destroying drudgery of a government office'.[6] Henry's second eldest son Cosmo supported this assessment of his father's 40-year career when he noted that 'his spirit of taking chances had been killed by heavy responsibility, the caution and timidity growing out of a painful knowledge of the risks and difficulties of life, and the undermining security of having sat all his working years in the safe cul-de-sac of a government office'.[7] There is the obvious contrast with the actions of Henry's sons who were part of the Diaspora of English men and women throughout the Empire and the Americas. Cosmo led a carefree but successful life in America, Frank emigrated to New Zealand after working as a plantation manager in West Africa, Arthur became an author and lived in America, and even Henry, who the younger brothers regarded as 'square', became a bank official in Argentina.[8]

---

[4] Gibbs, *The Pageant of the Years*, p. 6.
[5] P Gibbs (1923) *Adventures in Journalism* (London: Harper and Brothers Publishers), p. 151.
[6] Gibbs, *Adventures in Journalism*, p. 151.
[7] C Hamilton (1924) *Unwritten History* (London: Hutchinson and Co), pp. 8–9.
[8] M Gibbs (2000) *Seven Generations—Our Gibbs Ancestors* (London: Martin Gibbs), p. 17.

In the few descriptions Gibbs provided of his father, he portrayed him as a man whose literary ambitions far outstripped his opportunities, yet one who had gathered a circle of 'worshipful friends' around him. This literary circle became one of the dominant memories of his father, for despite coming to know many of the great writers of his age—GK Chesterton, EW Hornung, Bernard Shaw, Sir JM Barrie, HG Wells, and Sir Arthur Conan Doyle among them—Gibbs remembered a youth spent in the 'company of men and women of a literary turn of mind...a long portrait of authors, novelists, and journalists...utterly unknown to fame, and entirely without fortune'.[9] He referred ironically to men such as George Alfred Henty, George Manville Fenn, and Ascot Hope Moncrieff as literary giants, though his father's résumé of two novels and a number of articles published in the *Globe* would also be dwarfed by his son's prodigious output. Interestingly, for a man of liberal politics, Gibbs does not mention that Henty was, among other things, a war correspondent who later enjoyed enormous popularity amongst boys for his historical fiction. His books were 'cheerily bellicose tales of Empire' in which the hero reaps 'the bounty of a world earmarked for the profit of white men'.[10] Such a view would have been the antithesis of Gibbs' far more critical view of jingoism, particularly later in life.

There were other literary and theatrical diversions. As a result of his friendship with an Irish family, for a time Gibbs attended the Irish Literary Society and met WB Yeats, 'who looked more like a poet than any poet ought to look', and Algernon Percival Graves, father of Robert and Charles.[11] His love of theatre was nurtured by a childhood toy in the form of a wooden theatre three feet by one, replete with back scenes, wings, and cardboard characters which were drawn on and off by fixing them into metal slides. He performed *Miller and His Men* with his brothers and sisters reading the parts while concealed behind curtains. In the middle of the last act, the 'theatre' caught fire and it was only the prompt action of his father that contained the blaze. In time, the family graduated to a live performance of *Pygmalion and Galatea*, presented in their home to an admiring audience of friends and family. Outside of the home, the family attended performances of Gilbert and Sullivan by the D'Oyly Carte Company at the Savoy, as well as the comic opera *Les Cloches de Corneville*

---

[9] Gibbs, *Adventures in Journalism*, p. 151.
[10] S Mitchell (ed) (1988) *Victorian Britain* (London: Gailand Publications), p. 358.
[11] Gibbs, *The Pageant of the Years*, p. 15.

in Surrey for the princely sum of twopence. It was a period of his life which would later form the basis of his novel *Oil Lamps and Candlelight* (1962), which documented the story of a middle-class Victorian family between 1887 and 1902.

A trait that Henry shared with his famous son was an enduring interest in the stories and anecdotes shared with him by a large and eclectic group of acquaintances. Over the course of 30 years, Henry kept a written record of 'the strangest friendships' and 'surprising confidences' in a journal which became the basis for his novel *A Long Probation*. Though Gibbs recognized that they were not of 'riveting interest' and were primarily examples of the 'many sidedness of human nature', it is not difficult to see the genesis of Gibbs' own determination, often to the detriment of his political analysis, to cast himself as the mouthpiece of the ordinary man and woman. As a man who drew a clear line between the public and the private, he also noted that many of his father's stories were of a 'personal and intimate nature'.[12] Though Gibbs was reticent to provide public insights into the dynamics of his family life, in at least one piece of personal correspondence, he revealed the depth of his connection to his father:

> My taste for literature (such as it is) is by right of inheritance. I owe it all to my father. His influence pervades every line I write. The conversations we have had together a multitude of times, during long rambles in the country, or in his study, have moulded my character very much on his own pattern (as regards my literary predilections, at least) and many a time when I am writing I catch myself unconsciously using a phrase, or running in a quotation that I have heard time out of number upon his lips.[13]

Gibbs remembered his mother, with whom it appears he had even more in common, somewhat differently, although he wrote even more sparingly of her in his autobiographies. She was born in Liverpool, the daughter of a local merchant, but to Gibbs she was a saint and martyr, 'always sewing and mending and darning to keep the boys' clothes decent and to make frocks for the two girls'.[14] His reverence for her would later find

---

[12] Correspondence with Mrs Suverkrop. The date is uncertain but it was written from Lancashire, which places it sometime in the first half of 1901. *Philip Gibbs Letters, Special Collections Research Center, Syracuse University Libraries.*

[13] Correspondence with Mrs Suverkrop 22 June, 1901. *Philip Gibbs Letters, Special Collections Research Center, Syracuse University Libraries.*

[14] Gibbs, *The Pageant of the Years*, p. 27.

expression in his unashamedly romanticized treatment of women. Even when he found them sheltering in the rubble of their homes in Rheims in 1914, he pictured them 'preserving their dignity, and in spite of dirty hands [eating] their meagre rations with a stately grace'.[15] As Phillips and Phillips observed to the growing Victorian middle class, the mother was the 'counterpoint to the vigorous and vulgar, material and masculine world', one which offered a civilizing influence in a world that could be both cruel and hard. They also noted the home was a shrine to this Goddess of the hearth.[16] Such was his emotional connection to this family life, Gibbs would later suffer from homesickness during the first years of his marriage.

Gibbs' most revealing insight into his relationship with his parents appeared not in his autobiographies, but in one of his works of fiction. In *The Street of Adventure*, in which he appears as both himself and the main protagonist Frank Luttrell, he is remarkably candid about his parents and their impact on his own nature. Luttrell, like Gibbs, was the 'heir to his father's sensitive and shy nature, although underneath that shyness he had the gay imagination and the desire for companionship which belonged to his mother, who had faced a life of drudgery…with a sunny courage'. Between father and son, 'there was a friendship of rare tenderness', but it was one veiled by 'the reserve which was natural to both of them'. It was to his mother that he 'revealed himself as much as any boy will—and most boys are in hiding from those they love'.[17] Written two years after his father's death, this passage remained one of the most personal insights that Gibbs ever wrote. He may well have regretted the emotional distance which separated him from his father, for certainly his relationship with his own son Tony was particularly close, based as it was on an 'affectionate equality'. Gibbs was always remarkably at ease with young children, yet for Tony it was a mixed blessing. He believed that except for his father, he never really made a friend.[18]

In spite of a childhood surrounded by the trappings of middle-class England, Gibbs and his siblings were able to sustain the romantic notion that by tradition and blood they were members of the old aristocracy.

[15] P Gibbs (1915) *The Soul of the War* (London: Heinemann), p. 153.
[16] J Phillips & P Phillips (1978) *Victorians at Home and Away* (London: Croom Helm), p. 98.
[17] P Gibbs (1970) *The Street of Adventure* (London: Howard Baker), p. 16.
[18] A Gibbs (1970) *In My Own Good Time* (Boston: Gambit Incorporated), pp. 10–11.

The reality, however, was somewhat different. Gibbs' grandfather had been a Queen's messenger, while his own father was reputedly born in Windsor Castle, a claim later proven false by Philip's grandson Martin. His Aunt Kate, whose drinking problem was passed off as her being intermittently 'unwell', had nursed many of the royal children, and according to family legend had once spanked the Kaiser. Another aunt was rumoured to have had an affair with a Duke who was a descendant of Charles II. Both stories were family secrets, and though the children came to know of them, it set a pattern of clearly delineating between the public and private. Other stories were far less scandalous, yet they still added a sense of romance to Gibbs' family lore. William Gibbs, his uncle, had served in the American Civil War, although for romance sake, the Gibbs children preferred the erroneous belief that it had been in the service of the South. Although Gibbs saw this family history as little more than a 'calling back of ghosts', its effect on a youth possessed of a romantic and sensitive nature was clear in his later writing.[19]

In reality, however, Gibbs enjoyed a comfortable middle-class childhood, one financed by his father's annual wage of between £400 and £500. The family lived in an old house on the edge of Clapham Park, moving there when Gibbs was about ten years old. They could at all times rely on the presence of two maids to lighten any domestic load. Gibbs' memories of childhood were of a gentle, dignified world dominated by books, pictures, and music, a world as yet untouched by poison gas and the agony of the Somme and Flanders. Evenings were spent on the sofa reading *The Three Musketeers* or listening to his beloved mother playing Handel, Beethoven, Schubert, Chopin, and Mendelssohn. On another evening, he remembered laughing so much at his mother's reading of *Martin Chuzzlewit* that he begged her to stop. Other evenings were spent listening to his brother Cosmo singing, or to one of his other brothers playing the violin, or being entertained by a guest at their weekly 'At Home' evenings. Both this idealization of the institution of family and the leisure pursuits themselves were typically Victorian, and similar scenes would have been played out in thousands of similar homes on any given night.[20] Indeed, one commentator in the *Saturday Review* observed that

[19] Gibbs, *The Pageant of the Years*, p. 40.

[20] See P Bailey (1978) *Leisure and Class in Victorian England: Rational recreation and the contest for control, 1830–1855* (London: Routledge and Kegan Paul). Bailey argued that increasing space and comfort in middle-class homes led to a trend for entertaining guests,

'the cleverness and the laziness of the age [was] aptly typified...by its ingenious contrivances for getting rid of an evening'.[21]

Gibbs' eight siblings were also steeped in a love of literature and culture, although only two, Cosmo and Arthur, received more than cursory mentions in his autobiographies. His eldest brother Henry (1870–1948), a bank official, immigrated to Argentina in 1890, married and raised a family. Charles, or Cosmo (1871–1942), the sibling to whom Gibbs remained most attached, became a famous author and playwright in the USA. After his divorce from his second wife and the loss of all of his money in the Depression, he returned to England and lived close to Philip for the remainder of his life. Frank (1873–1953) worked as a plantation manager in West Africa, writing novels about his experiences. He married in Bombay and immigrated to New Zealand in 1911 where he worked as a farmer and raised a family of five children. His sister Helen (1874–1956) was a nun for several years, but later married and became a novelist. Philip's younger siblings tended to have markedly different life experiences than their older counterparts. Hypatia (Pat) (1879–1970) worked as a governess and never married; Katherine (1880) died of atrophy shortly after birth; Thomas (1886–1907) committed suicide, an issue which is dealt with in greater depth later in this narrative; and Arthur (1888–1964), who became an author, won the Military Cross in the First World War, immigrated to the USA where he married, and died two years after Philip.

For a man acknowledged to have conducted the first press interview with a pope and who was once included in an anthology of prominent Catholic authors, it is interesting that neither Gibbs nor his parents or his would-be wife were born Catholic. Martin Gibbs, his great grandson, speculated that Henry and Helen Gibbs may have been converted by their daughter Helen, who after being educated in a convent school became a nun. Alternatively, she may have been sent to the convent school after the conversion. What is clear, however, is the fact that at least three of the Gibbs children—Philip, Frank, and Helen—also became Catholics. Gibbs' wife to be, Agnes Rowland, the daughter of an Anglican minister, converted to Catholicism while attending the same convent school as Helen Gibbs. Despite her father's anger, Agnes remained a staunch Catholic her

particularly at dinner parties. The Gibbs' predilection for private theatricals and games was also typically Victorian.
[21] Bailey, *Leisure and Class in Victorian England*, p. 60.

entire life. Unfortunately, there is little concrete evidence to support any speculation as to why, or even when Gibbs converted, although it is possible that he did so in order to marry Agnes in a Catholic Church. The fact that Agnes was by far the more committed Catholic would tend to support the view that her conversion was a matter of faith while Gibbs' may have been motivated by more pragmatic considerations. This conclusion has the advantage of explaining Philip's reticence (or carelessness, depending on one's interpretation) in overtly identifying himself as a Catholic, though it rests on the threadbare evidence that Gibbs was able to marry in a Catholic Church.[22] The possibility also exists that the marriage may have taken place in a Presbytery, a development which may not have concerned Gibbs overly much, but would certainly have been a less than satisfactory arrangement for his far more religiously committed young wife. In keeping with his reticence concerning private matters, Gibbs did not mention the ceremony in any of his autobiographical writings.

Though Gibbs was occasionally identified as a Catholic author, the influence on his writing is just as difficult to quantify. He did not make an explicit public statement about his personal religious beliefs other than general references to Christian values. In an interview in 2009, his grandson Martin described him as 'only a very mild convert' and expressed doubt as to whether it was a major part of his grandfather's life. In contrast, he noted that his grandmother Agnes was a very passionate Catholic. Though it is possible that Gibbs may have used the term Christian in a careless manner as a synonym for Catholic, what is more certain is that he saw the term Christian as implying all that was civilized in human behaviour. It is of course possible that far from being careless in his use of the term Catholic, Gibbs might well have sought to avoid any professional or personal impediments due to anti-Catholic feeling at the time. There is no clear evidence to support or refute such an interpretation, other than speculating that he feared its impact on book sales or his growing social network. This must be balanced against the more concrete evidence of his condemnation of Britain's Irish policy, which he surely would have avoided if he was in fact seeking to hide his Catholicism. In the eyes of at least one Catholic author, however, Gibbs was a skilful evangelist. Matthew Hoehn

---

[22] It was only Philip and Agnes' son Tony who did not follow the trend, and actually broke with all organized religion when he married a divorced woman in 1928.

observed that Gibbs' fiction supported the belief that 'the only real sanity in the world is the philosophy preached by the Catholic Church'.[23]

Though Gibbs himself refrained from overt references to Catholicism, preferring instead the more general term Christian, he saw value in it as a belief system:

> All the experience of human life in history goes to show that mankind will not be obedient long to any law of self-restraint and self-denial unless it is imposed upon their conscience by a supernatural authority which they believe divine. Yet without self-denial, human society must cease to exist, even human life must end abruptly, because men and women will not continue to raise up children unless they are impelled by the fear of sin. For the pursuit of human happiness ends always in disillusion and despair, and without spiritual hope of some compensating life beyond the grave this earthly span will seem but mockery as always it has seemed in the past to thoughtful souls, balancing the debit and credit side of life's account.[24]

The only time in his vast body of work where there is any extended mention of Catholicism is in his revisionist history of the First World War, *Realities of War*. In war, he observed that many soldiers found solace in religion:

> Close to death, in the midst of tragedy, conscious in a strange way of their own spiritual being, and of spirituality present among masses of men above the muck of war, the stench of corruption, and fear of bodily extinction, they groped out toward God. They searched for some divine wisdom greater than the folly of the world, for a divine aid which would help them to greater courage. The spirit of God seemed to come to them across No Man's Land with pity and comradeship.[25]

Gibbs argued that the Catholic chaplains had an easier task than their Protestant counterparts. He believed that Catholic soldiers possessed a simpler, stronger faith which proved of greater solace than Protestantism, which in his view relied more 'on intellectual arguments and ethical reasonings'. As a result, Protestant clergy were confined to providing physical comforts to the men rather than the spiritual acts such as anointing and

[23] Matthew Hoehn (ed) (1947) *Catholic Authors 1930-1947* (Newark: St Mary's Abbey), p. 265.

[24] P Gibbs (1921) *More That Must be Told* (New York: Harper & Brothers), p. 120.

[25] P Gibbs (1936) *Realities of War* (London: Hutchinson), p. 479.

absolution. What all faiths shared, in Gibbs' view, was the common need to explain to their adherents the wartime contrast between Christian profession and Christian practice. For Gibbs though, this was not a call to reject mainstream religion, let alone to atheism, but rather proof of the relevance of Christ's teachings. Nevertheless, he did acknowledge that apart from a 'heroic and saintly few' most clergy 'subordinated their faith, which is a gospel of charity, to national limitations'. Without recognizing that it was a similar charge which would be levelled at journalists, he observed sadly that they were 'patriots before they were priests'.[26] Gibbs placed enormous value on personal conscience. Even late in life, he believed that the major shortcoming of the parliamentary system was that it reduced the responsibility of the individual members who instead 'became automata responding to the crack of the Whips, supporting any government measure if they are on that side whether they agree with it or not'.[27]

Gibbs' education was more idiosyncratic than his family's leisure pursuits. His father Henry believed that the private education provided by institutions grouped under the otherwise misleading descriptor 'public schools' were 'sinks of iniquity and most horrible dens of bullying and brutality'.[28] Most of the Gibbs children were educated at home, an arrangement which satisfied their father's philosophical objection to schools such as Marlborough, Rugby, and Winchester. It was a liberal education, free from formal lessons, resting as it did almost solely on Henry's ability to communicate his intellectual passions to his children. The children were encouraged to educate themselves by reading widely and studying foreign languages, and even 35 years later Gibbs recalled his father as always 'inspiring and encouraging'.[29] This freedom from the constraints of a formal education system suited Gibbs temperamentally, as he was a voracious reader and endlessly curious about the world in which he lived. It also shielded him from a system he was, by all accounts, ill-equipped to face:

> I was at that time a shy, sensitive lad, without any armour to protect myself against the brutalities, or even the unkindness, of the rough world about me. I blushed at any coarseness of speech. I had no toughness of fibre, none of the ease and assurance which are acquired by a public school education. I was deplorably self-conscious and diffident in company. Worse than that

---

[26] Gibbs, *Realities of War*, pp. 479–80.
[27] Gibbs, *How Now England?* p. 64.
[28] Gibbs, *The Pageant of the Years*, p. 7.
[29] *Lethbridge Daily Herald* 30 June, 1923.

for myself, I was far too sensitive to the tragedy of life and to other people's pain and suffering, so that I agonized over the martyrdom of man, and even over the imaginary tortures of fictitious characters in novels and plays. It took a long time to harden me in the Street of Adventure [Gibbs' term for Fleet Street] where most men get hardboiled. I am not quite hardened yet.[30]

In 1913, Gibbs was able to say that bullying 'in its barbaric forms has died a natural death. School life has become more easy, more comfortable, more cheerful'.[31] Yet in the same book, he added that the schools 'from which the New Men are produced have thrown away all the old-fashioned principles of education as useless lumber and superstitious nonsense. The masters are for the most part New Men themselves, and, having no respect for duty and discipline, for the virtues of obedience and honour, for the dignity and grandeur of knowledge and the deathless pursuit of truth, do not trouble to teach them to their scholars',[32] For a man who never attended school himself, Gibbs was always ready to pass judgement on their failings based on this recollection of his father's attitude and the stories his contemporaries shared with him of being 'unmercifully flogged' and who in 'this brutalising system' then meted out similar 'tortures' to younger students.[33] Gibbs' son Tony inherited this disdain for formal education, noting in his autobiography that 'of course I went to school, but as the whole process of education is peculiarly unpleasant, I prefer not to dwell upon it'.[34]

It is an interesting contradiction that Gibbs identified himself so closely with Victorian England, yet criticized one of the very means by which this society sought to perpetuate itself. Here again, we see the influence of his father. Henry worked in education and would have been aware that the decade before Philip's birth marked a watershed in the development of the public school system. By the 1860s, the influence of an 'imperialist and materialist industrialisation' had become the ruling educational dogma, a transition evident in the rise of the cult of Athleticism.[35] It was a system very different from Gibbs' view of education as a deathless pursuit of truth,

---

[30] Gibbs, *The Pageant of the Years*, p. 17.

[31] P Gibbs (1913) *The New Man: A Portrait Study of the Latest Type* (London: Sir Isaac Pitman & Sons), p. 33.

[32] P Gibbs, *The New Man*, p. 19.

[33] Gibbs, *The Pageant of the Years*, p. 7.

[34] Anthony Gibbs, *In My Own Good Time*, p. 7.

[35] See B Simon and I Bradley (eds) (1975) *The Victorian Public School: Studies in the Development of an Educational Institution* (Dublin: Gill and Macmillan).

for it was one which stressed 'the prevalent anti-intellectual bias, sounding the death knell of individuality in favour of conformity to a stereotype, substituting narrow moral aims by drying up a broad conception of human worth in favour of a philistine one, to sacrifice the professed moral end to the means'.[36] Other more personal objections may have ensured the survival of this family prejudice. There may have been an enduring sense of having been excluded from an education that, though increasingly driven by the middle class, was still perceived as an aristocratic institution. Early in his journalistic career, Gibbs recalled being unable to get a position on *The Times* because he had not attended university, a further reason to have nursed a grievance against formal schooling. This interpretation would help explain the later decision to send his son Tony to just such a school, although it was probably made by his wife Agnes rather than at Gibbs' behest. Gibbs' revulsion at the 'barbarity' that he believed dominated schooling during the period, a faint echo of his reaction to stories of German atrocities in 1914, would certainly have reinforced any prejudice. There would also have been the powerful incentive to defer to his father's opinion regarding the shortcomings of public schools, thereby de-emphasizing the practical impediment of cost and celebrating it as an ideological objection.

Though formal education may have been beyond the financial resources of the Gibbs family, they were nevertheless comfortably middle class, both in lifestyle and in aspirations. Many of their contemporaries, as Gibbs later acknowledged, faced financial pressures far more pressing than weighing the costs of education. In later life, he recalled being well aware of this disparity in wealth and the social ills created by poverty. As a disciple of Charles Dickens, he would have had an intellectual, if not a practical, exposure to the excesses of Victorian England. Although he may have exaggerated the extent of his adolescent awareness, he was too skilled an observer of his surroundings and too driven by an often overwrought, emotional empathy to have been entirely ignorant of the more public evidence of the plight of his countrymen. In a groundbreaking sociological study called *Life and Labour of the People in London* (1891–1903), written just as the young Gibbs was flexing his nascent literary talents, Charles Booth estimated that over 30 % of Londoners were living in poverty. At approximately the same time, the economist John Rae noted that government reports indicated that 5 % of the populace were paupers,

[36] Simon and Bradley (eds) *The Victorian Public School*, p. 8.

20 % were malnourished, and that the majority led 'a life of monotonous and incessant toil, with no prospect in old age but penury and parochial support'.[37] As a boy, Gibbs had seen what poverty was when he 'adventured' into the East End. Here, he witnessed 'much squalor and fierce and frightful drunkenness which was the only anodyne to misery among people living in foul conditions'. Gibbs remembered being horrified by the sight of 'poor wretched women mad drunk fighting the police until they were strapped down to police stretchers outside the gin palaces'.[38] Despite acknowledging that it had been a golden period 'only for those who had the gold', Gibbs mourned the passing of the 'quietude of family life in the prosperous middle class' and the 'elegance and charm among those who were called the gentlefolk, stately homes and lovely parks, a lot of character, and an age of genius which flowered into great art and literature'.[39] It was a world at that time blessed by peace 'without any dark forebodings of two world wars which some of us might have to endure'.[40]

While visiting Bruges and Brussels in 1892, Gibbs wrote to the Bentley family who had been guests at some of his family's 'at home' evenings. In his letters, he described the old canals of Bruges, the great belfry, the Beguinage, the lace makers, and the art galleries, and given his later penchant for personal sketches, inevitably he also described the people. The Bentley patriarch, who was the architect of Westminster Cathedral, read some of Gibbs' letters and noted the calibre of his writing. This was the first encouragement outside of his family that Gibbs had received concerning his writing. The following year, the *Daily Chronicle* published his first article, a vignette describing the sea gulls screaming over London Bridge on a winter's afternoon. He received the sum of seven shillings and sixpence for his efforts. Gibbs followed this success with a number of fairytales, published in *Little Folks*. During this period, Gibbs' sense of empathy with the poverty of 1890s London, combined with the heightened emotional state experienced during adolescence, resulted in an intensity of experience he recalled clearly over half a century later:

> I had moments of ecstasy or—shall I say—of being carried outside myself, which I have not known since, at least so intensely and poignantly. The

[37] G Craig (1966) *Europe Since 1815* (New York: Holt, Rinehart & Winston), p. 317.

[38] P Gibbs (1949) *Crowded Company* (London: Allan Wingate), p. 14.

[39] Gibbs, *The Pageant of the Years*, p. 1; p. 3.

[40] Gibbs, *The Pageant of the Years*, p. 1.

first May blossom, lying like snow on the branches of the trees on Surrey common, stirred me with a sense of earth's beauty and loveliness. It was perhaps a kind of pantheism when I felt myself to be part of this universe and of all life.[41]

This emotion was not confined to a love of the countryside, for the young Gibbs, like Dickens, was also fascinated by the drama and colour of London, a peacetime memory no doubt enriched by the later experience of seeing the city bombed:

> The human drama of London seemed to enter into me, and take possession of me, so that I was aware, as it seemed, of all the suffering, the agony, the heartbreak, and the hopes, of all those millions in this half sleeping city. It was an intense awareness of life and of the beating pulse of humanity of which I was one insignificant boy.[42]

Gibbs' only real exposure to the more martial aspects of Victorian society was through his family connection with the Artists' Rifles, one of the old volunteer regiments.[43] Drawing its members from citizens involved in creative pursuits such as painters, writers, actors, musicians, and architects, it had been formed in 1860 in response to a perceived threat from France. Gibbs' father, his three elder brothers, Henry, Cosmo, Frank, and his uncle Charles Hamilton and two of his sons were all members. As a child sharing a bedroom with two of his brothers, Gibbs watched in awe as they paraded in their uniforms. In their absence, he tried on their helmets and played with their rifles. Sixty years later, he recalled the 'smell of its oil is in my nostrils as I write, a lifetime afterwards'.[44]

In addition to the general childhood influences that helped to shape his world view, there was also an intellectual inheritance from two of the great writers of the Age. When William Shirer wrote his controversial, though immensely popular, *The Rise and Fall of the Third Reich*, he claimed that whoever wished to understand National Socialism must first understand Wagner.[45] Had Shirer turned his attentions to Gibbs, he

---

[41] Gibbs, *The Pageant of the Years*, p. 17.

[42] Gibbs, *The Pageant of the Years*, p. 17.

[43] As the 28th (County of London) Regiment, its members won eight Victoria Crosses during the First World War. It is now the 21st SAS Regiment.

[44] Gibbs, *Crowded Company*, p. 40.

[45] W Shirer (1964) *The Rise and Fall of the Third Reich* (London: Pan), p. 133.

may well have observed that to understand Gibbs one first had to understand Charles Dickens (1812–1870) and Thomas Carlyle (1795–1881). Both writers stood at the 'beginning of the Victorian Age like choruses to the drama, one in tragic, the other in comic masks' and they were part of the young Gibbs' first hesitant ideological steps.[46]

There is much more to Gibbs' connection to the world of Dickens than a childhood fascination carried through into adulthood. There are significant ideological links which bind Gibbs to Dickens in a way that is only hinted at by his constant referencing of the great man in his autobiographical writing. Though much is left to speculation, the parallels in their thinking are quite marked. Like Dickens, Gibbs' world view can be reduced to the basic contention that if men would behave decently, then the world would be decent.[47] Neither author confined his criticisms merely to an identification of the failings in the structures erected and maintained by society; both, instead, looked further and demanded a change of spirit.[48] For Dickens, it was a belief in the 'power of good heartedness to triumph over evil' and which took the form not of a political programme, but of personality, one based on the quality of benevolence.[49] For Gibbs, it was the essential decency of the common man. As George Orwell observed, Dickens was not the type of reformer 'who thinks the world will be perfect if you amend a few by-laws and abolish a few anomalies'.[50] This is as true of Gibbs as it is of Dickens, and his later frustration with the failures of the League of Nations were, like Dickens' criticisms of the worst of the excesses of Victorian England, essentially moral rather than political in nature.

Unlike Gibbs, however, Dickens' fiction became increasingly more complex as he matured, for as he sought to 'penetrate more deeply to seek answers to questions inherent from the start...he discovers the object of his search to be not social evil at all, but the everlasting existential questions that great art always leads to'.[51] In this development, Gold sees the influence of Carlyle, who had guided Dickens to the realization that 'middle class civilisation itself, and not its corrupt institutions, was the great evil'. Gone was the simplicity of analysis which permitted Dickens to

---

[46] AN Wilson (2007) *The Victorians* (London: Hutchinson), p. 14.
[47] G Orwell (1946) *Critical Essays* (London: Secker & Warburg) p. 10.
[48] Orwell, *Critical Essays*, p. 21.
[49] Wilson, *The Victorians*, p. 16.
[50] Orwell, *Critical Essays*, p. 9.
[51] J Gold (1972) *Charles Dickens: Radical Moralist* (Minneapolis: University of Minnesota Press), p. 5.

link social evils to 'individual villainy' and see in 'personal benevolence' a remedy.[52] Gibbs, however, never really moved beyond the simplicity of his understanding of good and evil. His fiction did not evolve, and was often merely a reworking of familiar ideas and settings, not all of which can be explained by the disparity in their respective talents. In Dickens, we see a great mind and talent evolving. In Gibbs, we see a respected journalist becoming increasingly moribund as he gazed, almost uncomprehendingly, at his world as it slipped away.

Where there is a marked similarity, however, is in characterization. For Gibbs shared with his hero a weakness for portraying benevolence; though in Dickens' case, he is far more successful with characters such as Pickwick than Gibbs could ever achieve with his brand of romantic melodrama. In a letter to his son Tony, also a novelist, Gibbs made a guarded criticism of his son's literary disdain for just this kind of heroic character:

> I notice that you have no 'heroes' in your novels. Or rather, your particular form of hero is an oddity who is probably rather ugly, with a stutter, or weak eyes hidden behind horners, or some absurdity of manner which makes him look foolish among his fellow men. You jeer—confound you—at the good looking young fellows who wander through my fiction.

Gibbs conceded that on the whole he was 'more kind to his characters', and was saddened by Tony's refusal to admit to the possibility 'of simple and straightforward emotion natural to the average man and woman as I know them'.[53] Gibbs' novels have all but disappeared from the modern consciousness. The only exception is *The Street of Adventure* which is still valuable for the insight it offers into pre-war journalism. His other works of fiction have proven to be ephemeral, too tied to current events, and too lacking in any complexity to attract modern readers.

Though Carlyle did not exert an influence on Gibbs as pervasive as Dickens, there is nevertheless a clear intellectual connection between the Scottish philosopher historian and the political mindset, which shaped much of his political commentaries. There was also a family connection, though a tenuous one. Henry Gibbs would often doff his hat to Carlyle when they passed each other on the street in Chelsea. After Carlyle's death

---

[52] Gold, *Charles Dickens*, pp. 9–10.
[53] Correspondence between Philip Gibbs and his son Tony, circa 1931. Courtesy Gibbs Family Archives.

in 1881, Henry wrote an article for the *Globe* pressing for the preservation of Carlyle's house. He would subsequently be installed as one of the founders of the Trust created in order to achieve that end. There is evidence of the influence of Carlyle in Gibbs' historical interests. One of Gibbs' earliest forays into historical research was his *Men and Women of the French Revolution*, perhaps inspired by Carlyle's own magnum opus *The French Revolution* (which Dickens claimed, 'jokingly', to have read 500 times).[54] In Gibbs' rejection of political extremism and his championing of the virtue of compromise, there is a sense that he shared Carlyle's abhorrence of the excesses of violent revolution.

In contrast to Dickens' lifelong 'veneration'[55] of Carlyle, 40 years after his father's death Gibbs conceded that his father's reverence was 'misguided'. He leaves no clue in his writing that would suggest why he had reached this conclusion.[56] Although it is pure speculation, it is quite possible that by 1946 Gibbs had firmly rejected any belief in the genius of the great men of history and was perhaps seeking an intellectual sanctuary in his oft-repeated faith in the intelligence and sincerity of the common man and woman. A century before, Carlyle had argued that history was the biography of great men who were 'lightning out of Heaven' while the rest of humankind 'waited for him like fuel and then they too would flame'.[57] Gibbs had seen the result of this fire, and chose to place his faith in the 'intelligence of the common crowd [and the] kindness, the humour, and the shrewdness of the ordinary folk'.[58] While visiting Berlin in February 1934, he had seen Hitler stir Germany by 'his flaming words' and 'with the eyes of the fanatic and the speech of a demagogue had put a spell on the people of all classes'.[59] Carlyle's biography of Frederick the Great, which Hitler was reading as the Red Army closed in on him in the ruins of Berlin, had as its integrating theme the power of a leader of genius to create a nation and a new moral culture out of chaos. Its appeal to Hitler is no less surprising than the rejection of its author by Gibbs who despite his own affection for some of the great men of the twentieth century, Lloyd George being just one example, knew as well as anyone the cost of such leadership.

[54] Gold, *Charles Dickens*, p. 20.
[55] M Goldberg (1972). *Carlyle and Dickens* (Athens: University of Georgia Press), p. 2.
[56] Gibbs, *Pageant of the Years*, p. 8.
[57] T Carlyle (1993) *On Heroes, Hero Worship and the Heroine in History* (Oxford: University of California Press), p. 13.
[58] P Gibbs (1934) *European Journey* (New York: The Literary Guild), p. 332.
[59] Gibbs, *European Journey*, pp. 226–7.

CHAPTER 2

The New Journalism: 1895–1912

In 1895, when still only 18 years of age, Gibbs began his career in the illustration department of Cassell & Company. A chance encounter with the Managing Director and Minister for War, HO Arnold-Forster, saw Gibbs promoted to department head with responsibility for the sale of educational books. Though this was the first professional advancement that Gibbs enjoyed, it was another meeting in the same year, which was to be the most momentous of his life. His sister Helen introduced him to a friend she had made while attending a convent school in Belgium. Agnes Rowland, the daughter of a country parson who had been a military chaplain in India, became the love of Gibbs' life. Her family background, however, was not as colourless as her father's profession might have suggested. While on a family sabbatical in England when she was seven, Agnes' mother, who Gibbs described as an 'incurable flirt', ran off with an Indian Army officer. The subsequent divorce and her remarriage ended the career ambitions of the Reverend William J Rowland, who was then temporarily exiled to the poor parishes of Somerset before finishing his days in charge of Clandon parish church in Surrey. Though he initially considered Gibbs to be beneath his daughter socially, a blow softened by Gibbs having already come to the same conclusion himself, in time the two men developed a friendship based more on intellectual connections than a ready affection.

© The Editor(s) (if applicable) and The Author(s) 2016
M.C. Kerby, *Sir Philip Gibbs and English Journalism in War and Peace*,
DOI 10.1057/978-1-137-57301-8_2

As an economy measure, Agnes was schooled at the convent in Belgium, and like her future sister-in-law she was sufficiently enamoured with Catholicism to convert. Her lifetime adherence to the faith began acrimoniously when her incredulous father first locked her in her room, then denounced the Catholic Church, and finally gave vent to his frustration in an angry letter to the Pope. Gibbs, whose own conversion to Catholicism failed to rate a mention in any of his autobiographical writing, fell in love at first sight. After first shrugging off the not insignificant competition posed by his brothers Cosmo and Frank, he and Agnes were married in the Roman Catholic Church in Sherborne, Dorset, in August 1898. Gibbs was 21 and his bride 2 years older, and though he noted that they were 'babes in the wood', they married with an audacity he later found 'superb'.[1] As an older man, and only after her death, he wrote movingly of their first meeting:

> As a young girl she had a rose like beauty, and it is among roses that I like to remember her for she tended them in many gardens. I saw her first among the roses in the garden of her aunt's house at Elstree, where in a white frock...and a big straw hat, she stood with a pair of scissors snipping off the dead blossom from a marvellous show of summer glory. Shyly I went towards her, and saw her laughing eyes, and heard her cry of 'Hello, Pip!'[2]

Agnes was her future husband's intellectual equal, a fact borne out in her position as head of the secondary school at St Andrew's Convent in Streatham, a post she held for the first 18 months of their married life. She later matriculated and became a student at King's College in London. Although poor eyesight prevented her studying medicine, she studied geology and graduated in 1932 at the age of 57. She subsequently worked at Imperial College in London and some of her detailed analyses of rocks and minerals were eventually published. Though a neighbour in Shamley Green remembered her as being 'Prussian' in her household arrangements, Gibbs described her as possessing the 'gift of laughter all her life, having a merry wit and a sense of humour'.[3] They enjoyed a belated honeymoon in Paris, staying at the Hotel du Dauphin in the rue St Roche near where Napoleon had fired his 'whiff of grapeshot'. As was the case with so many

---

[1] P Gibbs (1946) *The Pageant of the Years* (London: Heinemann), p. 27.
[2] Gibbs, *The Pageant of the Years*, p. 18.
[3] Correspondence between author and Michael Harding 31 March 2008; Gibbs, *The Pageant of the Years*, p. 17.

of Gibbs' continental wanderings, the trip coincided with political tension. Coming as it did during the major Anglo-French crisis remembered rather quaintly as the Fashoda Incident, the newly-weds were subject to overt hostility from Parisians angered by what they saw as British imperial arrogance. Nevertheless, they enjoyed themselves, visiting the Louvre and walking hand in hand through the parklands of the Bois de Boulogne. Gibbs' short description of his honeymoon, written in 1946, is one of the few intimate portraits of a marriage which lasted four decades. It began a lifelong love affair with Paris, though this was not a passion shared by his son with whom he otherwise had a great deal in common. Tony believed that there was nothing to do but 'saunter about, admire the perspectives, drift back to the Café Berri, buy an *Evening Standard* and take the first plane out'.[4]

In the same year that Gibbs married Agnes, Arnold-Forster commissioned him to write the first of three books in the Cassell's 'Our Empire' series. *Founders of Empire* was a collection of biographies of great Englishmen, covering a thousand years of history, ranging from Alfred the Great to Nelson and Wellington. It sold well and was used extensively in English schools. Gibbs saw his subjects as 'some of the greatest Englishmen—men who in their day, each in his different manner, contributed to make Britain great, good, glorious and free'.[5] *India: Our Eastern Empire* (1903) and *Australasia: The Britains of the South* (1903) followed five years later, but it was this first book which brought Gibbs to the notice of the reading public. In the book on India, Gibbs made his views on Empire explicit. In the Delhi Durbar of 1903, which was held to commemorate the coronation of King Edward VII and Queen Alexandra as Emperor and Empress of India, Gibbs saw the glory of Empire present in the form of the many 'proud and magnificent princes, and so many brave and warlike people', all ready to offer their lives in defence of their 'British rulers'. He felt immensely thankful that British rule had not 'bred hatred and malice, but splendid loyalty'.[6]

Despite the subject matter of these early books and his clear support for Imperial policy, it was not an ideology which he espoused consistently once he had seen the cost of jingoism on the battlefields of Europe. He was present outside the Guildhall when the Lord Mayor of London

[4] A Gibbs (1970) *In My Own Good Time* (Boston: Gambit Incorporated), p. 65.

[5] P Gibbs (1900) *Founders of the Empire* (London: Cassell & Co Ltd), p. iv.

[6] P Gibbs (1903) *India: Our Eastern Empire* (Ludgate Hill: Cassell & Co Ltd), p. 201.

announced the declaration of war against the Boers. In 1910, he characterized the patriotic fervour which accompanied the announcement as a Christian virtue drawing 'from all parts of the Empire a great host of young men ready to shed their blood in the service of that Empire'.[7] Years later, Gibbs remembered the event somewhat differently. He recalled that as a 'liberal minded youth hostile to the loud mouthed jingoism of the time', he was not enthused by what he believed was little more than a poor pastoral people being bullied by an Empire, a view he ascribed to the influence of Gladstonian Liberalism. When Gibbs wrote these words, he was in his late seventies, by which time this process of re-evaluation had seen him distance himself almost entirely from the militant nationalism that had brought so much tragedy to so many millions of people. By then, he had reinvented himself as one who had been 'pro Boer'.[8]

It is tempting to see in this a pattern of personal myth-making that would have gladdened the heart of his old sparring partners Lloyd George and Winston Churchill, themselves no strangers to selective recall in memoirs. Perhaps, like Shakespeare's Macbeth, he feared recognizing his own complicity and recoiled at his youthful support for a by-then-discredited war.[9] Though this is pure speculation, what is certain, however, is that over the course of four autobiographies, the first written in 1923 and the last in 1957, there is evidence, naturally, of an evolution in Gibbs' thinking. Read in isolation, each autobiography presents a relatively consistent view written by a skilful journalist. When read consecutively, and in concert with his political commentaries, they are clearly derivative, and are heavily shaped and coloured by his contemporary views, rather than providing a deeper insight into his thoughts and motivations at the time. Gibbs has been poorly served by writers seeking to understand his wartime record without contextualizing him, but he regularly committed the same offence against himself, particularly in regard to his work as a war correspondent. Critics of his dispatches simply place his observations next to what we know happened by virtue of exhaustive historical scholarship. When the shortcomings are inevitably exposed, some critics have seen them as proof of his complicity in a propaganda war. Yet in his autobiographies, he actually does not place himself sufficiently in context, and rarely in his

---

[7] P Gibbs (1910) *Knowledge is Power: A Guide to Personal Culture* (London: Edward Arnold) pp. 285–6.

[8] Gibbs (1957) *Life's Adventure* (London: Angus & Robertson), p. 99.

[9] *Macbeth*, Act II, Scene II.

post-wartime writing did he seek to mitigate the charges against him by encouraging an empathy with the conditions under which he worked. He instead defended himself by claiming an accuracy and truthfulness which was impossible, given the scope of the war and official censorship.

The inconsistency in his attitude to the Empire is again exhibited in his 1913 criticism of 'the new man', who in contrast to earlier generations did not get 'that thrill in his bosom and the lump in his throat experienced by his father when these words were uttered...Empire, Patriotism, Duty, Honour, Glory, and God'.[10] His despair at this loss of reverence extended to those who opposed war:

> He is, frankly, a peace at any price man, and is prepared to stomach an insult, to see his nation lose its influence in the council of nations, to be all things to all men, in order to avert the frightful catastrophe of war. He can see nothing which would justify the unsheathed sword between civilized nations...Not for him is the old faith that there are many things worse than death-national dishonour, national decadence, or individual dishonour and individual decadence.[11]

Though he may have had an ambivalent attitude to Imperial policy, particularly in the 1920s and 1930s, he certainly did not oppose either the Empire or the Monarchy as institutions. In 1957, he recalled witnessing the celebration of Queen Victoria's Jubilee in 1887. His description was pervaded by an idealization of both the Queen herself and the world she represented which was now lost. For it was 'in our days of imperial power when Britannia ruled the waves and vast areas of the earth were under our dominion'. In retrospect, Gibbs believed that the Queen 'would have dropped dead in her carriage had she foreseen for a moment the future of the Empire over which she ruled with the loyalty and reverence—the almost religious reverence—of her subject peoples. India has gone. Egypt has gone'.[12]

Gibbs' six-year stint with Cassells ended in 1901 when he accepted a position as editor of Tillotsons' Literary Syndicate in Bolton in Lancashire. Fiction syndication originated in France early in the nineteenth century but did not become common in England until the late Victorian

---

[10] P Gibbs (1913) *The New Man—A Portrait Study of the Latest Type* (London: Sir Isaac Pitman and Sons), p. 6.

[11] Gibbs, *The New Man*, p. 58.

[12] Gibbs, *Life's Adventure*, p. 91.

period. Tillotson and Sons pioneered the practice in 1868 and eventually extended their operation to newspapers throughout the country. Gibbs' letter of application succeeded because of the impact of the statement that he, like the younger Pitt, was 'guilty of the damnable crime of being a young man'.[13] The position required him to interview authors, acquire the rights to their books and articles, and then market these rights to publishers. He was initially unimpressed by his new industrial surroundings with its factory chimneys, blackened buildings, and the 'hideous architecture', but he quickly learnt that 'one can make one's own little paradise in the blackest environment'.[14] Faced with the need to supplement an income which barely covered living expenses, Gibbs wrote a series of articles titled 'Knowledge Is Power' which were syndicated in *The Weekly Scotsman* and later published in book form as *Knowledge Is Power* (1903) and *Facts and Ideas* (1905). In these articles, he undertook to answer any question posed by a reader, thus permitting him the opportunity to 'write about great books, and the wisdom of the ages, and the love of poetry and art and drama and all beauty'.[15] In public, he described the articles and their subsequent publication in book form as a means of inculcating a shared culture which would facilitate the raising of the 'standard of the race, to bring men a little nearer the angels, a little further from the brutes'.[16] In private, however, he derided them as 'second hand goods'.[17] Nevertheless, these second-hand goods helped to augment a rather small income, an increasingly more pressing consideration after the birth of his only child, a son named Anthony, in March 1902.

Just after Tony's birth, and having spent two-and-a-half years with Tillotsons, Gibbs wrote to Alfred Harmsworth seeking employment. He was offered editorship of the literary page of the *Daily Mail*, a relatively new paper established in 1896. Harmsworth, who would rise from genteel poverty to the summit of unelected power and influence, understood the growing influence of the politically unaligned middle to lower class whose members were unlikely to buy expensive papers such as *The Times*. He was rightly considered one of the geniuses of his age, for by running newspapers at a profit and freeing them of government influence, Harmsworth

---

[13] Gibbs, *The Pageant of the Years*, p. 31.

[14] Gibbs, *The Pageant of the Years*, p. 32.

[15] Gibbs, *The Pageant of the Years*, p. 33.

[16] Gibbs, *Knowledge is Power*, p. 4.

[17] Letter to Mrs. Suverkrop, 22 June 1901. *Philip Gibbs Letters, Special Collections Research Center, Syracuse University Libraries.*

'gave England the rare gift of a free press'.[18] He was, however, just as accurately described as a 'man who fed off power, needing it as a vampire needs blood, and [he was] prepared to destroy in order to get it'.[19] Regardless of Harmsworth's capacity to polarize opinion, Taylor was not all that wide of the mark in seeing him as both a harbinger of the future and a metaphor for the inventions and attitudes of the twentieth century itself.[20] Though not blind to Harmsworth's faults, Gibbs, however, saw him as the founder and pioneer of a new journalism and a man of quality and genius.[21] He noted that to Harmsworth, news 'meant anything which had a touch of human interest for the great mass of folk, any happening or idea which affected the life, clothes, customs, food, health, and amusements of middle class England'.[22] Gibbs did not explicitly make the link himself in any of his four autobiographies; he shared this understanding of the art of journalism, though he differed from Harmsworth in possessing an instinctive suspicion of invention and innovation:

> Everything in his paper had to be bright, sparkling, and pointed. He wanted his young writers to dramatise their news stories. In fact everything had to be a 'story' rather than a report. He sent them out to search for oddities of character, strange ways of life, out of the way adventures. In the description of an historic scene, or an affair of public ceremony, he gave his praise to the descriptive writer who had observed some little touch of oddity behind the scenes, or who had avoided the obvious by seeing the human stuff on the side walk while some pompous pageant passed.[23]

Gibbs thus entered Fleet Street, a world which exerted a hold on his imagination that would end only with his death. Working in turn for the *Daily Mail*, the *Daily Express*, and the *Daily Chronicle*, as well as a short stint with the ill-fated *Tribune*, it was a golden period, one which would assume added lustre once he had witnessed the horror of the Western Front. It was not without its pain, however, for there were sporadic periods of unemployment and a succession of personal losses which blighted a

---

[18] AJP Taylor (1965) *English History 1914–1945* (Oxford: The Clarendon Press), p. 187.

[19] AN Wilson (2005) *After the Victorians* (London: Hutchinson), p. 178.

[20] SJ Taylor (1996) *The Great Outsiders: Northcliffe, Rothmere and the Daily Mail* (London: Weidenfeld & Nicholson), p. 38.

[21] Gibbs, *The Pageant of the Years*, p. 40.

[22] P Gibbs (1923) *Adventures in Journalism* (London: Harper and Brothers Publishers), p. 9.

[23] Gibbs, *The Pageant of the Years*, p. 40.

period of professional success and personal contentment. In appearance a bookish, intellectual character, Gibbs was not immune to the possibilities for adventure offered by journalism:

> The thrill of chasing the new story, the interest of getting into the middle of life, sometimes behind the scenes of history, the excitement of recording sensational acts in the melodrama of reality, the meeting with heroes, rogues, and oddities, the front seats at the peep show of life, the comedy, the change, the comradeship, the rivalry, the test of one's own quality of character and vision, drew me back to Fleet Street as a strong magnet.[24]

The London that Gibbs returned to was without doubt the 'city of Empire' in which any visitor was daily witness to the 'the visible expression of a city of unrivalled strength and immensity'.[25] Even the architecture stood in mute celebration of 'British heroism on the battlefield, British sovereignty over foreign lands, British wealth and power, in short, British imperialism'.[26] For Gibbs and men of his ilk, London also offered more than just an abstract celebration of Anglo-Saxon greatness. There were also concrete opportunities:

> By 1900 the reader had a choice of well over 2000 monthly and weekly titles on the news-stands, and the capital supported more than a dozen daily newspapers. Collectively they consumed vast quantities of non-news material and an army of free lancers supplied it. It is true that the competition was ferocious [but] some of the weekly penny papers had circulations in the millions, and all were vying to get the best fiction, the most striking articles.[27]

Gibbs' Fleet Street career did not begin in an auspicious fashion, for having almost bankrupted himself moving back to London to a flat in the Prince of Wales Road overlooking Battersea Park, he discovered that in the interim Harmsworth had appointed Filson Young to the position. Though Gibbs viewed this as an oversight, Hamilton Fyfe believed that it was Harmsworth's practice to put two men into one position in order

---

[24] Gibbs, *Adventures in Journalism*, pp. 2–3.

[25] P Ackroyd (2000) *London: The Biography* (London: Chatto Windus), p. 717.

[26] J Schneer (2001) *London 1901: The Imperial Metropolis* (London: Yale University Press), p. 7.

[27] P Morton (2009) 'Australia's England, 1880–1950'. In P. Pierce (ed.) *The Cambridge History of Australian Literature* (Cambridge: Cambridge University Press), p. 261.

to play each off against the other, thereby ensuring maximum effort.[28] Despite what may have seemed an untenable situation, they worked well together until Filson Young assumed other duties, leaving Gibbs as the sole literary editor. Despite this slight, Gibbs both liked and respected Harmsworth. He was regularly impressed by the experience of watching him preside over the daily three o'clock staff meeting. Chairing the meeting in an easy and informal manner, Harmsworth encouraged all of his staff, including the most junior, to offer suggestions for the following day's paper. Such an inclusive process would have impressed Gibbs with its sense of democracy, but just as compelling was the dominating presence of Harmsworth himself.

The position brought with it significant responsibilities, but for a 23-year-old man with a family, this was more than compensated for by the salary of six pounds a week and a further three for any article he might write. In hindsight, he believed he was exposed to a profession and a city undergoing profound change:

> It was a world changing in social life, manners, and morals. In this country it was a change over from the Victorian era to the Edwardian, with an improvement in the conditions of the working class, with a better standard of education among the masses, and with less hypocrisy and smugness in the upper classes who did not know that their power, and wealth, and old tradition of elegance, splendour, and privilege, were in their last phase.[29]

Gibbs and Agnes lived near Battersea Park for three years in a ground-floor flat in Overstrand Mansions, one of three sections of high dwellings, the other two being Prince of Wales Mansions and York Mansions. Gibbs recalled that nearly all of the inhabitants were of 'literary, artistic, or theatrical avocations, either hoping to arrive at fame or fortune, or reduced in circumstances after brief glory'.[30] In the flat above lived GK Chesterton, then in the 'full glory of his girth, and in the springtime of his genius'.[31] Gibbs enjoyed the sense of intellectualism and urban colour and later wrote a book called *Intellectual Mansions, SW*. As a writer himself, Gibbs enjoyed the company of other authors, and given his capacity for

---

[28] H Fyfe (1935) *My Seven Selves* (London: George Allen & Unwin), p. 95.

[29] Gibbs, *The Pageant of the Years*, p. 37.

[30] Gibbs, *Adventures in Journalism*, p. 156.

[31] Gibbs, *The Pageant of the Years*, p. 46.

making and keeping friends, he socialized with many household names whose fame far outstripped his own. HG Wells, with his 'dynamic energy of mind'; John Galsworthy, possessed of 'a very human sweetness and sensitivity to all human suffering'; and Bernard Shaw, who had a 'pen like a sword as champion of justice and fair play against the monsters of greed and side whiskered humbug', were all either friends or acquaintances.[32] As a member of the Reform Club, he socialized with an even wider circle, which would come to include Arnold Bennett, AG Gardiner, editor of the *Daily News* and brilliant essayist, and W Somerset Maugham.

There are few surviving descriptions of Gibbs' life during this period other than those he penned himself, but one of the best is written by a colleague at the *Daily Mail*. Frank Dilnot recalled his time working with Gibbs in an article written as an introduction to his first American speaking tour in 1919. Dilnot recalled that 'despite his humour, he had that mark of reflectiveness and intensity which has since carried him to fame. I remember how in those far off days we active young barbarians of the reporter's room shook our heads quizzically at him because of a serious article a column long in which he fiercely and wittily protested against a certain type of man in the streets of cities who fancies he is fascinating and ogles girls with a view to casual flirtations'. Dilnot balanced this description of a serious-minded young man with the observation that he also possessed 'humour, clear vision and radiated companionship and helpfulness'.[33]

Gibbs impressed Harmsworth sufficiently to warrant an invitation to spend a weekend at Sutton Place, near Guildford, with a number of other Fleet Street identities. Harmsworth used the opportunity to sound Gibbs out concerning the secrets of syndication. He then offered Gibbs the leadership of a new literary syndicate, openly offering Gibbs the opportunity to 'smash the Tillotsons'. Harmsworth had the wrong man if he thought he could tempt this most gentle of men with visions of destroying the company which had given him such an important career opportunity. Gibbs was surer of his man when he realized that his hesitation would cost him dearly. For though he wrote a report concerning the project, Gibbs knew, even then, that Harmsworth 'wanted instant enthusiasm and the optimism of youth' for he 'who hesitated with Harmsworth was lost'.[34] His report was ignored and increasingly fault was found with his

[32] Gibbs, *Life's Adventure*, pp. 10; 16; 13.
[33] *New York Times*, 23 February 1919.
[34] Gibbs, *The Pageant of the Years*, p. 44.

editorial work. Gibbs anticipated the end of their association by handing in his letter of resignation. Though faced with unemployment, typically Gibbs parted from Harmsworth with no ill feeling, firm in the belief that his former boss harboured no ill will for him. On two later occasions, Harmsworth offered Gibbs employment, once before and once during the war. Gibbs declined the first offer because he was enjoying his work as a freelance, and the second because he felt that to change papers at that stage was akin to 'changing horses mid-stream'.

Following the trail blazed by other ex-employees of Harmsworth (it was often suggested that there was an underground passage between the *Daily Mail* in Carmelite House and the office of the *Daily Express*), Gibbs then found a position as special correspondent with the rival paper, then owned by Arthur Pearson. Gibbs did not admire Pearson, particularly at first, for he found him narrower in his outlook than Harmsworth. Typically, Gibbs still felt able to express a personal liking for him. Pearson later lost his sight to glaucoma and worked tirelessly for soldiers blinded during the First World War. His most notable achievement was the founding of St Dunstan's, a home for blinded soldiers which offered them vocational training. Gibbs believed that a speech Pearson gave in New York after the war in which he spoke about St Dunstan's was the most beautiful he had ever heard. He believed that blindness brought out all that was best in Pearson and that 'he found light in his darkness'.[35]

Gibbs spent only a few months at the *Daily Express* before he resigned on an issue of journalistic integrity. Pearson directed Gibbs to research and write a series of articles arguing that Shakespeare was a fraud and that his plays were in fact authored by Francis Bacon. Believing the hypothesis to be ridiculous, Gibbs resigned rather than write the article. Short of money with a young wife and child to support, it was a courageous decision made on a matter of principle. Gibbs believed that to write against one's convictions was bad morality, requiring as it did the 'prostituting of one's pen and the betrayal of truth itself. I have always refused to do so, and I refused Arthur Pearson then'.[36] Critics of his wartime dispatches have ignored the fact that Gibbs twice resigned positions on a matter of principle (the second time in 1921). He did stay long enough, however, to report on the Joseph Chamberlain-led campaign for tariff reform which was in Dangerfield's view 'heresy and defeatism to all but a few'

[35] Gibbs, *The Pageant of the Years*, p. 49.
[36] Gibbs, *The Pageant of the Years*, p. 48.

and condemned the Conservatives to a 'desolate political midnight'.[37] As a liberal, Gibbs was a supporter of free trade and believed that the issue had 'divided friend from friend, wrecked amenities of social life and started passionate arguments at every dinner table'.[38] Nevertheless, Gibbs came to admire Chamberlain's 'courage and hard sledge hammer oratory', though he later felt ideologically alienated from a man who he believed represented the 'old jingo strain of Victorian England in its narrow patriotism and rather brutal intolerance'.[39]

Politically though, Gibbs was able to enjoy the Liberal landslide in the 1906 election which he saw as the result of military incompetence and the casualty lists from the Boer War, as well as a more general 'weariness with bugle blowing, flag waving and false heroics'. In retrospect, it heralded eight years of peace, years 'of illusion, hope and confidence in a general advance of civilisation, intelligence and prosperity for all classes'.[40] Though Gibbs was committed to liberalism's agenda of economic freedom and its social justice initiatives, it did not demand of him an explicit ideological commitment. Liberalism was more accurately characterized as a 'state of mind' based on 'free speech, religious liberty, racial equality before the law and obedience to the law itself until it is altered by the will of the majority'.[41] In particular, Gibbs shared with it a rather nebulous understanding of the 'spirit' or 'soul' of the English people.[42] For as Bentley observed, any study of the primary material from the period 1914–1929 finds the pervasiveness of the explanatory language of 'mind', 'spirit', and 'outlook'.[43] To the liberal faithful, 'mind and religion were in fact hard to separate and both tended to be subsumed as a politics of faith',[44] an outlook evident in Gibbs' regular use of terms such as 'Christian', 'liberal', and 'civilized' as synonyms and without really ever

[37] G Dangerfield (1966) *The Strange Death of Liberal England* (London: MacGibbon & Kee), pp. 21–2.

[38] Gibbs, *Adventures in Journalism*, p. 95.

[39] Gibbs, *Adventures in Journalism*, p. 97.

[40] P Gibbs (1952) *The Journalist's London* (London: Allan Wingate), p. 123.

[41] P Gibbs (1924) *Ten Years After* (London: Hutchinson & Co), p. 183.

[42] For a selection of Gibbs' use of soul, one might look at 'the soul of the war', 'one's democratic soul', 'French soul', 'the soul of England', 'the wounded soul of the world', Lloyd George could 'risk his soul', the 'soul of men', while Germany could search 'for its soul'.

[43] M Bentley (1977) *The Liberal Mind 1914–1929* (London: Cambridge University Press), p. 2.

[44] M Bentley, *The Liberal Mind 1914–1929*, p. 3.

defining what he meant by them. This vagueness was again typical of liberalism itself, which was never a series of 'readily applicable maxims for use in a political manifesto'.[45] It was a political religion, not a concrete dogma, one which, as HG Wells noted, possessed a 'multitudinousness' that left it a 'vague and planless association'.[46] To other even less sympathetic eyes, liberalism appeared an 'irrational mixture of Whig aristocrats, industrialists, dissenters, reformers, trade unionists, quacks and Mr Lloyd George'. In the face of 'the destructive contradictions of daily reality', this eclectic group sought an intellectual safety in 'an almost mystical communion with the doctrine of laissez-faire and a profound belief in the English virtue of compromise'.[47]

The contradiction inherent in committing oneself wholeheartedly to such a nebulous belief system is brought into even starker relief when one considers the fact that Gibbs never actually exercised his right to vote in a general election, presumably even refraining from voting in the election contested by his son, albeit in a different district. Instead, he believed that 'a writing man should hold himself aloof from any party, not labelling himself or entering the political arena' and thereby remaining 'an observer, a critic and only sometimes a judge'.[48] Nevertheless, he himself saw no contradiction between his failure to participate in the democratic process, yet simultaneously describing liberalism as having once been the 'glory of the nation' and bemoaning its political emasculation as a tragedy because their 'moderate and reasonable philosophy' remained the most genuine expression of English national character.[49]

An example of this lack of a clear political or social agenda, which had as its natural consequence, contradictory impulses, is to be found in Gibbs' recognition of racial equality as a central tenet of the old liberalism which he espoused. He supported it with the cautious conservatism indicative of liberalism's 'profoundly conscience stricken state of mind'.[50] Yet Gibbs saw it as unnecessarily provocative for the French to use Senegalese and Moroccan troops in the occupation of German territory after the First

[45] M Bentley, *The Liberal Mind 1914–1929*, p. 3.

[46] HG Wells (1911) *The New Machiavelli* (London: John Lane), pp. 325–6. In S Hynes (1991) *The Edwardian Turn of Mind* (London: Pimlico), p. 12.

[47] Dangerfield, *The Strange Death of Liberal England*, p. 70.

[48] Gibbs, *Life's Adventure*, p. 51.

[49] Gibbs, *Ten Years After*, p. 23; P Gibbs (1958) *How Now England?* (London: Angus and Robertson), p. 68.

[50] Dangerfield, *The Strange Death of Liberal England*, p. 179.

World War. He was similarly critical of the English use of Indian troops and the American use of black soldiers. Gibbs also saw a threat which he described as the 'rising tide of colour' emerging from the 'massacre of the world war and some of its lessons and watchwords' which had 'aroused the passions and ambitions among the dark skinned races'.[51] One of the watchwords that this determined proponent of the League of Nations feared the most was 'the self determination of peoples'.[52]

Yet Gibbs was not racist in an extreme sense, finding much to admire in other peoples. He just preferred to admire them in their own country. Nor was he blind to the violence inflicted on indigenous peoples in the name of Empire, yet he saw that as a failing in human wisdom rather than an institutional flaw requiring radical change. He saw in the Empire a 'benevolent despotism' with 'responsibilities towards the coloured races which cannot be supported without force of arms'.[53] For men who believed in national liberty, and Gibbs numbered himself among them, there was, he felt, agreement that Western ideas of parliamentary democracy could not 'be translated into an Oriental country before centuries of education and preparation'.[54] Compromise, the English love of the underdog, and the cautious interference of the liberal would see most situations resolve themselves. This timidity in applying ideals to concrete issues was later evident in Gibbs' support of the suffragettes and his sympathy for the plight of the working class.

As liberalism was never a fully resolved ideological commitment for Gibbs, one looks in vain in the written record for a clear political statement in which he outlined a detailed and coherent exploration of his beliefs. When he used it as a descriptor, it was actually the expression of a very personal, deeply held, romanticized construct of England. It denoted a lifestyle as much, if not more, than a political viewpoint. When he returned from the Continent in the latter half of 1934, after two months abroad, Gibbs argued that England was the envy of her European neighbours, who were 'astonished by the stability, order and tranquillity of the English people'. In his celebration of these qualities, he wrote what was in effect an extended love letter to the land of his birth, a land free from 'tyranny' and 'civil strife' where 'one can talk without looking over

[51] Gibbs, *Ten Years After*, p. 151.
[52] Gibbs, *Ten Years After*, p. 151.
[53] Gibbs, *Ten Years After*, p. 155.
[54] Gibbs, *Ten Years After*, p. 151.

one's shoulder lest a spy should be about'. It was a world where a knock at the door did not herald an attack from political opponents, where one could cultivate one's garden without fear that local villagers were planning acts of violence and sabotage. Most of all, it was one devoid of 'political passion and without any apparent menace to its old tradition and ancient loyalties'.[55]

This devotion to liberalism left Gibbs, as it would the political party as a whole, 'squeezed between the Tory imagination of traditional English virtues…and the Socialist imagination of a planned and just society'.[56] Unable to shake his adherence to nineteenth-century laissez-faire individualism, yet cognizant of at least some of the major failings in a system whose history he viewed as a romantic pageant, Gibbs sought solace in a generalized faith in human nature. Drawing heavily on the virtues of English character, he developed an idealistic and often naive faith in the power of the common people to alter history. Repeatedly in his writing, Gibbs sought to generalize about vast political movements based on conversations with 'the man in the street', and in doing so he regularly failed to recognize that it is these very people who are swept along by the currents of history, subject to the whims of fate, chance, and, sadly too often, the machinations of those in power. He believed that the vast majority of people wished to be left to cultivate their gardens in peace, and if 'a man is seen stabbing another, the crowd rushes to intervene without enquiring into the causes. There is a policeman round the corner who says "What's all this about?" and takes action in the name of the law'. It was a wonderfully sincere, idealistic, yet utterly impractical transference of the lifestyle in an English village to international relations. Gibbs acknowledged the impossibility of such a system, but he paradoxically noted that there is 'no other way of avoiding this anarchy of nations'.[57]

The same fluidity which marked his liberalism was later evident in his ambiguous attitude to the War. The pre-war England for which he yearned might have destroyed itself in civil war had the struggle against Germany not united a society at breaking point. For Gibbs, the war, though terrible and clearly the antithesis of his own values, served as both the saviour and the destroyer of the England he had constructed for himself. At a personal level, this ambiguity extended beyond the

[55] P Gibbs (1934) *European Journey* (New York: The Literary Guild), p. 339.
[56] Hynes, *The Edwardian Mind*, pp. 56–7.
[57] Gibbs, *European Journey*, pp. 341–2.

large canvas of his world view to the more intimate change it wrought on his own person. Fame brought him a degree of financial security, the satisfaction of imperial honours, professional respect, and the friendship of the famous and powerful. But it also subjected him to daily visions of slaughter he was physically ill-equipped to face and temperamentally ill-suited to address with any degree of professional detachment. It was the very fluidity and ill-defined ideology that was liberalism which permitted him to move from a successful war correspondent to a peace activist without recognizing any inconsistency, let alone hypocrisy. Yet it was during the period between 1914 and 1929 that Gibbs, like the other 'custodians of traditional liberalism lost everything they most valued in political life'. Gibbs, who believed that his writing might help avert this catastrophe, was left, like other liberals, 'hoping for better things and lamenting lost virtues'.[58]

As he would all of his life, Gibbs continued to write during the pre-war years: his first two novels, *The Individualist* (1908) and *The Spirit of Revolt* (1908), as well as four historical books, *The Romance of Empire* (1906), *Men and Women of the French Revolution* (1906), *The Romance of George Villiers, First Duke of Buckingham* (1908), and *King's Favourite* (1909). *The Romance of Empire*, an illustrated history of the British Empire published by Edward Arnold, drew heavily on his previous books for Cassell. The other three were biographical works, the most notable being *Men and Women of the French Revolution,* published by Kegan Paul, which was illustrated with reproductions of rare eighteenth-century prints and measured an impressive 26 cm by 20 cm. In total, Gibbs made less than 300 pounds from his foray into historical research and quickly came to the conclusion that the writing of history was the most unprofitable branch of literature.[59] From 1923 onward, Gibbs entrusted most of his fiction to Hutchinson, replicating his arrangement with Heinemann, who were the preferred UK publisher of his non-fiction, a relationship cemented with the release of *The Soul of the War* in 1915.

It was also a period of considerable upheaval in the Gibbs' family. His father, Henry, suffered from tuberculosis and subsequently died of heart failure while a patient at the Holloway Sanatorium on 5 July 1906. It was a mental asylum for the lower middle classes, and though there is no evidence of what particular health problem he suffered, his grandson Martin

[58] Bentley, *The Liberal Mind*, p. 1; 2.
[59] Gibbs, *Adventures in Journalism*, p. 114.

Gibbs believed, not unreasonably, that it was a mental illness of some kind.[60] The only description Gibbs provides is a simple reference to the breakdown of his father's health.[61] The following June, Thomas Gibbs, one of Philip's younger brothers, shot himself dead in a railway carriage at Paddington Station. He was at that stage a 21-year-old art student. His death is not mentioned in any of Gibbs' autobiographies.[62] Gibbs' mother Helen died four years later in April 1911, a bereavement which again finds no place in her son's autobiographies.

Gibbs' silence about the suicide of his brother may merely have been the natural extension of his reticence to reveal matters that he considered private. It may, however, have stemmed from a peculiarly Victorian view of suicide. For though many Londoners of Gibbs' parents' generation would have readily conceded the concept of diminished responsibility and though there was a weakening of the view that it was a sin, suicide still remained a social disgrace. There was also the associated view, one that Charles Dickens used in his fiction, that it was the fitting end of a villain or perhaps in an unexpressed view of Thomas' death, a weakling.[63] Belonging to a class which celebrated the bonds of family, any taint of suicide would have been perceived as a negative reflection on the victim's family. Later, during the war, Cosmo described Gibbs as being a 'martyr to nervous breakdowns' during this period, and given his father's death in a sanatorium, it is unsurprising that he would decline to discuss any issue with even a hint of mental illness.

In 1906, Gibbs applied for the position of literary editor for a new daily Liberal paper called *The Tribune*. In a broad sense, the paper was an attempt to return to the old liberal mode of journalism which emphasized the newspaper's role in disseminating news and opinion as opposed to its value as a saleable commodity.[64] The owner, Franklin Thomasson, assembled a brilliant staff, and though it was a quality

---

[60] M Gibbs (2000) *Seven Generations—Our Gibbs Ancestors* (London: Martin Gibbs), p. 38.

[61] Gibbs, *The Pageant of the Years*, p. 30.

[62] In his most complete autobiography written in 1946, Gibbs states that there were seven children, not eight, thus leaving out either a sister who died shortly after birth or the unfortunate Thomas who committed suicide.

[63] See B Gates (1988) *Victorian Suicide: Mad Crimes and Sad Histories* (Princeton: Princeton University Press).

[64] A Lee (1973) 'Franklin Thomasson and the Tribune: A Case Study in the History of the Liberal Press, 1906-1908' *The Historical Journal*, vol. 16, no. 2, June 1973, p. 341.

publication, it failed to appeal to a broad demographic. Gibbs believed that it was too intellectual in its attempt to preach 'the gospel of liberalism'; however, there is some evidence to support the view that its failure was as much the result of commercial and political factors.[65] It closed after two years when belated attempts to broaden its appeal or to seek other financial backers failed. Unemployed with a young family, Gibbs decided to abandon journalism and instead work full time as a writer. In retrospect, he argued that journalism was 'merely a novitiate for real literature, a training school for life and character, from which I might gain knowledge and inspiration for great novels, as Charles Dickens had done'.[66]

Shortly after this decision and at his wife's insistence, Gibbs took his family on a month-long seaside holiday at Littlehampton. During this period, he raced through a 150,000-word manuscript with an industry and speed remarkable even for him. *The Street of Adventure*, destined to be his most popular, yet one of his least financially successful novels, was a thinly veiled description of his time at *The Tribune*. He wrote it with 'one purpose only—apart from an imaginative urge to tell the story of a Fleet Street romance—and that was to maintain the upkeep of a little house in Kensington'.[67] A number of his former colleagues felt libelled and threatened legal action, although only one case was pursued. A coincidental meeting on the day before it was due to be heard saw both parties share lunch and, as a result, the action was dropped. Though the book continued to sell well for decades, the royalties were lost to the legal bills accrued while preparing for the case.

Driven by the 'spur of poverty' and a sense that to any journalist a long absence from Fleet Street left him 'outside the arena of life', Gibbs became a special correspondent at the *Daily Chronicle*, probably early in 1909.[68] A decade and a half later, he still believed that it was 'one of the best games in the world for any young man with quick eyes, a sense of humour, some touch of quality in his use of words, and curiosity in his soul for the truth and pageant of our human drama'.[69] In the few years before the outbreak of war, he covered events as diverse as the fraudulent discovery of the

---

[65] Gibbs, *Life's Adventure*, p. 13; Lee, *Franklin Thomasson*, p. 359.
[66] Gibbs, *Adventures in Journalism*, p. 109.
[67] Gibbs, *Life's Adventures*, p. 35.
[68] Gibbs, *The Pageant of the Years*, p. 71.
[69] Gibbs, *Adventures in Journalism*, p. 3.

North Pole by Dr Cook,[70] the death of King Edward VII,[71] King George V's Coronation,[72] Blériot's flight across the Channel,[73] the trial of Doctor Crippen,[74] and the Battle of Sidney Street.[75] He revelled in the drama of Fleet Street and being so near to the 'pulse of life'. After the day's labour, which had often continued well into the night, 'there is a lull' followed by 'an earth tremor below them. There is a murmurous, throbbing noise, like the beating of a mighty heart. The day's paper is being born'.[76]

Arriving at his office in Fleet Street, his 'own little kingdom', at ten in the morning, and normally remaining there until at least midnight, Gibbs was responsible for the magazine page which he believed was, by general consensus, 'the best of its kind in English journalism'.[77] He was nominally in charge of three artists who illustrated the page with black-and-white drawings. One of them, Edgar Lander, later travelled with Gibbs through western and central Europe in 1934 while he gathered research for his book *European Journey*. Never a robust, overtly masculine figure, Gibbs was nevertheless able to indulge in the kind of 'horseplay' his home education had denied him. Wrestling matches on the floor of his office offered something of a relief from the pressure of constant deadlines and long hours. Another seemingly trivial episode provides a further insight into Gibbs' character. Ernest Perris, then the news editor, but later the

---

[70] Frederick Cook (1865–1940) claimed to have reached the North Pole in April 1908, a year before Robert Perry. His claim is still clouded in controversy (as is Perry's), although Gibbs, who broke the story, was convinced that he was a fraud.

[71] King Edward VII (1862–1910).

[72] King George V (1865–1936) was crowned in 1910.

[73] Louis Bleriot (1872–1936) achieved the first heavier-than-air flight over a large body of water on 25 July 1909 when he crossed the English Channel.

[74] Dr Crippen (1862–1910) was executed for the murder of his wife. He and his lover were the first criminals to be apprehended with the aid of wireless communication.

[75] In January 1911, Peter Piatkov (Peter the Painter) and some fellow Latvian anarchists were caught by police trying to tunnel into a jeweller's shop in Houndsditch, East London. Two policemen and one of the burglars were killed, with the remainder returning up the tunnel to their quarters in 100 Sidney Street. A siege ensued, and the then Home Secretary, Winston Churchill, gave the authority for the use of the Scots Guard in the Tower and the Horse Artillery from St John's Wood barracks. The anarchists set fire to the house, and police subsequently found three corpses in the gutted building. The episode gained notoriety because Churchill hurried to the scene himself, not so much in spite of the danger but because of it, and his subsequent unsuccessful introduction of amendments to the Aliens Act to forbid the carrying of firearms by aliens.

[76] Gibbs, *The Journalist's London*, p. 15.

[77] Gibbs, *The Pageant of the Years*, p. 55; Gibbs, *Adventures in Journalism*, p. 100.

managing editor, wagered 10 pounds on the result of a 40-mile walk. Opening the wager to all comers, a party of six, Gibbs included, set off from Marble Arch at 6 a.m. one morning. Gibbs came second, despite being so dazed that by the 30-mile point he was observed walking like a ghost and singing nursery rhymes. Later that evening, Gibbs had to be carried up the steps of Baker Street Station by his five companions, at least one of whom had stopped at an inn for afternoon tea. It was clear, however, that behind his physical frailty there existed a man of iron will, one who would later call on hitherto unsuspected reserves of willpower and dogged determination during almost four-and-a-half years on the Western Front.

The only real 'scoop' of Gibbs' career came courtesy of Frederick Cook, an American explorer who fraudulently claimed to have reached the North Pole in April 1908. As Cook approached Copenhagen in September 1909 on his return from the Pole, Gibbs arrived in the city seeking an interview some days after most of his competitors. In an amazing coincidence, and certainly much to Gibbs' good fortune, he met the wife of Dr Rasmussen, an earlier colleague of Cook's, at a restaurant. She and a friend were preparing to board a launch which would rendezvous with Cook prior to his arrival in Copenhagen. They offered him the slim chance of being included in the party if he accompanied them to Elsinore, of *Hamlet* fame. Although his new friends were themselves denied passage, Gibbs was able to make the rendezvous. With an understandable sense of his own good fortune, Gibbs was able to clamber aboard the *Hans Egede*, and, in the company of a couple of other reporters, who could not speak English, was able to conduct the first interview with the new hero. Though Gibbs acknowledged that he knew nothing of polar exploration and that he was at first completely accepting of the claim, the defensive and truculent attitude of Cook when asked for his diary led him to suspect the explorer of a massive fraud. It was a suspicion which Gibbs felt was in part due to his 'sensibility to mental and moral dishonesty'.[78]

His scepticism was further justified when the ship arrived in Copenhagen and, with a hero's welcome waiting, Cook cowered in his cabin. He appeared, in Gibbs' view, like a criminal who had lost his nerve. Having been sued once already for libel, Gibbs nevertheless took his career in his hands and wrote a number of articles which cast doubt on the veracity of Cook's claim by emphasizing inconsistencies in his account and the lack

---

[78] *Salt Lake Tribune*, 20 May 1923.

of any substantive proof. They were written against the tide of popular opinion and for a time made him the most unpopular man in the city. The newspaper *Politiken* described him as 'the liar Gibbs', a slander which they later withdrew with an apology.[79] Even a lecture given by Cook in the presence of the Crown Prince, during which he was evasive and uncooperative, which Gibbs believed proved conclusively that his claim was a 'fairy tale', was not enough to immediately dissuade his diehard supporters.[80] Despite being the earliest and perhaps most courageous of the sceptics, Gibbs felt no personal animosity for Cook, but rather felt a 'profound admiration' for his 'iron nerve' and 'miraculous self-control'. He should, in Gibbs' view, be assured immortality as one of the 'great impostors of the world'.[81] Gibbs' vindication was, as one commentator noted, a 'triumph of sheer intuition in the first instance and dogged persistency and remarkable courage'.[82]

It was also an age of changing technology, a fact evident in Gibbs' presence at a number of the first aviation meetings where he recalled waiting for hours and sometimes days for men like White,[83] Latham,[84] Blériot, Cody,[85] and Hamel[86] as 'they tinkered with their machines, stared at the wind gauge, would not risk the light breeze that blew, or rose a little, after moving like lame ducks around the field and crashed again like wounded birds'.[87] The first inkling that Gibbs had of the enormous possibilities of powered flight was at another meet at Doncaster when Cody flew despite the assembled reporters having laughed 'long and loud' at the first sight of his aeroplane.[88] When Cody's plane rose 'gracefully and gently as a butterfly', Gibbs and an excited crowd ran after him, shouting and cheering.[89] Minutes later after the aeroplane crashed, he helped drag the bloodied but triumphant Cody from the wreck. Gibbs then travelled straight from Doncaster to Blackpool where he saw Latham, who he considered the

---

[79] Related by Gibbs in the *Salt Lake Tribune*, 20 May 1923.
[80] *New York Times*, 8 September 1909.
[81] *New York Times*, 9 September 1909.
[82] G Overton (1924) *Cargoes for Crusoes* (New York: D Appleton & Company), p. 20.
[83] Claude Grahame-White (1879–1959).
[84] Hubert Latham (1883–1912).
[85] Samuel Franklin Cowdery later known as Samuel Franklin Cody (1867–1913).
[86] Gustav Hamel (1889–1914).
[87] Gibbs, *Adventures in Journalism*, p. 168.
[88] *Syracuse Herald*, 1 July 1923.
[89] Gibbs, *Adventures in Journalism*, p. 170.

greatest daredevil of the early aviators, fly in such appalling weather that Gibbs believed it to be the most astounding flight made up to that time.

Nevertheless, Gibbs could not hide his suspicion of the new technology when he described the first day of the 'first aviation week in England' in October 1909 as a 'most dreary and depressing, melancholy and mournful affair I have ever seen in connection with merry sports and pastimes'.[90] Hampered by poor weather, Gibbs passed the long hours by counting the crowd in the stands which had been expected to reach 100,000. At one point, with a most un-Gibbs-like derision, he noted that crowd numbers jumped from six to seven before dwindling to three and then finally settling on one. The following day, blessed with better weather and a crowd of 50,000, Gibbs could report that 'for the first time in English history and above English ground two men were seen flying in the air together'.[91] In later life, Gibbs could not recall attending more than a handful of these meetings where there was not at least one fatality. Again with a knack of being in the right place at the right time, at least in a journalistic sense, Gibbs was at Bournemouth when Charles Rolls[92] became the first Briton to be killed in an aircraft accident.

By a further stroke of luck, Gibbs was present in Dover when Blériot crossed the Channel. This achievement had come down to two fliers, in this instance Latham and Blériot. Over a two-week period, Gibbs crossed the Channel almost every day, and having guessed correctly was there to welcome the French aviator. In an interview conducted almost immediately after Blériot landed, Gibbs heard a story that was 'thrilling and romantic to those who can read between the lines of a narrative told simply and straightforwardly by the hero of the adventure'.[93] At a banquet given for Blériot by Alfred Harmsworth and the *Daily Mail*, there was much excited talk of 'the dawn of a new era' and of 'man taking to himself wings like the gods of Greek mythology'. For Gibbs, however, there could never be a celebration of technology without an acknowledgement that change brought with it pain. In 1949, he felt compelled to point out that 'nothing has done us so much injury, or caused so much death, or destroyed so much beauty. Lovely old cities, the treasure houses of history,

---

[90] *Daily Chronicle*, 16 October 1909.
[91] *Daily Chronicle*, 18 October 1909.
[92] The Hon. Charles Stewart Rolls (1877–1910).
[93] *Daily Chronicle*, 26 July 1909.

the shrines of civilisation, have been smashed into dust'.[94] For the English, this flight robbed them, 'for all time [of] our island security'.[95] In taking to the sky, humanity 'rose very high and fell very low'.[96]

Gibbs also reported on some of the early races, the first being one from London to Manchester in late April 1910 between White and Paulhan.[97] The second was the All-around England race, which became a duel between two famous French aviators, Vedrines[98] and Beaumont.[99] Vedrines was a 'rough, brutal, foul mouthed mechanic with immense courage and skill', while his opponent was a 'charming and gallant' naval officer.[100] When Vedrines arrived to discover that he had been beaten, he clenched his fists and swore. He then asked if there was a woman prepared to kiss him, an appeal answered by a young French woman who perhaps understood her countryman better than Gibbs and the assembled throng. The shattered mechanic threw his arms around her, kissed her, and burst into tears. Gibbs found it characteristic of the 'French soul that in this moment of tragic disappointment he should have sought a woman's arms'.[101]

There were other more mundane stories which did not bring Gibbs either fame or fortune. He was sent to Holland on what he believed to be a ludicrous mission to report on the birth of Queen Wilhelmina's first child during which Gibbs spent most of his time sightseeing. As the Queen had miscarried in 1901 and 1906 and had given birth to a stillborn son in 1902, the event was eagerly anticipated by her subjects, not the least for the fact that the next in line to the throne if she failed to produce an heir was a German. When the news finally broke in the early hours of 30 April 1909, Gibbs and Hamilton Fyfe (who Gibbs would later alienate when he accepted a knighthood) ran down the street leading to the post office shouting 'princess, princess'. It was during the ensuing celebrations that Gibbs was involved in his first and only fight. A Dutch photographer climbed onto their cab which lurched to and fro as a result of his considerable size and refused Gibbs' entreaties to remove himself. The photographer attacked Gibbs who promptly felled his assailant. Fyfe, who described

[94] P Gibbs (1949) *Crowded Company* (London: Allan Wingate), p. 39.
[95] Gibbs, *Adventures in Journalism*, p. 177.
[96] *Syracuse Herald*, 1 July 1923.
[97] Isidore Auguste Marie Louis Paulhan (1883–1963).
[98] Jules Vedrines (1881–1919).
[99] Jean Louis Conneau (1880–1937) flew under the pseudonym Andrew Beaumont.
[100] Gibbs, *Adventures in Journalism*, p. 175.
[101] Gibbs, *Adventures in Journalism*, p. 175.

the fight as a battle between a white rabbit and a Dutch boar, laughed delightedly. According to his version, which Gibbs neither confirmed nor denied in his own light-hearted retelling, Gibbs landed the only real punch of his life firmly to the groin of the unfortunate photographer.

Royal events closer to home had a more personal effect on Gibbs. He was one of the first people to hear of the death of King Edward VII on 6 May 1910. He and another reporter had hired a four-wheeled cab to take them to the Palace gates and await news of the stricken King. Being familiar with one of the King's detectives, Gibbs and his companion were the only pressmen allowed to park in the grounds. While keeping vigil, Gibbs saw members of the Royal family arrive and guessing at the signifi-cance of this development ran to the equerry's entrance where he heard the news. He had liked the King, for despite the 'heady indiscretions of youth' he had 'played the game of kingship well and truly, with a desire for his people's peace and welfare, and had given a new glamour to the Crown which had become rather dulled and cobwebbed during the long widowhood of the old Queen'.[102] Obtaining permission to see him lying in state, Gibbs believed that this solemn moment was marred by an 'out-rageous invasion of vulgarity'. The King had hated photographers in life, and, now in death, he was surrounded by a dozen of them in what Gibbs, in his outrage, later described as a 'photographers' orgy'.[103]

As an incurable romantic with a keen sense of history, Gibbs was always susceptible to the effect of place. Even in his mid-fifties, he admitted that he walked around foreign cities and old English towns with a sense of 'an intimate relationship with the past'. He felt able to 'see old ghosts' and 'touch old stones and get a thrill out of them because of other hands which have touched them'.[104] It is not surprising, therefore, that the coro-nation of King George V remained the most impressive ceremony that Gibbs ever witnessed. Held in Westminster Abbey, 'that ancient shrine of history where many ghosts walk—the ghosts of lion men and tiger men, of saints and sinners, of kings and princes, queens and princesses, heroes and villains, martyrs and traitors', the coronation was an event steeped in history and myth.[105] It was a ceremony that moved Gibbs not in spite of

[102] Gibbs, *Adventures in Journalism*, p. 27.

[103] Gibbs, *Adventures in Journalism*, p. 28.

[104] Correspondence between Philip Gibbs and his son Tony, circa 1931. Courtesy Gibbs Family Archives.

[105] Gibbs, *Life's Adventure*, p. 26.

its ancient origins, but because of them. It was a call to his sense of connection with the past, and, though he cloaked his reaction in the language of intellectualism, his reaction was emotional, almost primal:

> And the coronation of an English king, in its ancient ritual, blots out modernity, and takes one back to the root sentiment of race which is our blood and heritage. One may, in philosophical moments, think kingship an outworn institution, and jeer at all its pomp and pageantry. One's democratic soul may thrust all its ritual into the lumber room of antique furniture, but something of the old romance of its meaning, something of its warmth and colour in the tapestry of English history, something of that code of chivalry and knighthood by which the king was dedicated to the service of his peoples, stirs in the most prosaic mind alive when a king is crowned again in the Abbey Church of Westminster.[106]

Though not referring specifically to Gibbs, Dangerfield also understood the appeal. He observed that 'one English Coronation is very like another; each has the same backward look. Each is a celebration of the past. Each rehearses, for a long hour or two, the glory that has departed'.[107] In 1952, with the coronation of Queen Elizabeth II imminent, Gibbs showed that he shared this view. Though he acknowledged that by then the ceremony had become an anachronism, it was a glorious anachronism. For if one has 'any spirituality at all, one has this wonderful sense of being in touch with the past, a ghostly yet living past', one in which the very stones of Westminster Abbey 'vibrate with the wavelengths' of a tumultuous history.[108]

Census records indicate that by 1911 Gibbs was living at 36 Holland Street, Kensington, although he made reference to living at that address as early as 1908. Years later, he recalled the excitement and charm of life in those last years of peace. On Mondays a Punch and Judy show, on Tuesdays a German band, on Wednesdays an Italian organ grinder, and at dusk every day a muffin man heralded his approach with a bell. Almost 40 years later, he could still recall the small flat being overcrowded with friends every Saturday and Sunday afternoon. As an insight into the extent that Gibbs saw this as a golden period and how grief-stricken he was when Agnes died in 1939, late in life, Gibbs would walk down Holland Street

---

[106] Gibbs, *Adventures in Journalism*, p. 30.
[107] Dangerfield, *The Strange Death of Liberal England*, p. 49.
[108] Gibbs, *The Journalist's London*, p. 68.

and stand opposite his former home and feel that both he and the woman he loved, and their friends, were all ghosts. Typically, he credited this network of friends to people falling in love with Agnes.

In October 1910, the revolution in Portugal saw King Manuel II deposed and the monarchy replaced by a republic. It gave Gibbs his first opportunity to work abroad as a special correspondent in difficult, though not overtly dangerous circumstances. Interestingly, Gibbs never carried a weapon, believing that the safest defence in any company was to be unarmed. English public opinion had been mobilized by reports from the Duchess of Bedford concerning the mistreatment of royalist prisoners by the new regime. Lord Lytton engaged Gibbs to travel to Portugal in 1911 to ascertain 'the true facts, uncoloured by prejudice'.[109] He found that part of the pressure to alleviate the sufferings of the royalist prisoners emanated from a young woman who Gibbs identified only as 'Miss Tenison',[110] who was in touch with many of the royalist families in Portugal. Whatever the altruistic motivations driving her, there was also a significant element of romanticism, a quality she shared with the 34-year-old Gibbs. He found her living with two elderly aunts in a remote part of England in a 'very ancient little house, unchanged by any passing of time through many centuries...haunted I am certain, by the ghosts of Tudor and Stuart England'. Always susceptible to atmosphere, he found her to be 'so delicate, so transparent, so spiritual, that I had the greatest difficulty in accepting her as an inhabitant of this coarse and material world'. He left her with a promise of support and a sense of beginning a romantic adventure, one in which he would play the part of the Scarlet Pimpernel.[111]

Armed with a bag of gold sovereigns hidden beneath his shirt and the letters of introduction so beloved of Englishmen abroad, Gibbs visited a few of the houses of the old nobility in Lisbon. Meeting women of the old regime in poorly lit mansions where they agonized over the fate of loved ones while surrounded by all the accoutrements of upper-class life would have been enormously appealing to Gibbs on almost every level. His sense of chivalry regarding women, his middle-class reverence for titles, and his innate humanitarianism would have rendered the assurances from Lady Bedford concerning the apolitical nature of his mission superfluous. He was now committed.

---

[109] Gibbs, *Adventures in Journalism*, p. 137.
[110] Eva Mabel Tenison.
[111] Gibbs, *Adventures in Journalism*, p. 138; Gibbs, *The Pageant of the Years*, p. 109.

After frequent visits to the Foreign Office, he received permission to visit two prisons, the Penitenciaria, a 'model prison', and the Limoeiro, which was rather 'old fashioned'. The model prison appeared to Gibbs as though it had been 'specially and beautifully designed to drive men mad and kill their humanity'.[112] It was spotlessly clean, but it kept prisoners 'entombed' in solitary confinement, preferring death to further terms of incarceration. The political prisoners were also united in their anger that the government had treated them like common criminals rather than having them shot and permitting them to 'die as gentlemen'.[113] They had their heads shaved, wore prison uniforms, and were forced to wear a hood with eyeholes. Gibbs always sought company in his own life, and it is not surprising that solitary confinement filled him with 'a cold horror'.[114] The old-fashioned prison, despite its unsanitary and crowded conditions, seemed far preferable to Gibbs because prisoners were able to mix openly. He also bribed his way into a prison called Forte Monsanto, located on a hill some distance from Lisbon. Located underground, its dungeons were the most awful Gibbs had ever seen, and he preferred not even to imagine what went on in 'the darkness of those men's souls'.[115]

Gibbs believed that the real indictment of the government was that, 'under the fair name of liberty, they had overthrown the monarchical regime and substituted a new tyranny'.[116] Gibbs' articles were published in the *Daily Chronicle* and many newspapers on the Continent. There was, however, some criticism of Gibbs' ready acceptance of the allegations and exaggerated interpretations provided by the monarchist lawyer Jose Soares da Cunha e Costa. Severe pressure was brought to bear on the new government of Portugal by a 'lurid British press and humanitarian campaign'. The agitation 'which put into shadow even the British protest over slavery in Portugal West Africa' was underwritten by veiled threats of British intervention and a break in Anglo-Portuguese relation.[117] Perhaps as a combined result of these pressures, a few months after his return to England, the Portuguese government declared a general amnesty. In 1923, Gibbs admitted that he had no idea whether his articles had influenced this

---

[112] Gibbs, *Adventures in Journalism*, p. 141.
[113] Gibbs, *Adventures in Journalism*, p. 142.
[114] Gibbs, *The Pageant of the Years*, p. 113.
[115] Gibbs, *Adventures in Journalism*, pp. 145–6.
[116] Gibbs, *Adventures in Journalism*, p. 146.
[117] D Wheeler (1999) *Republican Portugal* (Madison: University of Wisconsin Press), pp. 98–9.

decision. However, in 1946, he wrote that his articles had alarmed the government which was anxious to remain on good terms with England and thus felt compelled to release the aristocrats.[118]

Though Gibbs later gently denigrated his pre-war reporting as inconsequential, he actually wrote about many of the most pressing issues facing England during the first decade of the twentieth century. He was aware that 'the years before 1914 seem, to those of us who remember them, a happy time in history, though now, in writing this, I doubt whether they were as happy as we think they were'.[119] Nevertheless, it was a 'brief but brilliant period of liberal optimism, when Edwardian creativity flowered, and the liberation of England from the repressions of the past seemed possible'. Yet the Liberal Party, which might have transformed English society, was consistently hampered by the disorderly state of progressive thought. It was thus incapable of effectively combating a 'fierce and mindless hostility to change' which was a symptom of the 'ossification of conservatism at the time'.[120] Gibbs was also aware of the issues that later writers such as Dangerfield and Wilson saw as the profound challenges of this time—potential revolution in English factories, disorder in Ireland, the militant suffragettes, political upheaval in England, and instability in Europe. Dangerfield described it, with ample justification, as a world of 'political furies, sex hatreds [and] class hatreds'.[121] Gibbs, however, felt that the 'spirit of England was, in the mass, rooted to its old traditions, and its social habits were not overshadowed by any dread'.[122] Dangerfield dismissed views such as this by observing that these years were 'golden only in the harsh reflected light of the Western Front'. He characterized it as 'a cruel, selfish and backward age, wedded to social and philosophical attitudes which no longer made sense'.[123] In Gibbs' defence, he was certainly aware of 'undercurrents beating up below all this fair surface of tranquillity', and given what he saw on the Western Front, it is understandable that he saw pre-war England enveloped in the golden glow of nostalgia.[124]

[118] Gibbs, *The Pageant of the Years*, pp. 115–6.
[119] Gibbs, *The Pageant of the Years*, p. 123.
[120] Hynes, *The Edwardian State of Mind*, p. 13.
[121] Dangerfield, *The Strange Death of Liberal England*, p. 298.
[122] Gibbs, *Adventures in Journalism*, p. 206.
[123] Dangerfield, *The Strange Death of Liberal England*, p. 12.
[124] Gibbs, *Adventures in Journalism*, p. 207.

Gibbs reported on these great issues in exactly the manner one would have expected of a middle-class liberal with a marked propensity for snobbishness.[125] He supported the suffragettes from the beginning, for he saw in their demands for political equality an elementary justice, but was often shocked and distressed by the violence. He abhorred the class consciousness of the police, who handled upper-class protesters with reasonable gentleness but were brutal in their treatment of the working-class suffragettes. Yet the more militant actions of the suffragettes could never have received complete support from a man who viewed the fairer sex in such an idealized manner:

> The suffragette movement kept me in a continual state of mental exasperation, owing to the excesses of the militant women on one side, and the stupidity and brutality of the opponents of women's suffrage on the other... I became a convinced supporter of 'Votes for Women,' partly because of theoretical justice which denied votes to women of intellect, education, and noble work, while giving it to the lowest, most ignorant, and most brutal ruffians in the country.[126]

Gibbs betrayed his middle-class snobbishness and his Victorian morality by idealizing upper-class women denied the vote. Yet he still saw a link between militant political action and sexual promiscuity. For he found the methods employed by the militants outrageous to the extent that they 'loosened...some of the decent restraints of the social code, for which we had to pay later in a kind of sexual wildness of modern young women'. Gibbs, a shy and gentle man, found something hysterical and dangerous in their passionate fanaticism.[127] Yet he also found mitigating circumstances for them in the 'deliberate falsity and betrayal of members of Parliament' who had reneged on their commitment to women's suffrage.[128] When the first female parliamentarian took her place in the House of Commons in 1919, Gibbs was able to trumpet it as a 'revolution'. Lady Astor[129] would have appeared to Gibbs as eminently suitable for the role of heroine, and

---

[125] That said, the Liberal Party itself was not necessarily any more pro-feminist in its outlook than the Tories.

[126] Gibbs, *Adventures in Journalism*, p. 215.

[127] P Gibbs (1931) *Since Then* (London: Heinemann), p. 368.

[128] Gibbs, *Adventures in Journalism*, p. 215.

[129] Lady Astor would later ask Philip and Agnes to receptions, in his view, to convert them to Christian Science.

no doubt remembering the violence of the suffragette movement, he wrote that 'today the gates were stormed not by violence, but by a change in the spirit of the people…Barriers of prejudice were removed without any sound of a crash'.[130]

Present at the trial of Emmeline Pankhurst and her daughter Christabel,[131] Gibbs later saw their jailing as not 'altogether reassuring as a demonstration of British Justice'.[132] Yet for all his natural sympathy for the individuals involved, his views on women would not appear modern to a contemporary audience nor even particularly consistent. In *The New Man—A Portrait Study of the Latest Type*, he revealed that though he might support women's right to vote, he was not proposing equality. For the weakness he observed in politics, social customs and home life was 'due to man's admission to the women's point of view, or at least to his lack of resistance to it. Many of the virtues of the time and some of its vices are caused by the conquests of the women's spirit over the mind of man'.[133]

In the same work, which one reviewer felt had been written as though Gibbs had been 'staying with an elderly aunt in the country and listening to her dirges on the changes about her from the days when she was young', he made his attitude to relations between the sexes even clearer.[134] *The New Man*'s 'acquiescence in the emancipation of women has upset the balance of human nature in which, after all, man should be still the lord and master'.[135] In his book *The Eighth Year*, Gibbs belittled the motives of many suffragettes as merely a reaction to marital dissatisfaction which left them vulnerable to 'crystal gazing, drugs, intrigues, divorce [and] feminism'.[136] Nevertheless, he wrote a novel based on the suffragette movement—*Intellectual Mansions, SW*—in which the death of one of the female characters at a demonstration was portrayed as martyrdom for an ideal, one which showed the necessity of granting women the vote. It was sufficiently sympathetic to the movement that the suffragettes bought numerous copies of the book and bound them in their colours of

[130] *New York Times*, 2 December 1919.
[131] Emmeline Pankhurst (1858–1928) and her eldest daughter Christabel (1880–1958).
[132] Gibbs, *The Pageant of the Years*, p. 128.
[133] Gibbs, *The New Man*, p. 4.
[134] *Times Literary Supplement*, 9 October 1913.
[135] Gibbs, *The New Man*, p. 87.
[136] *New York Times*, 9 November 1913.

white and green.[137] Gibbs believed that the unpopularity of the suffragettes destroyed whatever chance the book had of making money. Half a century later, Gibbs remembered it as a very bad novel, an unduly harsh assessment of a work of fiction comparable in quality to most of his other offerings.[138]

Gibbs offered the same idiosyncratic sympathy to the poor who struggled to survive in a society where the disparity between the classes has been described as 'grotesque'.[139] In the financial year 1903–1904, it was estimated that the national income was 1710 million pounds. Of this sum, 830 million pounds was taken by 5 million people, and 38 million people shared the remaining 880 million pounds.[140] Gibbs recalled seeing, beneath the pleasure and pageantry and sport, a different England:

> Labour for millions of men and women by whom the wealth of the nation is made was underpaid, overworked, and insecure. The Welsh miners rioted at Tonypandy. I saw them marching down the Rhondda valley. I saw baton charges not pleasant to see. My sympathies were with these men, knowing something about the miserable conditions in which they worked, underpaid and housed worse than cattle, in such foul slums as Merthyr Tydfil. There was a general strike in Liverpool to which I was sent. It was as near to revolution as anything I have seen in England…The situation was alarming and not without brutality among the strikers, whose passions were aroused.[141]

Yet as he showed with his conditional, almost reluctant support of the suffragettes, Gibbs was far more prepared to side with the working class in the abstract rather than the concrete. In the right to strike, he saw the 'power of laziness' wielded by a class 'perfectly aware that the Governing classes are afraid of him and throw him sops to keep him quiet. He accepts the sops, and utters new threats. At present he is preparing for a general advance all along the line to ensure himself a minimum wage for a minimum amount of work'.[142] His experiences in England and Ireland convinced Gibbs that if ever there was revolution in England, 'it would not be

[137] Gibbs, *Life's Adventure*, p. 104.
[138] Gibbs, *Life's Adventure*, p. 104.
[139] Wilson, *After the Victorians*, p. 52.
[140] Chiozza Money, quoted in Wilson, *After the Victorians*, p. 55.
[141] Gibbs, *The Pageant of the Years*, p. 125.
[142] Gibbs, *The New Man*, pp. 99; 112.

made with rose water', though he reassured himself at the time with the thought that the working class were out for revolution, not violence.[143]

In February 1912, Gibbs travelled to Belfast to report on a speech extolling the virtues of Home Rule delivered by Winston Churchill, then First Lord of the Admiralty. Due to Protestant opposition, a suitable venue became problematic, finally necessitating the hiring of a marquee and its erection on the Celtic Football Ground. Gibbs felt that Churchill's preparedness to face his enemies was brave but rash. Nevertheless, the future prime minister was compelled, against his own instincts, to leave by a circuitous route to avoid further protest. Unfortunately, Gibbs arrived at his hotel in a car of a similar make and colour to that used to transport Churchill, and the crowd, still unaware that the object of their ire had long departed, descended on him in their thousands. Gibbs, who looked nothing like Churchill, was engulfed by an angry crowd before making a less than dignified escape.

One story that does not even rate a mention in *Adventures in Journalism* or *The Pageant of the Years* is the remarkable success of his report on the sinking of the *Titanic*. *The Deathless Story of the Titanic* proved to be one of the most influential of the early reports on the loss of the White Star Liner and over 1500 of her passengers in the early hours of 15 April 1912. Gibbs' relative silence on the subject is not surprising, as it was symptomatic of the general loss of interest when war broke out in August 1914 and offered a much larger tragedy and a more universal taste of loss and grief. What is significant in his report is not only its commercial success but also the fact that the style, tone, and discourse are exact blueprints for his later dispatches from the Western Front, even down to some of the phrasing. It is also indicative of the extent to which the tone and content of Gibbs' reports reflected contemporary sensibilities. For regardless of whether he was reporting on a maritime disaster or a poorly conceived and executed offensive on the Western Front, to Gibbs, tragedy was transient when contrasted with a glory which would ensure immortality.

There were more subtle thematic devices at work than merely the romantic view that in the face of glory, death must give way. In a view as yet untested by war, Gibbs saw a man's reaction to danger as more than a mere test of masculinity. It was a call to the 'old qualities of nobility', a veritable harkening back to the past for some great shared unconscious to

[143] Gibbs, *Adventures in Journalism*, p. 214; Gibbs, *The New Man*, p. 98.

'the old traditions of race and manhood'. This shared heritage had 'for a time seemed sleeping', but in these hours of tragedy 'all the great virtues of the soul...leapt forth, as though to the call of God, like a "sunburst in the storm of death"'. Gibbs revealed this ideological commitment in his choice of a poem by Harold Begbie as an introduction. More than merely providing a convenient opening, it is a precursor to an articulate, passionate, almost overwrought 40-page celebration of those whom Begbie believed had chosen to die 'like men'.[144] Yet as Howells argued in his excellent study *The Myth of the Titanic*, Gibbs thus joined almost all of his contemporaries in celebrating what was in effect a passive rather than an active heroism. Only for Captain Smith, for whom there are five competing versions of his final minutes, does Gibbs present a more active and 'sublime heroism'.[145] For the rest of the male passengers, writers such as Gibbs offered an 'imperceptibly smooth transition between praise for action, praise for behaviour, and praise for manner'. In the context of the *Titanic* disaster, it was therefore possible to display manly heroism simply by 'taking it well' and 'dying with dignity'.[146] This does not denigrate the courage of those who gave, and subsequently those who obeyed, the much-celebrated order that women and children would go to the lifeboats first. The order was indeed given. It was generally obeyed. To Gibbs, and to most, if not all of his readership, this was as it should be. Such a scenario reflected deeply held views about gender shared by the passengers themselves, by writers such as Gibbs, and the audience for whose tastes they catered.

Far from being a tomb for so many hundreds of men and women, the *Titanic* therefore became a 'shrine of many miracles'. For to Gibbs, there was no greater miracle than 'that a man should lay down his life for a friend' or that 'weak women should suddenly be uplifted from their weakness, and become strong to suffer and to dare'. In facing death as they did, these men and women obeyed 'to the last letter the great code of honour'.[147] Yet there was more to Gibbs' description than just issues of gender. It was not enough to celebrate the heroism of those who died as men, for it was also important to memorialize those who faced death as

[144] P Gibbs (1912) *The Deathless Story of the Titanic* (London: Lloyd's of London Press Ltd), p. 14.

[145] Gibbs, *The Deathless Story of the Titanic*, p. 16.

[146] R Howells (1999) *The Myth of the Titanic* (New York: St Martin's Press), p. 69.

[147] Gibbs, *The Deathless Story of the Titanic*, pp. 1–2.

'gentlemen'. This is particularly evident in the story of American million-aire Benjamin Guggenheim who after having declined a place in the boats changed into evening wear and went to his death dressed in the uniform of his class. Gibbs went further than most in this process. He extended the status of a gentleman to everyone who died courageously and as a result would have their names 'written in gold'. For 'whatever their condition', these passengers all 'died like noble gentlemen and ladies of quality'.[148] As a member of the middle class, working in what many considered a disrepu-table vocation, it was easy for Gibbs to believe that courage, chivalry, and honour came naturally to those of the higher classes.

The following year, Gibbs travelled to Germany on a journalistic mis-sion to assess the extent of a war climate. He found a disturbing level of militant nationalism amongst those in power, but as he would do so often, he turned to the common man for reassurance. Among businessmen, railway porters, labourers, hotel waiters, and university students, Gibbs found 'utter incredulity regarding the possibility of war between England and Germany and contempt for the sword rattling and "shining armour" of the Kaiser and the military caste'.[149] Though he wrote this ten years later after a world war and by then deeply immersed in the promotion of peace, Gibbs was adamant that the German people as a whole did not want war 'until their rulers persuaded them that the Fatherland was in danger, called to their patriotism, and let loose all the primitive emotions, sentiments, ideals, passions, and cruelties which stir the hearts of peoples, when war is declared'.[150]

As someone standing near him observed as King Edward lay dying, it was the end of peace. The world Gibbs had loved would soon be con-sumed by blood and fire, or drowned in the mud of countless battlefields. He would mourn its death, yet to the end of his life he would display a remarkable fidelity to this construct of England which was in its death throes even before the guns of August. Years later, Gibbs recalled this period before the war with unabashed nostalgia, for he had always believed that London was a city made for journalists. He never felt devoid of inspira-tion while exploring the backstreets of the capital, travelling either on foot or in horse-drawn omnibuses which 'lurched down Fleet Street and the Strand with a thunder of hooves', or better still, in a hansom cab 'driving

---

[148] Gibbs, *The Deathless Story of the Titanic*, p. 28.
[149] Gibbs, *The Pageant of the Years*, p. 223.
[150] Gibbs, *The Pageant of the Years*, p. 225.

through Victorian London, before world wars and all that, with a pretty lady by one's side, holding her gloved hand on the way to St James' Hall or the old Empire'.[151] He worked in the company of men 'who were the chroniclers of history day by day' and, though not a rambunctious character himself, Gibbs found them 'to be a first class lot, not without odd and even fantastic characters among them, keen eyed, humorous, cynical'. These 'Peeping Toms' were engaged in what at times could be a 'squalid adventure' for the reporter was 'the slave of Fleet Street, bound by an unwritten law, unwritten but almost unbreakable, never to let his paper down'.[152] It meant long hours away from Agnes, often missing meals, and the comforts of home, in search of a story that might not get published, or might be mutilated by an editor harried by a late breaking story and a shortage of space. Yet for all the stress and long hours, Gibbs mourned that this world, like the liberal England he later yearned for, could not last. Fleet Street, he observed in 1952, had lost the 'riot and ribaldry...as they have gone from London itself, in which there is less laughter as well as less dirt, less poverty, and less of the picturesque among crowds all dressed alike in mass produced clothing'.[153]

Gibbs' first introduction to the work of a war correspondent was during the Balkan War of 1912, an opportunity he saw at the time as the 'crown of journalistic ambition, and the heart of adventure and romance'. Gibbs was designated 'artist correspondent' by *The Graphic* and the *Daily Graphic*, a task which placed few demands on his elementary artistic skills. He was to provide only rough sketches and an artist in England was to 'work them up'. By the time war broke out on 8 October 1912, with Montenegro's declaration of war against Turkey, to be followed within a week by Bulgaria, Greece, and Serbia, Gibbs was already in Belgrade. Within a month, every Turkish Army in Europe was defeated, and by December the belligerents had accepted an uneasy peace. The second Balkan War between the former allies of the League in June of the following year showed that simmering tensions in the Balkans remained and that any future conflagration would almost inevitably involve the Great Powers. Only a few hours after arriving, Gibbs received an introductory lesson in military censorship. While sketching a group of reservists waiting to entrain, he was arrested as an Austrian spy. While recounting the story

[151] Gibbs, *The Journalist's London*, p. 1.
[152] Gibbs, *The Journalist's London*, pp. 4–5.
[153] Gibbs, *The Journalist's London*, p. 14.

years later, he was able to joke that 'the sketch was what alarmed them, as well it might have done, if they had any artistic sense'.[154]

Gibbs spent only a few hours in custody and was released in time for the outbreak of war later that evening. He spent a further few days in Belgrade before travelling to Sofia, the capital of Bulgaria, as an accredited correspondent with the Bulgarian Second Army. Once there, he and his fellow correspondents faced further delays. There was a wall of censorship which forbade any description of the disposition of troops, the names of generals, the names and number of the wounded, the success or failure of Bulgarian troops, the state of their health, or the climate. When he asked the chief censor what he could actually report on, he was nonplussed to receive the suggestion that Bulgarian literature was of some interest. Eventually, Gibbs and many of the other correspondents were permitted to travel to Stara Zagora where King Ferdinand had established his head-quarters. Here, the correspondents received the welcome news that they would travel to Mustapha Pasha and witness the siege of Adrianople.

Gibbs soon discovered that the correspondents were to be hampered by severely restrictive censorship which left them virtually unable to report on the war at all. Even seemingly harmless descriptive articles about the scenes behind the lines were viewed as dangerous. In response, Gibbs and two companions regularly evaded the authorities and smuggled out arti-cles which he later conceded 'was extremely rash'.[155] In spite of the official promises, Gibbs and his companions saw little of the conflict, and after being expelled and then readmitted, Gibbs ultimately returned to England frustrated at the severity of the censorship. He learnt little of war during this first sojourn, a shortcoming recalled in a humorous but otherwise lau-datory speech given by his fellow correspondent Henry Nevinson in 1917. Nevinson viewed the correspondents as 'a ménage—I ought to almost say menagerie—not seen since the days of Noah's Ark. In this Ark I always privately regarded Philip Gibbs as the dove. I call him the dove because he was then absolutely ignorant of war; he did not know a horse from a gun or a Staff Officer from a fool'.[156] Interestingly, Gibbs also offered a mixed

---

[154] Gibbs, *Adventures in Journalism*, p. 192.

[155] Gibbs, *Adventures in Journalism*, p. 201.

[156] Commemorative booklet for a dinner given in Gibbs' honour at the Savoy Hotel, 27 December 1917. Gibbs Family Archives.

assessment of the correspondents. At different times, he described them as 'vultures', 'good friends all', and 'a wild horde'.[157]

Gibbs was not so much angered by the imposition of censorship as by the fact that the Bulgarians promised access to the front, and then stalled, obstructed, and finally reneged on this promise. The final indignity for a man of Gibbs' upbringing was that his antagonists forgot that they were dealing 'not with truant boys or with ticket of leave convicts, but with gentlemen, among them being the most brilliant men in Europe...They subjected men who were superior to them in education and social rank to petty insults and irritating humiliations'.[158] Yet Gibbs retained a strangely ambiguous attitude towards censorship, one which he was to maintain throughout the course of his life. Despite being angered and frustrated by this experience in the Balkans, Gibbs believed that conflict was not 'a theatrical exhibition, nor a peep show, for descriptive journalists and men of literary attainments. It was a business in which great nations had staked all they had'. Gibbs argued that it was a nation's right to regard a war correspondent as a potential spy and to limit his access to the facts by severe censorship and strict regulations.[159]

As a well-read man, Gibbs was able to contextualize the conflict in the broader sweep of European affairs. He remained, however, dismissive of the people and their politics, seeing the war as a gathering of semi-civilized peoples allied against Turkey.[160] He wrote that the Turks 'have paid the price of their old sins, of their old cruelties, of their long record of misgovernment, corruption and tyranny'.[161] Of Turkey's opponents, he observed that:

> The liberation of Macedonia from Turkish rule was the watchword adopted by the rulers of the Balkan States to give righteousness to their cause, and to gain the sympathy of other Christian people. That each of the States, now joined in an offensive and defensive alliance had other and more selfish interests to serve, was perfectly clear to all but the simplest of souls. Servia had long set her heart upon an open window on the shores of the Adriatic, Montenegro coveted the Sanjak of Novi Bazar, Bulgaria was ambitious to

[157] Commemorative booklet, pp. 12; 25; Gibbs, *Adventures in Journalism*, p. 196.

[158] P Gibbs (1913) *The Balkan War: Adventures of War with Cross and Crescent* (Boston: Small Maynard and Company), p. 115.

[159] Gibbs, *The Balkan War*, p. 113.

[160] Gibbs, *The Balkan War*, pp. 191–2.

[161] Gibbs, *The Balkan War*, p. 5.

bring within her frontiers the rich country of Thrace, and to thrust the Turk back into Asia Minor, Greece would not be baulked of Crete, and all these allies in the Balkan confederation had old scores which they were eager to wipe out in Turkish blood.[162]

Gibbs believed that there was 'a devil's brew to poison the system of international relations, and behind the scenes corrupt interests of armament firms, Jewish money lenders, international financiers, were working in secret, sinister ways for great stakes'.[163] He often saw the influence of shadowy groups conspiring in private for questionable ends. In 1913, in a sustained criticism of English society, he described 'the real business of politics (being) conducted behind the scenes, by secret negotiations between the leaders, by bargaining and bribing between various groups and interests, and by compromise and diplomacy. This is also a game—a game of poker—but it is played for high stakes'.[164]

In his brusque critique of the war aims of the belligerents lies the genesis of his perceived failings on the Western Front. Bulgaria was not his country, and the Bulgarians were not his people. Correspondents such as Max Hastings observed during the Falklands War in 1982 that reporting on your own nation at war is a different proposition from wars which involve people with lives totally foreign to the correspondent.[165] In the Balkans, Gibbs had no vested interest in either the outcome or the people involved. When war involved those he loved, however, in his own cultured and gentle way, he was as patriotic as those

men of intelligence, who have spent their lives scraping at the soil, laying by little savings after long days of labour, and proud of their small possessions, in farms and homesteads, (who were) not only willing but eager, and delirious almost with enthusiasm, to abandon their work, to give up their oxen and their carts, to leave behind them all that they hold dear in life, and to go at the word of command, from men they have never seen, to fight a death struggle with unknown enemies.[166]

---

[162] Gibbs, *The Balkan War*, p. 9.
[163] Gibbs, *The Balkan War*, p. 190.
[164] Gibbs, *The New Man*, p. 205.
[165] P Knightley (1989) *The First Casualty* (London: Pan Books), p. 481.
[166] Gibbs, *The Balkan War*, p. 3.

Almost immediately after his return from the Balkans, Gibbs turned 'this squalid adventure'[167] into the first of his seven war memoirs. The product of a collaboration with Bernard Grant, who had been a correspondent with the Turkish Army, *Adventures of War with Cross and Crescent*, did not, however, make any pretence of being a history of the war: 'Neither my friend or I, nor any other correspondents, were allowed to see very much of the fighting [but] as some historians of war forget, the real enduring drama of it is to be found not in military facts and figures, but in the human side of it'.[168] While it is true that much of the drama is indeed to be found in the human side of war, it is these very facts and figures which permit a nation's people to make an informed judgement about the conduct, or even the morality of a war. Yet it cannot be assumed that Gibbs was alone in this view. In its review of the book, the *New York Times* noted, with no observable sense of irony, that though in many respects it was a fine book, 'yet when all they can tell is summed up it amounts to very little',[169] The *Times Literary Supplement* agreed, describing it as a 'readable story, if not of war, at least of the condition of a region when war has swept over it'. Yet as the reviewer pointed out 'military exigencies are, after all, a matter for the combatants themselves'.[170] The general acceptance of censorship by two such influential papers lends credence to any claim that far from being self-serving, or even idiosyncratic, Gibbs' understanding of censorship reflected widely held views.

[167] Gibbs, *Adventures in Journalism*, p. 191.
[168] Gibbs, *The Balkan War*, p. 1.
[169] *New York Times*, 23 February 1913.
[170] *The Times Literary Supplement*, 26 December 1912.

CHAPTER 3

Free Lance War Correspondent: 1912–1915

Although he was already a prolific writer and a respected journalist prior to 1914 (he was described by Overton as 'one of the greatest reporters the press has ever had'), Gibbs owes his fame to his work as a war correspondent on the Western Front.[1] By the time the guns fell silent in 1918, he had established for himself a vast audience on both sides of the Atlantic and throughout the Empire. It would bring with it a commensurate improvement in his social standing and influence. Yet it is this very profile that has drawn critics to both the content and tone of Gibbs' war dispatches, the veracity of which he defended stoutly, with one major concession in 1946, for the remainder of his life.[2] Nevertheless, there is evidence of profound failings in his dispatches, some institutional and others personal. The nature of the relationship between politicians and the press, the evolution of military thinking regarding the press, and the changing role of the foreign correspondent exerted considerable influence on the articles he submitted and his later justification of them. Just as vital in shaping the dispatches, however, was his romanticism, his credulity, and his patriotism. It was the interplay of these forces, some far beyond Gibbs' control, which encouraged the writing of dispatches that refrained from

[1] G Overton (1924) *Cargoes for Crusoes* (New York: D. Appleton & Company), p. 25.
[2] M Farrar (1998) *News from the Front: War Correspondents on the Western Front* (Phoenix Mill, Gloucestershire: Sutton Publishing) and P Knightley (1989) *The First Casualty* (London: Pan Books).

© The Editor(s) (if applicable) and The Author(s) 2016   59
M.C. Kerby, *Sir Philip Gibbs and English Journalism in War and Peace*,
DOI 10.1057/978-1-137-57301-8_3

criticism of British generalship and was consistently too optimistic and prone to an unsubtle deification of the common soldier. Yet the accusation that Gibbs was knowingly part of a grand conspiracy or, as Knightley described it, part of a 'meta system of propaganda and myth making' is absurd.[3] There is nothing in Gibbs' character or his writing that would support such a claim. It was a far more nuanced situation than Knightley's broad brush strokes would suggest.

On 27 July 1914, with Britain's involvement in a continental war now almost inevitable, arrangements for the accreditation of war correspondents began. At a conference with the War Office and the Admiralty, the press assented to a voluntary code of censorship which covered the reporting of troop movements and shipping. This decision of newspaper proprietors to acquiesce to government control and to cooperate in disseminating propaganda brought them the rewards of social rank and political power.[4] The War Office subsequently released 'Regulations for Press Correspondents Accompanying a Force in the Field'. It in turn led to the creation of a register of approved correspondents who were authorized to travel with the army. Even after consultation between the press and the War Office, a prospective correspondent still had to be approved by the Army Council before a licence was granted and their name added to the register. This left the correspondent not only answerable to his newspaper but also subject to the dictates of the military, the very organization whose successes and failures he sought to report.

To complete the removal of any remaining vestige of independence, the Chief Field Censor attached to General Headquarters (GHQ) became their commanding officer. In Farrar's view, from the very outset, the aim was to both limit the number of correspondents and ensure that those chosen were completely compliant with the needs of officialdom.[5] Any communication between the correspondent and his paper would have to be submitted in duplicate to the Chief Field Censor via the Press Officer. It was forbidden to mention, let alone discuss, morale, casualties, troop movements, or their strength, location, or composition. To protect those who oversaw their nation's war effort, criticism or praise of those in a

---

[3] Knightley cited in M Farish (2001) 'Modern Witnesses: Foreign Correspondents, Geopolitical Vision, and the First World War' *Transactions of the Institute of British Geographers*, vol. 26, no. 3, pp. 273–87; 274.

[4] Knightley, *The First Casualty*, 80–1.

[5] Farrar, *News from the Front*, p. 4.

position of authority was also forbidden. In any event, it was all essentially a smokescreen, one which left the correspondents who waited for official accreditation exercising their horses in Hyde Park as the German Army crashed through Belgium.

As an English journalist, Gibbs and his colleagues were servants of a free press which supported the war from the outset. This support was 'openly arrived at [and despite] Party differences...the press leaders reached unanimity by individual routes'. This was in direct contrast to the German experience, where unity was imposed hierarchically from above, a contrast which reflected profound differences between the two countries.[6] Various attempts at a heavy-handed official censorship, which were not dissimilar to the German method, were stillborn. Instead, what evolved was a very English style of control relying heavily on self-censorship, one strangely suited to both the political system and public sensibilities. It was broad, but unobtrusive, based as it was on a close control of the news at its source combined with a tight-knit group of press lords.[7] Newspaper owners and editors were part of the ruling elite and regularly mixed socially and professionally with leading politicians. Members of the same clubs, guests at the same dinner parties, and active members of the same political parties offered their support freely without need of coercion. Their restraint and belief in 'loyal opposition' somehow became identified with 'gentlemanliness', and doing the right thing became a matter of fulfilling obligations to fellow members of the club rather than meeting a professional responsibility of informing readers.[8] As Koss observed, what might have appeared from a distance as an adversarial relationship between press and politics was in effect a 'network of uneasy and transitory alliances'.[9]

If this network failed to control dissent, there was the additional safeguard of the *Defence of the Realm Act* (DORA) which was enacted on the fourth day of the war. It granted the State unlimited power to control the dissemination of information. Any opposition to the war, in any form, potentially became a criminal offence. The legalities were, however, an irrelevancy for Gibbs, for in all his written work he never made a single reference to the threat of serious repercussions for those who did not toe

[6] A Marquis (1978) 'Words as Weapons: Propaganda in Britain and Germany during the First World War' *Journal of Contemporary History* vol. 13, no. 3 July, p. 472.

[7] Marquis, 'Words as Weapons', p. 476.

[8] Marquis, 'Words as Weapons', p. 485.

[9] S Koss (1984) *The Rise and Fall of the Political Press in Britain Vol. 2: The Twentieth Century* (London: Hamish Hamilton), p. 249.

the official line. He did not need to be compelled. Yet as late as 2009, Nicholson in her otherwise excellent study of Britain in the immediate post-war years wrote about journalists such as Gibbs that they 'fear[ed] prosecution if they told the truth'.[10]

Nevertheless, such unanimity made it impossible for any 'rebellion' against censorship to succeed if it emanated from the level of the correspondent. It would have to start at the top, a reality evident in Harmsworth's campaign against Lord Kitchener during the 'Shell Scandal' which was in part responsible for the fall of the Asquith government.[11] Even had the correspondents and the newspaper proprietors been unified in their opposition to the war or its execution, they would, as Moorcraft and Taylor observed, have found it almost impossible 'to sail against the tide of national fervour'.[12] Gibbs and his fellow correspondents thus worked in a profession and served a cause which saw the pursuit of victory and the role of the press in the propaganda war as a just and moral activity.

Gibbs and the correspondents were certainly not alone amongst the nation's writers in accepting that their talents and their profession would find a legitimate and honourable role in the war against Germany. For example, within a month of the outbreak of war as Gibbs wandered about France looking for a German Army to write about, a meeting took place at Wellington House in London under the direction of CFG Masterman, the recently appointed Chief of British war propaganda.[13] Present were 25 of Britain's most respected authors, including HG Wells, Thomas Hardy, John Masefield, Ford Madox Ford, Sir Henry Newbolt, GK Chesterton, Sir Arthur Conan Doyle, and John Buchan. Without need for coercion, and without any sense of being morally compromised, to a man they indicated their preparedness to participate in a propaganda war. As Peter Buitenhuis observed, 'seldom in recorded history have a nation's

---

[10] J Nicolson (2009) *The Great Silence: Britain from the Shadow of the First World War to the Dawn of the Jazz Age* (New York: Grove Press), p. 19.

[11] J Hohenberg (1964) *Foreign Correspondence: The Great Reporters and Their Times* (London: Columbia University Press), p. 217.

[12] P Moorcroft & P Taylor (2008) *Shooting the Messenger—The Political Impact of Reporting* (Washington: Potomac Books), p. 43.

[13] See P Buitenhuis (1987) *The Great War of Words: British, American and Canadian Propaganda and Fiction, 1914-1933* (Vancouver: University of British Columbia Press), p. xv–aviii<AU: Please clarify whether the page number is correct.>; GS Messinger (1992) *British propaganda and the state in the First World War.* (Manchester: Manchester University Press), pp. 24–52.

writers so unreservedly rallied round a national cause'.[14] It also raised what Messinger saw as the 'ancient problem of the individual thinkers need[ing] to balance obligations to state and society against allegiance to personal perceptions of rightness and the truth'.[15] That view is, of course, predicated on the assumption that a balancing act is required, for there is no evidence that Gibbs was conscious of the moral implications of what he wrote or what he refrained from writing. He was painfully conscious of his privileged position as a writer, but never conceded he was anything but honest in his writing within parameters that he publically acknowledged.

Five days later, on 7 September 1914, Masterman chaired a second meeting which in its own way lost nothing in comparison to his gathering of writers. The list of invitees was a gathering of the most influential editors in the English-speaking world: Sidley Brookes, Sir Edward Tyas Cook, Robert Donald (the *Daily Chronicle*), AG Gardiner (the *Daily News*), JL Garvin (the *Pall Mall Gazette*), the Hon. HLW Lawson (the *Daily Telegraph*), Sidney Low (the *Standard*), Thomas Marlowe (the *Daily Mail*), Sir William Robertson Nicoll (the *British Weekly*), Geoffrey Robinson (*The Times*), J Alfred Spender (the *Westminster Gazette*), St Loe Strachey (*The Spectator*), Fabian Ware, AS Watt, and the Under Secretary for Foreign Affairs.[16] Broadly speaking, the group committed themselves just as willingly as their literary counterparts. Masterman himself eschewed the fabrication of news, preferring instead the careful selection and presentation of facts. Despite Masterman's own preference for secrecy, the press support for the war effort was still far from being a criminal conspiracy arrived at in a clandestine manner. For by subsequently drawing the press lords into the government, this system was subject to considerable public debate and scrutiny. The decision that the exigencies of war required such a merging of press and politics was thus an open one, and one that rendered the question of official censorship and the press largely a 'dead letter'.[17] The whole fabric of news gathering was thus enlisted in the war effort, and it does critics well to remember that Gibbs actually had to operate in a system that had given itself over, unashamedly and in many cases as the result of sincere conviction, to the successful prosecution of the war.

[14] Buitenhuis, *The Great War of Words*, p. xv.
[15] Messinger, *British Propaganda*, p. 25.
[16] Messinger, *British Propaganda*, p. 36.
[17] Marquis, 'Words as Weapons,' p. 474.

The subsequent attempts at censorship were ad hoc and, in the case of Sir George Riddell's weekly rounds of the Press Bureau, Admiralty, War Office, Foreign Office, and other departments and his subsequent disseminating of his findings at a weekly news conference, strikingly informal. When a Department of Information was formally organized in January 1917 under Colonel John Buchan and coordinated by the First Lord of the Admiralty, Sir Edward H Carson, the advisory board included Lord Harmsworth; Lord Burnham, managing proprietor of the *Daily Telegraph*; Robert Donald, editor of the *Daily Chronicle*; CP Scott; Lord Beaverbrook; and Sir George Riddell. It was, as Bruntz observed, a roster of British press lords.[18] In February 1918, the Foreign Office was given control of propaganda with Robert Donald, Gibbs' superior at the *Daily Chronicle*, in charge of propaganda in neutral countries. When it was centralized the following month under Lord Beaverbrook, the question was asked in Parliament whether there were dangers inherent in the blurring of the lines between press and politics, even though it was merely part of a process which regularized a pre-existing relationship.

There were, however, muted criticisms of censorship, some emanating from Gibbs himself. Yet the one quality that most of these criticisms shared is that they were invariably 'less doctrinaire and focused upon the anomalies'.[19] Lord Burnham of the *Daily Telegraph* was angered by the emasculation of reports 'when war correspondents were locked up in stalls by a corporal's guard' while *The Times* felt hampered by a 'vigorous censorship' administered by officials whose 'incompetence' exceeded their 'common sense'.[20] Like Gibbs' complaints about censorship during the Balkan War in 1912, these criticisms say as much, if not more, about issues of class and attitudes to bureaucracy than being in any way representative of a wider dissatisfaction with government/press relations or the need for censorship. More in keeping with the general sense of national submission was the admonishment of the Liberals by Gibbs' own paper, the *Daily Chronicle*:

> Liberals who are inclined to wax warm (as we notice some are) on behalf of the abstract freedom of the Press would do well to ask themselves whether

[18] Bruntz (1938) *Allied Propaganda and the collapse of the German Empire in 1918.* (California: Stanford University Press), pp. 22–3.

[19] Koss, *The Rise and Fall of the Political Press*, p. 242.

[20] History of the Times, IV, part 1, p. 220. Quoted in Koss, *The Rise and Fall of the Political Press in Britain*, p. 241.

the way to make Liberalism and democracy triumph in the world is to impose on Liberal democracies in war-time such a gigantic military handicap as an uncensored Press would be.[21]

The extent to which the press was complicit in the control of the news is evident in the fact that the one major exception to the tendency of the government to steadily tighten its control over society was actually in the area of press censorship.[22] At the end of 1915, the legal responsibility for censorship was handed to the newspapers themselves, who by then had proven their loyalty. Gibbs was a servant of a system, therefore, which was committed to the defeat of Germany and cognizant of the role it was expected to play. Closer to the truth than the simplistic criticism of the honesty of the correspondents is the inescapable conclusion that Gibbs, like the bulk of English society, supported the war effort. He was an ideological devotee. He was not bribed. He was rewarded for serving England in a manner he saw as moral and just. As was the case with his fellow correspondents, Gibbs railed against the stupendous cost of the war and though he recognized shortcomings in its execution, in his view, Germany had to be defeated. It is in the very nature of human fallibility that we are all condemned to work in systems that are imperfect.

It was not merely systemic faults which militated against accurate reporting, nor even the obsolescence of the role of the correspondent. It was also the very language used by the correspondents. In representing the war using the traditional rhetoric, a 'set of abstractions that expressed traditional martial and patriotic values', the correspondents, as Hynes observed, misrepresented it. It was not as a significant proportion of pre-war society had expected, an adventure or crusade, but rather a 'valueless, formless experience that could not be rendered in the language, the images, and the conventions that existed'. Hampered by this increasingly outmoded rhetoric, the correspondents gave the war 'meaning, dignity, order, greatness'.[23] The truth, which Gibbs came to understand, was that all too often it was futile, undignified, disordered, and petty.

[21] *Daily Chronicle*, 9 November 1915.

[22] See Koss, *The Rise and Fall of the Political Press*, p. 245.

[23] Samuel Hynes (1991) *A War Imagined: The First World War and English Culture* (New York: Atheneum), p. 108.

Fussell saw this failure of rhetoric as a 'collision between events and the language available—or thought appropriate—to describe them'.[24] He posed the rhetorical question of whether there is, in fact, 'any way of compromising between the reader's expectations that written history ought to be interesting and meaningful, and the cruel fact that much of what happens—all of what happens?—is inherently without "meaning"'.[25] Confronted with the need to write about events which were part of an 'all-but-incommunicable reality', writers appealed to the sympathy of their readers 'by invoking the familiar'. They were thus consigned to the unenviable task of describing a new and terrible reality using 'the available language of traditional literature'. The same author identified an 'atmosphere of euphemism as rigorous and impenetrable as language and literature skilfully used could make it' and the almost antithetical use of unashamed sentiment and utter sangfroid as supporting players in efforts to make sense of the war.[26] In one report on 18 July 1916, Gibbs actually resorted to all three means in a single description of street fighting in the town of Ovilles. In the hand-to-hand fighting in the rubble and cellars of smashed buildings, there had been 'no sentiment', a euphemism which is only half resolved by the additional description that the soldiers 'had flung themselves upon each other with bombs and weapons of any kind'. The question remains as to what Gibbs wished to communicate—is he referring to the ferocity of the fighting, the brutality of using ad hoc weapons, which may or may not have been clubs, shovels, and rocks, or does it hint at a refusal to take prisoners in the heat of battle. Perhaps it was nothing more than Gibbs' own imaginative reconstruction of what it may have been like, but he clearly and with intent left part of his job to the readers' imaginations. Once combat is complete, however, he reverts to sentiment in his description of the eventual surrender of the 'last of the German garrison [a descriptor which gives the desperate defence an ordered and meaningful character] being received with the honours of war, and none of our soldiers denies them the respect due to great courage'. Finally, Gibbs celebrated the sangfroid, or what Fussell described as the 'British Phlegm'

[24] P Fussell (2000) *The Great War and Modern Memory* (Oxford: Oxford University Press), p. 169.
[25] Fussell, *The Great War and Modern Memory*, p. 172.
[26] Fussell, *The Great War and Modern Memory*, p. 174.

by quoting a participant in the fighting observing that the Germans had 'stuck it splendidly'.[27]

Regardless of the literary tools which Gibbs made ample use of, it was, nevertheless, a war which appeared to the greater part of Western Europe and the British Empire as one that had to be won. It was a view which Gibbs shared, and it is simplistic to write of the lies of the correspondents as though the tragedies of the Somme and Flanders might have been averted if only they had told the 'truth'. Gibbs was conscious that he was working in a flawed system and was always open about what he was free to describe. Any regular reader of his dispatches should have been aware that the articles were subject to the dictates of officialdom. Though he wore a uniform and had the honorary rank of captain, he had no military training. Even with greater access to the Front, he needed to gain experience to make sense of what he observed. The war was initially beyond the understanding of the military, and to expect a journalist to unravel its mysteries and interpret it in a manner accessible to the public at large is absurd. Gibbs did not understand the fighting on the Somme in July 1916 any more than the military caste who misdirected it so calamitously. The British Army, which reached Mons in November 1918, bore only a passing resemblance to the one which had fought there four years before. Gibbs' correspondence had also evolved, and it is simplistic to criticize his work without recognizing that he too had been altered by his experience of war.

Even writers such as Moorcraft and Taylor who argued that censorship forced the press to 'peddle fantasies' added as way of mitigation that many of the correspondents were 'psychologically numbed by the vast landscapes of horror caused by total war'.[28] Gibbs also came to this realization in the immediate post-war years, for, by 1920, he acknowledged that he had been 'overwhelmed' by the 'vastness and horror'.[29] Gibbs was equally aware of other pressures, which the same authors saw as nothing less than the correspondents being 'traduced by a sense of duty, patriotism, and front line bonding' and thus succumbing to the most 'corrosive dictatorship of all: self-censorship'.[30] This was a process repeated in

---

[27] Fussell, *The Great War and Modern Memory*, p. 175; P Gibbs (1916) *The Battles of the Somme* (London: William Heinemann), pp. 136–7.

[28] Moorcraft, *Shooting the Messenger*, p. 43.

[29] P Gibbs (1936) *Realities of War* (London: Hutchinson & Co Ltd), p. 70.

[30] Moorcraft, *Shooting the Messenger*, p. 43.

the press' initial treatment of political issues on the domestic front, during which there was a 'clear editorial determination to maintain national solidarity'.[31] This was itself an extension of the political truce between the parties agreed upon on the outbreak of war. The unintended consequence of this uneasy truce was that the press become the forum in which politicians vented political antagonisms. To their great discredit, this was an activity pursued with the 'connivance of top ranking parliamentarians and often at their instigation'.[32] The abrogation of the responsibilities of a free press and the attempted suspension of party politics were widely perceived as being in the national interest. Such a surrender, though freely offered, is indicative of the difficulties faced by a democracy when waging war against a more autocratic government.

Though it is simplistic to refer to the press as a homogeneous whole, as a group, they did grow increasingly impatient with this political and military stalemate, seeing both a need and an opportunity to seize the initiative. Added to this was the interplay of events in late 1914 and early 1915—the push for conscription, the munitions scandal, the Bryce Report into German atrocities, the sinking of the *Lusitania*, and the resignation of Lord Fisher as First Sea Lord—which saw the press cease its attempts to galvanize the government and look instead to transform it, a shift which contributed to the eventual formation of a coalition government.[33] The conditions which had rendered the nation's politicians more 'reticent, owing to their determination to foster a spirit of unity', had quite the opposite effect on domestic journalism. For all their support of the war effort generally, by the first decade of the twentieth century, fewer newspapers could be readily pigeonholed as organs of any political party. It left the fourth estate 'more anxious, more presumptuous, and more reckless'.[34] Yet at the same time, the official accreditation of the correspondents ensured that they were less anxious, less presumptuous, and far less inclined to offer a dissenting voice. The correspondents found themselves tied, by instinct, temperament, personal conviction, and if need be, the law, to the one group which could lay claim to each of their loyalties—the army. It was the one organization which appeared a truly national

---

[31] Koss, *The Rise and Fall of the Political Press in Britain*, p. 243.
[32] Koss, *The Rise and Fall of the Political Press in Britain*, p. 238.
[33] Koss, *The Rise and Fall of the Political Press in Britain*, p. 275.
[34] Koss, *The Rise and Fall of the Political Press in Britain*, p. 275.

institution and was thus able to lay claim to their loyalty far more bindingly than a mere political connection.

Beyond even that, there was also what Koss termed a 'popular pressure'. When the *Daily Mail* railed against Kitchener's 'latest tragic blunder' in May 1915, copies were burnt at the London Stock Exchange, and copies 'banished' from the Service Clubs in Pall Mall. More pressing than the ceremonial rebukes was the loss of revenue judged to be in excess of £100,000. Wartime shortages in machinery and newsprint ensured that newspapers were involved in their own battle for survival, a situation that made it unlikely for them to pursue any course of action other than offer their submission. As Koss observed, 'collusion, if it could be obtained, was always preferable to collision'.[35] The First World War brought particular problems for the rapidly developing modern British press. Both the Admiralty and the War Office censored war news from the beginning, and soon there was an Official Press Bureau to which editors had to submit all controversial items for scrutiny. The press remained both independent and commercially acute, however. Marwick argued that far from being a question of the correspondents colluding with the army or even the government, the press merely continued its old habit of going in for 'stunts and sensationalism rather than calculated brainwashing. Headlines got bigger and bolder, effecting a permanent change in newspaper presentation, but the patriotic rubbish printed remained the invention of proprietors and editors rather than of governments'.[36] Though the axiom that the British Army was comprised of lions being led by donkeys has maintained a remarkable currency, it is too simplistic to really serve a useful analytical purpose. It might have been more prudent to state that the British soldiers fought better than their government or military leaders deserved, a far less polemic argument. One might also argue that for all their faults, Britain was better served by her correspondents than any country with so submissive a population and so compliant a press could legitimately demand.

The very role of the foreign correspondent proved an unsuitable vehicle for the dissemination of war reports. During the rush to gain accreditation as an official correspondent, Gibbs observed at the War Office a procession of 'literary adventurers...lost somewhere between one war and another [with] claims of ancient service on the battlefields of Europe when

[35] Koss, *The Rise and Fall of the Political Press in Britain*, pp. 243–5.
[36] A Marwick (1965) *The Deluge: British Society and the First World War* (London: Bodley Head), p. 51.

the smell of blood is scented from afar; and scores of new men of sporting instincts and jaunty confidence eager to be in the middle of things'.[37] These men were the dying echoes of the golden age of the foreign correspondent, whose dispatches prior to the war, 'though they hinted at travels through "dangerous" and "exotic" landscapes...were frequently scripted from a position of moral and physical distance'.[38] This age of the journalist as spectator had been personified by men such as William Howard Russell of *The Times*, George Warrington Steevens of the *Daily Mail*, Arthur Conan Doyle, and Rudyard Kipling, who all had reported on Britain's imperial exploits. They were, as Bruno observed, both voyeurs and voyagers, and though they were not the 'key actors in life's innumerable dramas, they were witnesses whose writings were the product of embodied proximity and disembodied detachment'.[39] Gibbs acknowledged this when he described himself in the immediate pre-war period as an 'outsider and looker on following the Edwardian pageant'.[40] The notion of detached analysis was rendered not only obsolete but was reduced to an irrelevancy by the demands of the Western Front and a national call to arms in a way it could never have been by the odd calamity such as an Isalandwana or a fall of Khartoum. As wars grew in scale and censorship restrictions inhibited reportage, these correspondents were challenged by immobile interpreters, making use of the telegraph to write reports from London. Clearly, it was not only military tactics which were to prove unsuitable in this new war.

The correspondents were therefore hampered in their attempts to describe the titanic struggles on the Western Front which involved their countrymen in a war of national survival within this 'prescribed set of possibilities, embedded in a system of conventions and limitations'.[41] As a result, some reporters, and Gibbs must be numbered among these, wrote 'graphic, theatrical, action and actor focused dispatches that appealed to a burgeoning readership'.[42] It was this paradigm and the presentation of battle as an extended heroic narrative which informed the work of the

---

[37] Gibbs (1915) *The Soul of the War* (London: William Heinemann), p. 5.

[38] Farish, *Modern Witnesses*, p. 273.

[39] G. Bruno (1977) 'Site seeing: architecture and the moving image'. Wide Angle, vol. 19; Farish, Modern Witnesses, p. 276.

[40] P Gibbs (1949) *Crowded Company* (London: Allan Wingate), p. 21.

[41] J Crary (1990) *Techniques of the Observer: On Vision and Modernity in the Nineteenth Century* (Cambridge, MA: MIT Press), p. 6.

[42] Farish, *Modern Witnesses*, p. 276.

correspondents when they were thrust into a war they could see little of and understand even less. Critics of the war dispatches often ignore this context and instead offer critiques more informed by modern sensibilities than those existing in 1914. For in the same way antiquated notions of warfare hampered the military, this older paradigm of reporting constrained the correspondents.

Gibbs' dispatches were even less likely to survive scrutiny by audiences in post-war assessments because by then his staunchly liberal view of England, which was at the core of his world view, was increasingly an anachronism. For by the interwar years, liberalism, as a philosophy, 'had lost its cohesiveness and much of its relevance to the problems of the age' and was thus rendered unable to consistently offer voters a credible third option to the Conservatives and the new labour parties.[43] Certainly, by the mid-1930s, it had been reduced 'to a forlorn remnant of its former self' whose eventual departure from government 'was a drawn out and not especially dignified affair'.[44]

When assessing the work of the war correspondents, it is also important to remember that there was no consistent pattern in their treatment. Censorship as a whole reflected the wartime fortunes of the belligerents— in Britain it became progressively more organized after a chaotic start, while in Germany, it disintegrated as her war effort collapsed. But more specifically, the place of the English correspondent had three major phases.[45] Between August 1914 and May 1915, they were outlaws, liable to arrest on sight. From May 1915 to April 1917, there was some acceptance of their role, but they were closely controlled and hampered by attempts to waste their time. From April 1917 until the Armistice, the war correspondents were valued as weapons in the propaganda war and the military went to great lengths to grant them access to the Front. The detail in their reports, which increased exponentially during the third phase of this relationship, is actually quite striking. Gibbs' reports from his period as a 'freelance' prior to official accreditation were action and actor-focused dispatches, and though they never lost this quality, as the war progressed, there was almost an avalanche of detail which would have overwhelmed any correspondent. After the embarrassment of heralding the battle of

[43] G Craig (1966) *Europe since 1815* (New York: Holt, Rinehart & Winston), p. 264.

[44] D Powell (2004) *British Politics, 1910-1935: The Crisis of the Party System* (London: Routledge), p. 176.

[45] Farrar, *News from the Front*, p. x.

the Somme as a victory, there was also greater care to avoid premature celebrations of victory.

It is against the background of these pressures that many of Gibbs' increasingly frustrated contemporaries waited for official accreditation in the weeks and months after the outbreak of war. For his part, Gibbs was already describing events in a style he had honed in peacetime. His wartime writing would exhibit the same tone of heroic narrative that made his descriptions of the *Titanic* disaster so popular. Though it was a style which was soon to be rendered inadequate as an explanatory tool by the scope of the conflict, it was still clearly evident in one of Gibbs' earliest descriptions of an England now at war. Though he had gently mocked those with claims of 'ancient service' on the battlefields of Europe, there was nothing modern in Gibbs' description of the approach of war:

> What man may lay bare the soul of England as it was stirred during those days of July when suddenly, without any previous warning, loud enough to reach the ears of the mass of people, there came the menace of a great bloody war, threatening all that had seemed so safe and so certain in our daily life? England suffered in those summer days a shock which thrilled to its heart and brain with an enormous emotion such as a man who has been careless of truth and virtue experiences at a 'Revivalist' meeting or at a Catholic mission when some passionate preacher breaks the hard crust of his carelessness and convinces him that death and the judgement are very near, and that all the rottenness of his being will be tested in the furnace of a spiritual agony.[46]

Ten years after the outbreak of war, Gibbs still believed that it was 'as though the nation had been shaken by a great wind in which the voice of God was heard'. He saw in the call to arms a 'nobility of purpose' which only the newspaper press 'vulgarized and degraded' by its appeal to 'blood lust and its call to hate and many frantic lies'.[47] Gibbs' words echo Rupert Brooke's belief that youth had been 'wakened...from sleeping' and could now turn 'from a world grown old and cold and weary'.[48] It was also a view which had a strong thematic link to the work of the Victorian social critics such as Carlyle who had helped shape Gibbs' ideology prior to the

[46] Gibbs, *The Soul of the War*, p. 1.
[47] P Gibbs (1924) *Ten Years After* (London: Hutchinson & Co), pp. 18–20.
[48] Rupert Brooke, 'Peace'. In M Harrison & Stuart Clark C (1989) *Peace and War* (New York: Oxford University Press), p. 38.

War. Social critics had observed an increasingly plutocratic and industrialized England, yet one which possessed an ever more alienated urban poor which had little share in the growing affluence. This knowledge contrasted with an idealized view of the past dominated by a 'lost, rural England that had been simple and more decent and, somehow, more English'. It was a mix of social guilt and nostalgia which Carlyle described as 'the Condition of England problem'. War, with its discomfort, its male asceticism, and its sacrifice, was the physical as well as the spiritual opposite of Edwardian luxury. War might both cleanse and purify, becoming in the process a cure for this 'condition'.[49]

Though in his late thirties, and possessing a frail physique and a temperament he himself recognized as too sensitive, Gibbs won a roving commission, first as artist correspondent to *The Graphic*, and a few days after the declaration of war as correspondent for the *Daily Chronicle*. He left for Paris without official accreditation on the night of 29 July, still incredulous that war might actually break out and that Britain 'might be engaged in the greatest war since the Napoleonic era, fighting for her life'.[50] He described the next seven months as a period of freelance adventure, ended only by the belated granting of official status as a war correspondent in May 1915. Outwardly, there was little evidence that Gibbs was equal to a task, which he later described as the 'most stupendous experience of life'.[51] One of his fellow correspondents remembered him at Charing Cross Station prior to his departure for the Continent and expressed surprise that he had survived the war:

> Anxious, he didn't know where he was going; for the matter of that he rarely does. Like a sound modern journalist he gives himself into the charge of events, to let them do what they like with him. He hands himself over to luck and trusts solely to Joss...Philip Gibbs still goes on, pallid as ever, tense, frail, his small mouth a little open like the beak of a startled bird. He always reminded me of a bird, acting by instinct, quick, capricious, uncertain whether he was on the right perch, apparently delicate, but able to travel further than a locomotive.[52]

[49] For a sense of this as a theme in Edwardian England, see CFG Masterman's *The Condition of England* (1909), HG Wells *Tono-Bungay* (1909), EM Foster's *Howard's End* (1910), and E Gosse *War and Literature* (1914). For a discussion of the effect on English thinking at the outbreak of war, see Hynes (1991) *A War Imagined*.

[50] P Gibbs, *Realities of War*, p. 22.

[51] P Gibbs (1923) *Adventures in Journalism* (London: Harper and Brothers Publishers), p. 260.

[52] *New York Times*, 21 September 1918.

His old neighbour and friend GK Chesterton, who believed him to be 'perhaps the first and finest war correspondent', also commented on his bird-like appearance:

> His features are very fine after the fashion of what I can only call a delicate falcon—a falcon not in the best of health...He looked like a grave and gifted man of letters: but he looked superficially at least, as if he were rather for the study than the stage, as the bad writers say about Shakespeare.[53]

Six years after the war ended, Overton sought to balance the sensitive, fragile Gibbs with the one able to endure the horrors of the Western Front. In his view, Gibbs was 'both timid and bashful; yet like many men of his stamp, he was to show on many occasions a lion like courage'.[54] His bother Cosmo also understood how ill-suited Gibbs first appeared for the role of war correspondent:

> Only the official war correspondents who watched his feverish work under the handicap of continual nervous strain upon a constitution that was only held together by a determined mastery of mind over matter and a high sense of duty, could give a true picture of this man during all those years—the master pacifist in uniform, tapping nightly on his typewriter those documents of human effort and almost indescribable suffering that were read with such emotion and exaltation by the English speaking world.

Cosmo's description, one of the rare insights into Gibbs' pre-war life, included the observation that his 'delicate' and 'fragile' younger brother had been a 'martyr to nervous breakdowns before the war'. Nowhere else in any published work is there reference to Gibbs having struggled with what might be termed a mental health issue. Cosmo does not explore this issue, using it only as a vehicle to emphasize that there was 'something a little misleading in his ascetic face and small frame, because he was capable, then at any rate, of greater physical and mental strain than men of far stronger physique, and every time he ought by rights to have been dead he was up and at it again and yet again'.[55]

As if determined to appear the innocent abroad, Gibbs arrived in Paris clad in a lounge suit and carrying a walking stick. Here he witnessed the

---

[53] *New York Times,* 22 October 1916.
[54] Overton, *Cargoes for Crusoes,* p. 17.
[55] C Hamilton (1924) *Unwritten History* (London: Hutchinson & Co), p. 161.

first scenes of mobilization, but found in the French Ministry of War an organization equally opposed to war correspondents as their British counterpart.[56] In contrast to his attitude after official accreditation, Gibbs was quite open in his criticism of censorship, writing as he was with the freedom of the outsider. He believed that 'by one swift stroke of military censorship journalism was throttled...Pains and penalties were threatened against any newspaper which should dare to publish a word of military information beyond the official communiqués issued in order to hide the truth'.[57] Yet even when confronted by this determined attempt to curtail the freedom of the press, Gibbs noted that it was by 'fair and courteous words'.[58]

Frustrated by official opposition and sensing that beyond Paris 'history was being made', Gibbs boarded a train to Nancy with the first of the French reservists on the night of 2 August.[59] In Nancy, he interviewed Foch's Chief of Staff, but then returned to Paris to seek official sanction to report on the approaching conflict. No doubt chastened by his earlier experiences in the Balkans, Gibbs waited in Paris only a few days before setting out in search of the German Army which was then storming into Belgium.[60] As the British Expeditionary Force (BEF) did not begin mobilizing until 5 August and did not see action until 23 August, Gibbs spent most of the early weeks of the war almost exclusively with the French and Belgians. Regardless of the subsequent controversy over official censorship, his early reports were indeed a 'triumph of enterprise and insight', achieved as they were in the face of significant official opposition.[61] Gibbs rightly described the correspondents as 'outlaws, subject to immediate arrest (and often arrested) by any officer, French or British who discovered us in the war zone'. He was ill-suited to the role of a rebel, however, and in 1923 criticized Kitchener's refusal to sanction the scheme which would

---

[56] In 1914, the French Army numbered 736,000, with a potential strength of 3.5 million. During the opening campaigns, France would commit 1.65 million men to battle.

[57] Gibbs, *The Soul of the War*, p. 40.

[58] Gibbs, *The Soul of the War*, p. 45.

[59] Gibbs, *The Soul of the War*, p. 45.

[60] The German war plan, named for its architect, Count Alfred von Schlieffen, called for them to stand on the defensive in the east and on their left flank in the west, while four armies struck through Belgium, Luxembourg, and Northern France on their right. It was the violation of Belgian neutrality which ostensibly brought Britain into the war.

[61] *The Times*, 12 March 1962.

have dispatched a small body of war correspondents 'whose honour and reputation were acknowledged'.[62]

Much of the early discussion concerning war correspondents became purely academic on 5 August 1914, when Lord Kitchener assumed the post of Secretary of War and banned the war correspondents from entering a military zone around the BEF and placed the War Office firmly between the correspondent and the public by demanding that dispatches be submitted to them for authorization. Kitchener's contempt for the war correspondent was firmly engrained. In the Sudan, his tactics were to make the 26 correspondents with him 'run exactly the same risks as his soldiers, to limit their telegraphic facilities to 200 words a day, and to give them no help, no briefings, no guidance, and little courtesy. It was not surprising that they hated him, and his disdain for them was behind what was to happen over war news at the outbreak of the First World War'.[63] Kitchener was not content with merely reacting to the work of the correspondents, but also sought to take the battle to the enemy. He created a Press Bureau under FE Smith[64] whose task it was to censor news reports from the army and then to issue information to the domestic and international press. These reports were intentionally devoid of any real news and, as Farrar noted, sought merely to limit or remove the power of the correspondent and provide the newspapers with a distraction.[65] The first report released on 11 August 1914 by the Bureau contained out-of-date information presented in a bland fashion which was unlikely to meet the growing clamour for news from the Front. This was only part, however, of a much wider process centred on DORA which drastically increased the government's ability and legal right to control the dissemination of news. It was effective enough to apparently warrant favourable comment in *Mein Kampf*. Even before Hitler's unwanted endorsement, the English had reached the same conclusion. Out of a mixture of 'moral repugnance' and a growing concern about the power of the press barons, allied with the much more practical considerations of post-war relevance, much of this infrastructure was dismantled almost immediately the war was won.[66]

[62] Gibbs, *Adventures in Journalism*, p. 236.

[63] Knightley, *The First Casualty*, p. 54.

[64] Frederick Edwin Smith, 1st Earl of Birkenhead (1872–1930). In 1917, the Press Bureau was subsumed into the Department of Information which was made a full ministry the following year.

[65] Farrar, *News from the Front*, p. 7.

[66] Moorcraft, *Shooting the Messenger*, p. 35.

Yet it was not as intrusive as critics of censorship might have it. As an institution, it was quite deservedly characterized as a 'meddlesome woman' who, 'though not lacking teeth, had no real need to bite'.[67]

The complicity of the newspapers themselves in the subsequent censorship is well documented in the *Daily Chronicle's* mission statement which was published in the first week of the war. It left Gibbs answerable to both his employer and to the army; although given the close alliance between the two, this did not prove as untenable a situation as it might now appear. Once he was officially accredited, the army assumed the role of a de facto employer, removing any real chance of a correspondent being hampered by divided loyalties:

> A newspaper's duty is to give news, but at times of war it has a patriotic duty as well. It must give no news which would convey information of advantage to the adversary. Throughout this war the *Daily Chronicle* will refrain from indicating the location and movements of warships and units of the army. At the same time the *Daily Chronicle* has taken complete and energetic measures to supply its readers with full intelligence from every part of the war areas. The censorship that we exercise over our news will not affect its value to the ordinary reader of the paper. The special correspondents of the *Daily Chronicle* are men of worldwide repute, experienced in war, vivid descriptive writers and brilliant news-getters.[68]

Temperamentally and ideologically, Gibbs was well suited to this style of reporting. For example, his description of the young men of France answering the call to arms is classic Gibbs—emotive, broadly religious, and delivered with an eye for the personal:

> Fate had come with the little card summoning each man to join his depot, and tapped him on the shoulder with just a finger touch. It was no more than that—a touch on the shoulder. Yet I know that for many of those young men it seemed a blow between the eyes, and, to some of them, a strangle grip as icy cold as though Death's fingers were already closing round their throats…The French women gave their men to 'La Patrie' with the resignation of religious women who offer their hearts to God. Some spiritual fervour, which in France permeates the sentiment of patriotism, giving a beauty to that tradition of nationalism.[69]

[67] Koss, *The Rise and Fall of the Political Press*, p. 240.
[68] *Daily Chronicle*, 7 August 1914.
[69] Gibbs, *The Soul of the War*, pp. 23–6.

In a 'prolonged nightmare' of ten weeks, Gibbs, like the other corre-spondents, wandered back and forth between the west coast ports and the Allied armies, relying on luck to stumble across something newsworthy.[70] William Beach Thomas, who was also knighted at the end of the war, was then also involved in 'the longest walking tour of my life, and the queer-est'. Like Gibbs, he saw nothing of the actual fighting and instead also cov-ered many 'human stories'.[71] Gibbs travelled with two colleagues, who he initially identified as 'the philosopher' and 'the strategist' (in *Adventures in Journalism* he identified them as Henry Major Tomlinson and WM Massey). Given that Tomlinson was an avowed pacifist, it is unsurprising that Gibbs would characterize him as a philosopher. In contrast to Gibbs, who never quite lost his idealism, Tomlinson was disillusioned prior to his experiences on the Western Front. Yet for some, however, he was the best of the war correspondents.[72] This did not save him from being recalled to England in the spring of 1917 on the grounds, he believed, of his humani-tarian leanings.[73] Not surprisingly, Tomlinson was overlooked for a knight-hood when the other correspondents were, in Knightley's view, rewarded for their silence. Gibbs, who had enormous respect for Tomlinson, felt that the war 'scorched his soul. The agony of it, the waste of it—all that young life—ate into his heart. The terror of it, the fury of it, the filth of it, the moral insanity of it, was to him the abomination of desolation in a world gone mad'.[74] Beach Thomas felt that it was a liberal education to hear Tomlinson tell 'a high Tory General that he, the General, was a cog in a marvellously socialist State, paid by the State, fed by the State, given a particular job with other men all fed, paid and compelled by the State to do particular work in a national cause'.[75]

In the 'vortex of the French retreat', conditions were far too chaotic to enforce the draconian decrees restricting correspondents.[76] Gibbs was able to blend in with the thousands of refugees, trusting to his charm

---

[70] Gibbs, *The Soul of the War*, p. 45.

[71] William Beach Thomas (1925) *A Traveller in News* (London: Chapman and Hall), p. 59.

[72] Arnold Bennett, in Stanley Weintraub (1971) *Journey to Heartbreak: The Crucible Years of Bernard Shaw 1914-1918* (New York: Weybright & Talby), p. 216.

[73] Henry Tomlinson, 'Adelphi Terrace'. In HJ Massingham (ed) (1925) *HWM: A Selection from the Writings of HW Massingham*, New York: Harcourt Brace), p. 121.

[74] P Gibbs (1949) *Crowded Company* (London: Allan Wingate), p. 126.

[75] Beach Thomas, *A Traveller in News*, p. 133.

[76] Gibbs, *The Soul of the War*, p. 72.

and luck while waving a pass stamped by French Headquarters permitting
him to receive the daily communiqué from the War Office in Paris and
dozens of other passes and permits from local authorities and police. It
was, as Farrar argued, a hit-and-miss approach which ensured that articles
were dominated by descriptions of the effects of battle rather than first-
hand accounts of the fighting.[77] This physical separation from the action is
reflected in Gibbs' reports when they were published in book form in *The
Soul of the War*, which did not document even a single first-hand account
of the fighting. Gibbs' publisher, William Heinemann, nevertheless felt
that it was a 'dangerous book', and both he and Gibbs were surprised that
it escaped censorship. Later in the war, Gibbs found that the censors and
some of the commanding officers he encountered owned a copy. At least
one reviewer felt that the passion of his language suited both the material
and the avowed purpose of its author:

> One may feel at first that in his anxiety, his extreme eagerness to make us
> see and feel what he has seen and felt, he writes in too fevered a style, but
> gradually one realizes that this is not from any cheap striving for effect; it
> comes from a hopeless struggle to find words that shall be adequate. At the
> end of the book, when one knows what Mr Gibbs's experiences have been,
> and realizes, too, the passion that is behind his purpose—so to shock us
> that we may make this war the end of militarism...he cannot write calmly.
> All through the book there is that refrain, the protest of the sensitive man,
> quivering and hurt by what is around him, against the senselessness of war.[78]

Although Gibbs did not witness fighting first hand, he was able to document the retreat of the Allied armies, grimly evidenced in the hundreds
of thousands of refugees pouring down from the north 'out of the black
shadow creeping across the sunlit hills of France, where the enemy, whom
no fugitives had seen, was advancing like a moving tide'. Gibbs also began
to hear that the newly arrived BEF was engaged at Mons and witnessed
for the first time 'English boys, crippled and broken, from an unknown
battle'.[79]

On 30 August 1914, a dispatch written by fellow war correspondent
Arthur Moore which made public the retreat from Mons appeared in *The
Sunday Times*. It was to alter the future of the war correspondents in

---

[77] Farrar, *News from the Front*, p. 25.
[78] *Times Literary Supplement*, 17 June 1915.
[79] Gibbs, *The Soul of the War*, p. 59.

France. Prior to being published, it had been censored by *The Times* and then sent to FE Smith at the Press Bureau, who proceeded to subedit it in an 'after dinner haze'.[80] He reinstated the deletions, rewrote the conclusion to include a call for reinforcements, and returned it for publication. Interestingly, Smith declined to present the dispatch in a coherent form, choosing instead to include ellipses to suggest that the reality of the retreat was even worse than the uncensored dispatch indicated. The public awareness of censorship could not be clearer.

To defend the official reports, which were at odds with Moore's dispatch, the Press Bureau was compelled to point out that 'no correspondents are at the Front, and their information, however honestly sent, is therefore derived at second or third hand from persons who are often in no condition to tell coherent stories'.[81] The Amiens dispatch, as it became known, had a twofold effect. The Press Bureau was caught out withholding bad news, and in compelling it to defend the veracity of its reports, it inadvertently highlighted the continuing refusal to accredit war correspondents, some of whom were still waiting with growing impatience in London. Gibbs felt that the dispatch, which he attributed to Fyfe,[82] was marred by being 'over coloured', but acknowledged that it awakened England to the growing threat:

> As it happened, Massey, Tomlinson, and I had covered the same ground as Fyfe and his companions, had seen the same things, and had agonized with the same apprehension. But owing largely, as I must say honestly and heartily, to the cool judgement and fine faith of Tomlinson, our deduction from those facts and the spirit of what we wrote was far more optimistic—and future history proved us to be right—*so that they helped to restore confidence in England and Scotland when they appeared on Monday morning, following Fyfe's terrible dispatch* [author's italics].[83]

The italicized reference to Gibbs' dispatch serving a purpose other than the unbiased provision of news underlines the fact that there was a widespread openness, perhaps even agreement, about the role of the

---

[80] C Hazlehurst (1971) *Politicians at War July 1914 to May 1915* (London: Jonathan Cape), p. 149.

[81] *The Times*, 31 August 1914.

[82] Fyfe did not write the Amiens dispatch, but rather was the author of a similar article which appeared the following day in the *Daily Mail*.

[83] Gibbs, *Adventures in Journalism*, p. 243.

press in the war. In his own dispatch, published under the headline 'The 100 Hours Fight, Full Story of Mons', Gibbs wrote authoritatively as one who had been in the 'middle of this real business of war'. He noted that it was nevertheless difficult to 'piece together the various incidents and impressions and to make a picture of them' for it seemed 'a jigsaw puzzle of suffering and fear and courage and death—a litter of odd, disconnected scraps of human agony and of some big grim scheme which, if one could only get the clue, would give a meaning'. Yet the tone was clearly one of reassurance, for despite acknowledgement of the large numbers of wounded 'our main forces...succeeded in withdrawing in good order without having their lines broken, while inflicting terrific casualties on the German right'. In a guarded admonishment of those who were seeing in the retreat a rout, he added that 'retreats which seem fatal when seen close at hand and when described by those who belong to the broken fragments of extended sections are not altogether disastrous in their effect when viewed in the right perspective'.[84]

Two years later, Chesterton, himself a participant in the propaganda war in a manner quite different from Gibbs, supported his friend's assessment, though he was less forgiving of the authors of the dispatch. Nothing in their reports had been as 'admirable' as Gibbs' tone, which had served as a 'corrective to such pessimist hysteria'. For when 'the line of the great alliance went down at Mons' and 'an armed empire seemed bearing down on Paris like a doom', Gibbs had refrained from adding even a single 'needless word to make us despair of it'. In a clear and measured rebuke of those who he felt had added to the hysteria, Chesterton credited Gibbs with the foresight and skill to describe what was a retreat rather than a rout. Chesterton considered it 'one of the blackest marks upon our history that during the strained and difficult operations after Mons the end of the British Army was practically announced in a British Newspaper'.[85] In contrast, Chesterton described Gibbs' style as 'sober exaltation' in which he had been able 'to keep that human detachment...in dealing with the most frightful facts as in dealing with his own fancies'.[86]

By the time Moore's article was published, Gibbs was travelling westward towards the English Channel accompanied by Tomlinson and Massey. They had resolved to get their dispatches to England and then return to

[84] *Daily Chronicle*, 31 August 1914.
[85] *New York Times*, 22 October 1916.
[86] *New York Times*, 22 October 1916.

Paris and report on the expected siege from inside the city. On a train crowded with refugees, Gibbs was tempted to yield up his place. He felt it cowardly to do otherwise, but consoled himself with the thought that 'I had a message for the English people. They too were in anguish because the enemy had come so close to Paris in pursuit of a little army which seemed to have been wiped out behind the screen of secrecy through which only vague and awful rumours came'.[87] Faced with the possibility of the Germans cutting the rail line west of Paris, and perhaps conscious of being an able-bodied man travelling with refugees fleeing the fighting, he melodramatically described his fears of being captured and executed.[88]

Even when Gibbs was able to get dispatches back to England, they were still heavily censored. In Beach Thomas' view, the principle which appeared to underline censorship was that 'the censors would not publish any article if it indicated that the writer had seen what he wrote of. He must write what he thought was true, not what he knew to be true'.[89] Even when a dispatch was written, the difficulty of getting it back to England was ever present. Sometimes, Gibbs was forced to entrust his dispatches to any chance acquaintance headed for England, or at other times he was compelled to journey to the coast and bribe a purser on a cross chan-nel steamer. On three occasions, Gibbs even had dispatches delivered by King's messengers who innocently carried them in their bags, addressed to the *Daily Chronicle*, care of the War Office. Eventually, the newspapers organized for their own couriers to operate between England and France, although they would be sent home once official opposition became more effective.

In a wartime conversation, Gibbs outlined his own philosophy regard-ing the focus of his dispatches. He believed that 'the big things belong to history and will be familiar enough, but afterwards the next generation will search for the intimate records and the psychology of the men who served'.[90] It was a theme which he expanded on at the end of the war when he wrote that '[I] was more interested in the things I had seen than in map references and divisional boundaries'.[91] It was a quality known to his contemporaries, for as Pound suggested, as a novelist Gibbs was

---

[87] Gibbs, *The Soul of the War*, p. 94.
[88] Gibbs, *The Soul of the War*, p. 95.
[89] Beach Thomas, *A Traveller in News*, p. 80.
[90] J Bickersteth (ed) (1995) *The Bickersteth Diaries 1914-1918* (London: Leo Cooper), p. 69.
[91] Gibbs, *Realities of War*, p. 36.

an excellent journalist. It could also be argued that as a journalist he was an excellent novelist. 'Observant, quick witted, and sympathetic' he also possessed 'an unerring eye for the human essentials in any incident and a gift for discovering the significant in the commonplace'.[92] This ability is evident in Gibbs' description of Paris when he returned there from the coast. On 2 September 1914, utterly exhausted and emotionally spent, he found the city seemingly deserted, but still in Allied hands. He wept for a city 'in which so many human hearts have suffered and strived and starved for beauty's sake, in which there have always lived laughter and agony and tears, where Liberty was cherished as well as murdered, and where love has redeemed a thousand crimes'.[93] Gibbs' skill as an observer is further demonstrated when he described the flight of the tens of thousands of refugees:

> It was a pitiful thing to see the deserted houses of the Paris suburbs. It was as though a plague had killed every human being save those who had fled in frantic haste...Roses were blowing in their gardens, full blown because no woman's hand had been to pick them, and spilling their petals on the garden paths...Packing cases littered the trim lawns and cardboard boxes had been flung about. In one small bower I saw a child's perambulator, where two wax dolls sat staring up at the abandoned houses. Their faces had become blotchy in the dew of night, and their little maman with her pigtail had left them to their fate.[94]

His exhaustion was such that he had to be carried to bed by Tomlinson and Massey, for 'we had worn down our nervous strength to what seemed the last strand, yet we went on again, in the wagons of troop trains, sleeping in corridors, the baggage rooms of railway stations, or carriages crammed with French poilus, who told narratives of war with a simplicity and realism that froze one's blood'.[95] One of his companions remembered that we had 'wondered whether we should be found holding his lady like hands and trying to catch his last whispered word when the boche arrived next day. But since then he has got his second wind and has continued in

[92] R Pound, 'Gibbs, Sir Philip Armand Hamilton (1877–1962)', rev. AJA Morris, *Oxford Dictionary of National Biography*, Oxford University Press, 2004, www.oxforddnb.com/view/article/33387, Date retrieved 29 January, 2008.

[93] Gibbs, *The Soul of the War*, p. 103.

[94] Gibbs, *The Soul of the War*, p. 99.

[95] Gibbs, *The Soul of the War*, p. 238.

a way which is nothing less than miraculous to those who think they know him'.[96] Gibbs recovered sufficiently to characterize the experience of the armies holding the road to Paris as an 'heroic story which may be read by any man now living' for he had seen them 'always retiring before an over-powering and irresistible enemy, but never in actual retreat, never fighting a rear-guard action with their backs to the foe, but always face forward, yielding every mile with stubborn and sublime gallantry'.[97] Later when the Germans began to retire eastward, Gibbs saw little of this sacrificial quality in their deaths, for many were 'stabbed in the back as they fled'.[98]

Discontent now became so great at the unnecessary state of ignorance in which the public was being kept that it was decided to compromise with a half measure.[99] War correspondents were still forbidden to visit the Front, but their place was to be taken by an officially sanctioned officer who would provide information to them. The appointment on 7 September 1914 of Colonel Sir Ernest Swinton to the staff of the commander-in-chief to report on the progress of the war under the alias 'Eyewitness' was not indicative of a softening of official opposition. Swinton's reports were first censored in France and then by Kitchener himself, ensuring in his words that he 'could not have given away anything useful to the enemy if I had tried'.[100] Rather than indicating a significant shift in official policy, this was in the view of one writer, the 'start of a period of conspiracy, of deliberate lies, and the suppression of the truth; the foundations of a propaganda process with which we are familiar today'.[101] The inadequacy of these reports is best summed up in the response of one editor—'Eye wash would have been a better pseudonym'.[102] In time, Gibbs also became aware of the general failure of the press during this period. A decade later, he observed that 'reading the English newspapers in those early days of the war, with their stories of starving Germany, their atrocity-mongering, their wild perversions of truth, a journalist proud of his profession must blush for shame at its degradation and insanity'.[103]

[96] *New York Times*, 21 September 1918.
[97] *Daily Chronicle*, 3 September, 1914.
[98] *Daily Chronicle*, 15 September 1914.
[99] E Swinton (1932) *Eyewitness* (London: Hodder & Stoughton), p. 52.
[100] Swinton, *Eyewitness*, pp. 31–2.
[101] Farrar, *News from the Front*, p. 24.
[102] Knightley, *The First Casualty*, p. 86.
[103] Gibbs, *Adventures in Journalism*, p. 233.

It was not until 10 September 1914 when Sir John French's report was published that the English people received official details concerning the retreat from Mons. By that stage, the BEF was fighting on the Marne. Though he was still unable to describe the actual fighting, Gibbs had been able to follow the line of the German retreat to the Marne which had begun on 9 September. He admitted that he had not yet seen 'the real work of war',[104] but here along the line of the retreat Gibbs was truly confronted with the 'misery and death which [had] flung its horror across the fair fields of France'.[105]

> Nature itself was fouled and the old dwelling places of peace were wrecked. Fighting their way back the enemy had burned many villages, or had defended them against a withering fire from the pursuing troops, so that their blackened stumps of timber, and charred, broken walls, with heaps of ashes which were once farmhouses and barns, remained as witnesses of the horror that had passed. Along the roadways were the bodies of dead horses. Swarms of flies were black upon them, browsing on their putrefying flesh, from which a stench came poisoning the air and rising above the scent of flowers and the sweet smell of hay in eddying waves of abominable odour.[106]

Until this point, the closest encounter he had with the war was witnessing the lines of refugees and walking wounded. Near the village of Rouville, on or about 23 September, he walked for a time in the company of the village policemen who had been employed in a burial party. While walking through fields strewn with the bodies of French and British soldiers, Gibbs witnessed the burning of the German dead. While he chose not to openly criticize the conduct of the war or the generals who directed it, descriptions such as the following bore testament to his sensibilities:

> No individual corpse among them could be brought in guilty of the crime which had caused this war, and not a soul hovering above that mass of meat could be made responsible at the judgement seat of God. They had obeyed orders, they had marched to the hymn of the Fatherland, they believed as we did, in the righteousness of their cause. But like the dead bodies of the Frenchmen and the Englishmen who lay quite close, they had been done

---

[104] Gibbs, *Adventures in Journalism*, p. 233; Gibbs, *The Soul of the War*, p. 121.
[105] Gibbs, *The Soul of the War*, p. 124.
[106] Gibbs, *The Soul of the War*, p. 119.

to death by the villainy of statecraft and statesmen, playing one race against another as we play with pawns in a game of chess. The old witchcraft was better than this new witchcraft, and not so fraudulent in its power of duping the ignorant masses.[107]

During its advance through Belgium, the German Army was responsible for the deaths of 5000 civilians who were 'shot as guerrilla fighters, as hostages or simply because they got in the way of a victorious army in which not every soldier was a saint'.[108] Through the use of propaganda, the Allies turned this into a deliberate and systematic campaign of barbarism. The publication of the soon discredited Bryce Report saw allegations of rape, mutilation, and murder that were, in the main, complete fabrications. The most enduring myth was the amputation of the hands of Belgian children. Though Gibbs was generally contemptuous of the atrocity stories used by the Allies in their propaganda war, he was not above repeating them. In particular, he seems to have felt a particular revulsion for any atrocities involving women. Given his reputation for honesty, it seems unlikely that he invented the stories, and as a journalist, he had a responsibility to record events he believed to have happened. Yet his melodramatic descriptions of bestial soldiers 'who would have their kisses even though they had to hold shrieking women to their lips' do little justice to heinous crimes.[109] More disturbing for a man of considerable humanity is his reference to a woman, raped at gunpoint in front of her mother-in-law and eight-year-old child, as having insufficient pride or courage to resist.[110] He contrasts her fear with another woman who had fought like 'a wild thing'. Her courage was not rewarded, however, for 'no one would court her after the lesson they had given her'.[111] For Gibbs, death was preferable to this defilement:

It was better for women and children to be in Arras under continual shell fire than in some of the villages along the valleys of the Marne and the Meuse...it was a nicer thing to be killed by a clean piece of shell than to suffer the foulness of men whose passions had been unleashed by drink and the devil and the madness of the first experience of war, and by fear which made

[107] Gibbs, *The Soul of the War*, p. 125.
[108] Knightley, *The First Casualty*, p. 83.
[109] Gibbs, *The Soul of the War*, p. 141.
[110] Gibbs, *The Soul of the War*, p. 142.
[111] Gibbs, *The Soul of the War*, p. 141.

them cruel as beasts...stained the honour of their race in the first phases of the war...These bald headed officers in pointed helmets, so scowling behind their spectacles, had fear in their hearts and concealed it by cruelty.[112]

An interesting correspondence is hinted at between Gibbs and Ralph Blumenfeld, editor of the *Daily Express*, in the form of two hastily scribbled notes, although at the time Gibbs' dispatches were being published in the *Daily Chronicle*. In one dated 9 September 1914, there is clear evidence that Gibbs was aware both of the constraints imposed by censorship and the extent of the reverses suffered in the first month of the war. On a personal level, the few hurried lines entrusted to a chance acquaintance highlight the pressures under which Gibbs operated during the opening months of the war:

Just arrived. I have interviewed one journalist but I did not commit myself as I did not think he was enterprising enough but this afternoon I am meeting a man who has been [illegible] at my request by the Commercial attaché here and I will fix him up till I return. I will return as soon as I can but progress is very slow, must motor everywhere. I am sending this by a motor cycle corps going to the coast and I think it will reach you in case not I cannot tell you all I [illegible] there is strict censorship on all letters if discovered. Sifting all the evidence I am satisfied we have been badly let down everywhere [illegible]...Est losses French 120 000, British 37 000. 2 Calvary Regts, 9. 18 about 100 odd left after. I am driving from [illegible] with HE and meeting the Russian Ambassador and Minister for War so will know a great deal more then. Meanwhile I doubt if I hear from you as all telegrams and letters are censored. I am collecting lots of news [illegible] only be very [illegible] about where it comes from.[113]

The continuing campaign for greater access to the Front was attracting support, or at least a lessening of opposition, from some varied quarters. In October 1914, Sir John French indicated to the Secretary of State that 'accredited journalists of good type, under control, would be less harmful than irregular correspondents'.[114] Even Kitchener came to see the potential for news reports to help shore up support from the Home Front in the face of mounting casualties, although he did not pursue the idea due to

---

[112] Gibbs, *The Soul of the War*, p. 139.

[113] Blumenfeld Papers, Parliamentary Archives, London.

[114] James Edmonds (1986) *The Official History of the Great War; Military Operations, France and Belgium. December 1915-1st July 1916* (Woking: Shearer Publications), p. 145.

what he felt were insurmountable difficulties in corroborating details.[115] The question of accrediting correspondents was also raised in the House of Commons in late November, which reflected not only a desire to hear about the British Army now fighting at Ypres, but also the anomaly that it was easier for an English civilian to get information about French and Belgian troops than their own countrymen.

In early October, Gibbs returned to Dunkirk and then Calais in an attempt to obtain a pass authorizing him to cross the Belgian frontier and enter the battle zone. Since late September, the BEF had been moving northward from the Aisne to Flanders, thereby shortening its line of communication and supply. Though they were saved from the stress and uncertainty of wandering all over northern France in search of the war, the war correspondents were now much easier to locate and arrest. A chance encounter with Lady Dorothie Feilding, who Gibbs had known in England, saw him cross into Belgium with a convoy of ambulances.[116] He left Tomlinson and Massey with a hasty handshake. In Belgium, in the town of Furnes, Gibbs saw the King of the Belgians, now 'sanctified by sorrow and crowned with martyrdom…he seemed to be the type of early kingship, as it was idealized by poets and minstrels…(the) supreme type of hero'.[117]

For a week, Gibbs worked to help set up an English hospital with a 'flying column', even accompanying it into *Dixmude* under heavy shellfire to retrieve the wounded. To Gibbs, it seemed the 'open mouth of hell', an impression no doubt reinforced when a piece of shrapnel narrowly missed his head.[118] For all his emotive descriptions of courage, which seem so antiquated to a modern reader, Gibbs showed himself equal to the task of enduring shellfire and controlling his fear. That evening he noted 'a strange excitement', which though an obvious reaction to stress, may well have been the thrill of having displayed courage rather than just witnessing it in others. In his fourth and final autobiography, Gibbs noted that 'I have been an onlooker of life. Since I was a very young man I have been watching, listening, recording, among many people in many scenes,

---

[115] Swinton, *Eyewitness*, p. 89.

[116] In September 1916, Lady Dorothie Feilding (1889–1935) was the first Englishwoman to be decorated with the Military Medal.

[117] Gibbs, *The Soul of War*, p. 172.

[118] Gibbs, *The Soul of War*, p. 180.

but never as one of the actors in its drama'.[119] For once, at least, he was a participant, and he both revelled in it and suffered because of it:

> That courtyard in the convent at Furnes will always haunt my mind as the scene of grim drama...I used to look up at the stars and wonder what God might think of all this work if there were any truth in old faiths...I helped to carry (a) body out, as everyone helped to do any small work if he had his hands free...It was the saving of one's sanity and self-respect. Yet to me, more sensitive perhaps than it is good to be, it was a moral test almost greater than my strength of will to enter that large room where the wounded lay.[120]

After a short return to England in late October to replace clothing caked in mud and blood, Gibbs learnt that an order for his arrest had been issued by Kitchener. He was also angered when a 'genial sub editor', recalling the traditional peacetime welcome for a returning journalist, asked if he had had a good time. In time, Gibbs would come to express a hatred for 'the people who had not seen and were callous of the misery... the dreadful, callous, cheerful spirit of England at war'.[121] The months in France and Belgium had given Gibbs a sense of having been a participant and he welcomed this growing sense of separation from civilian England. Though not yet in uniform himself, he was now unable to offer, or even recognize the need for any sense of professional detachment. He had 'walked in the red fury of war' and was eager to return.[122] Showing the same resourcefulness that had carried him further and longer than even he might have anticipated, he returned to France as a special commissioner acting on behalf of the Red Cross. As a sign that the authorities were getting more serious in their opposition to war reporting, this subterfuge, which would have been successful a few months before, failed utterly. Gibbs was arrested even before disembarking, incarcerated for 10 days, and then returned to England. Such was the official antipathy to reporters that General Bruce Williams, the British officer in command of the base at Le Harve, talked openly of having correspondents shot. While it is unlikely that this was a serious threat, he was clearly expressing the spirit, though not the letter of the law regarding correspondents.

---

[119] P Gibbs (1957) *Life's Adventure* (London: Angus & Robertson), p. 9.
[120] Gibbs, *Life's Adventure*, p. 192; 194.
[121] Gibbs, *Realities of War*, pp. 49–50.
[122] Gibbs, *The Journalist's London*, 4.

The constant stress of wandering 'about the countryside with only the vaguest idea of the direction in which the enemy may appear' found voice in a reasonably extended criticism of censorship in early October.[123] To Gibbs, it appeared 'senseless that the greatest war in history should be fought behind a veil of absolute secrecy'. With an eye already on posterity, he feared that if the correspondents were pursued as criminals, 'thousands of facts would be lost forever and many things will be hidden which should see the light'. As a 'chronicler of human events' he was clearly frustrated at being so close to the biggest news story in history, yet being thwarted by those whose cause he had made his own:

> It is no joke for the special correspondent. I can only see flashes of humour in dodging arrest at every crossroad and plunging across country towards the firing line with the uneasy thought that if one's papers are not in order— they never are—one risks more by capture in the Allied lines than by a chance encounter with the enemy's patrols...It is demoralising to a man with a comparatively blameless record.[124]

October brought a more personal loss for Gibbs. Though he did not identify him as such until 1952, and then in a book on the history of London journalism, Alphonse Courlander, a Jewish journalist and author working for the *Daily Express*, was Gibbs' best friend in Fleet Street. Gibbs mentions him in two of his autobiographies, yet the significance of this friendship is easily overlooked in books laden with references to people he had worked with, reported on or met socially. Although Courlander had seen war as a correspondent in the Balkans in 1912, as a result of what Hamilton Fyfe described as succumbing to 'the prevailing epidemic of fright', he fled to London and, perhaps shamefaced at abandoning his post, committed suicide on 23 October 1914.[125] Gibbs believed that the sudden terror of war had been too much for Courlander's nervous imagination, though initially he could not bring himself to use the word suicide, choosing instead the euphemism 'a tragic end'. Four decades later, Gibbs recalled

> talking together for hours at a time on books, plots, the marketing of library wares, the quality of genius, style and construction...I have still a great affection for his memory and for his sparkling sense of humour, beneath which,

---

[123] *Daily Chronicle*, 12 October 1914.
[124] *Daily Chronicle*, 8 October 1914.
[125] H Fyfe (1935) *My Seven Selves* (London: George Allen & Unwin), p. 176.

as often I perceived, there was a dark melancholy and fear and uneasy conscience (though there was no cause for that) revealed if he had a few drinks,
as if he looked at his naked soul with sadness, until his mood changed to
hilarity in some tavern on the left side of the Seine or in Dublin's fair city
where its girls are so pretty.[126]

Courlander's death came only days after Gibbs' first experience under
shellfire. Having proven himself, the mix of anger, grief, and shame at his
friend's inability to endure what was essentially a fear of war rather than an
experience of it, would almost have certainly left its mark. If nothing else,
it would help explain the regular motif of suicide in a number of his novels. By mentioning Courlander, when he declined to do the same for his
brother Thomas, or indeed even his beloved mother Helen whose death
was more conventional, Gibbs was perhaps seeking to posthumously redress
what may have been a mixed response to his friend's suicide. Given Gibbs'
emotional reticence to discuss such personal issues, his desire to record his
friend's life flies in the face of his pattern of seeing grief as a very personal
issue. He was left to observe that, sadly, his good friend, whose most successful novel was inspired by Gibbs' *Street of Adventure*, was 'forgotten
now poor lad, as we all get forgotten'.[127]

The First Battle of Ypres, which raged from 12 October to 22 November
1914, cost the BEF 58,000 casualties.[128] Of the battalions which had
fought at the Marne as well, there remained, on average, 1 officer and
30 men who had landed in August. Steps were taken, therefore, to create the country's first mass citizen army. By November 1918, 22 % of
the adult male population, or 5.7 million men, had served in the army.
The nationalization of the conflict brought with it even more pressure for
reliable news. Developments far away from the Front now set in train a
series of events which would see Gibbs return to France not merely as an
accredited war correspondent, but in an officer's uniform with the honorary status of captain. In spite of the increasing pressure to allow some
news from the Front, there was still a very strong desire on the part of the
War Office to fight the war without press scrutiny. But it was an interces-
sion far from the 'immense anxiety of a nation' which, when added to

---

[126] Gibbs, *The Journalist's London*, p. 135.

[127] Gibbs, *The Journalist's London*, p. 135.

[128] At the outbreak of war, the regular army numbered 247,500 men, a third of whom
were stationed in India.

other pressures, probably led to a change.[129] On 22 January 1915, former American president Theodore Roosevelt wrote to the Foreign Secretary, Sir Edward Grey, criticizing the Allies' failure to permit, let alone aid the work of the war correspondents:

> There has been a very striking contrast between the lavish attention showered on war correspondents by the German military authorities and the point blank refusal to have anything to do with them by the British and French governments...the only real war news, written by Americans who are known to and trusted by the American public comes from the German side. If you think public opinion should be taken into account, then it is worth your while considering whether much of your censorship work and much of your refusal to allow correspondents at the front has not been a danger to your cause from the standpoint of the effect on public opinion without any corresponding military gains.[130]

Prime Minister Asquith, reacting to discussion in the House of Commons in early February 1915, made further concessions. Sir John French's dispatches became biweekly reports from 17 February 1915, and four correspondents, including Gibbs, were invited to British GHQ for a tour during the Battle of Neuve Chapelle (10–12 March 1915).[131] It was, as Farrar observed, a strange coincidence that four of the most prominent British correspondents were invited just as a major battle was to commence.[132] The subsequent refusal to facilitate coverage of any of the actual fighting on the absurd premise that the correspondents might impede the movement of reinforcements displayed how the war correspondents could be thwarted more successfully by removing their outsider status and absorbing them into the system.

Though the first wave of the attack was generally successful, the gain of a stretch of mud 2000 yards wide and 1200 yards deep was hardly commensurate with 7000 British and 4000 Indian casualties.[133] Gibbs

---

[129] Gibbs, *The Soul of the War*, p. 244.

[130] H Lasswell (1927) *Propaganda Technique in the World War* (London: Kegan Paul), p. 136.

[131] The correspondents were Gibbs (*Daily Telegraph* and *Daily Chronicle*), Valentine Williams (*Daily Mail* and *Daily Mirror*), Henry Nevinson (*The Times* and the *Daily News and Leader*), and Ernest Townley (*Daily Express* and the *Morning Post*).

[132] Farrar, *News from the Front*, p. 52.

[133] In a more pleasant contact with the Indian troops on the Western Front, Gibbs and his fellow correspondents played a game of cricket with KS Ranjitsinhji, His Highness the

described it as 'a victory' albeit one bought at a 'fearful price'.[134] Again, Gibbs interviewed prisoners of war and the wounded, but his dispatch on the second day of the first British offensive on the Western Front showed how effectively the correspondents had been muzzled. 'How the striking power of the Armies is organized' is a headline hardly indicative of a new policy of openness regarding press coverage. There were signs of a thawing of relations between the press and the Military which were nevertheless more impressive in appearance than substance. Gibbs recalled crowding around a table where a staff officer, having spread out his map, proceeded to show the correspondents the general disposition of the troops engaged in the operation:

> The vague tremor of distant guns gave a grim significance to his words and on our own journey that day we had seen many signs of organized activity bearing upon the attack...I went back to my billet in General Headquarters wishing that I had seen something of that affair which had netted all these men. It had been a 'day out' for the British troops, and we had not yet heard of the blunders or the blood that had spoilt its success. It was hard to have seen nothing of it though so near the front.[135]

The loss of freedom was clearly not just a literary one, but also a limitation in the freedom to move and the freedom to see.[136] This situation was repeated even as recently as the Second Gulf War when embedded reporters found that they were confronted with remarkably similar difficulties.[137] They were unable to travel independently but were tied to the military as their major source of information which had banned the publication of 19 different types of information. At a human level as well, there was the influence which Gibbs had found all pervasive—the very closeness of the reporter's contact with the troops made self-censorship a powerful force. Embedded reporters tended to present the war from the viewpoint of the unit they are with. As Gibbs had quickly found, they too came to identify

Maharajah Jam Sahib of Nawanager (1872–1933). The scorer of 72 first-class hundreds, he was revered as one of the most brilliant batsmen of the age. Using a makeshift bat, Ranjitsinhji was bowled first ball by Tomlinson, before using the club 'like a sword' in the second innings (Gibbs, *The Pageant of the Years*, p. 177).

[134] Gibbs, *The Soul of the War*, p. 357.

[135] *Daily Chronicle*, 15 March 1915.

[136] Farish, *Modern Witnesses*, p. 276.

[137] See S Fahmy & T Johnson (2007) 'Embedded Versus Unilateral Perspectives on Iraq War,' *Newspaper Research Journal*, vol 28, no 3, Summer.

with the men and women with whom they shared common goals, the most basic of which was a shared desire to survive. These shortcomings were compounded by the fact that unlike the war in the Gulf where the legality of Allied involvement was openly questioned, each of the correspondents supported both the legality and morality of their nation's war effort, if not always the means by which it was pursued.

While Gibbs was in no position to forcibly make his way towards the fighting or to have his reports published even if he did, he opened himself to later criticism for adding in the same dispatch that 'few things have been hidden from us'. Gibbs was a man of considerable honesty and conviction and it is unlikely that he would have knowingly lied in a dispatch. Far more likely was a decision to omit details rather than an outright fabrication of them, an act which Gibbs would have seen as a patriotic and military necessity. It was also one which would not, in his view, have been dishonest, for he had always been quite open about being subject to censorship. Later when he had gained in experience and might have been in a better position to make a more accurate assessment of the conduct of the fighting, his commitment to the cause and the strictures of official censorship made this impossible. During a tour of the First Army, Brigadier General Charteris, who later as head of military intelligence would become the correspondents' commanding officer, was surprised at how little they actually understood about modern warfare:

> The first batch of correspondents had to be treated gingerly. I doubt whether they will really be much wiser after their visit. They arrived, accompanied by three officers from the WO [War Office], who themselves were quite as ignorant of what was actually happening as the correspondents... There were many well-known names among the correspondents. They were all most amazingly ignorant, but that was the real justification for their mission as opposed to the official 'Eyewitness'. It is impossible for us here to realize how ignorant the public must be, and in writing copy that the public requires, one must begin with the knowledge of how little they know.[138]

In March, Gibbs also saw Ypres, 'a town which will for ever be haunted by the spirit of those men' for the first time. By the time he returned, two months later, the 'devil had come to Ypres' in the form of a German gas

---

[138] John Charteris (1931) *At GHQ* (London: Cassell), p. 79.

attack. It was now a 'city of ruin' which during the remainder of the war changed only in the degree of its disintegration.[139]

Against the backdrop of the failures at Neuve Chapelle and Aubers Ridge, in May, and the subsequent Shell Scandal[140] which compelled Asquith to form a coalition government, five correspondents received their long-awaited accreditation. John Buchan, Percival Phillips, Herbert Russell, and Valentine Williams joined Gibbs at GHQ, although over the course of the war they would be replaced or joined by William Beach Thomas, H Perry Robinson, Basil Clarke, HM Tomlinson, Hamilton Fyfe, Filson Young, Percival Gibbson, George Dewar, Prevost Battersby, Frederick Palmer, and Henry Nevinson.[141] Farrar saw this as an opportunity for the correspondents to make amends for earlier failures and to restore the reputation of their profession. He argued, however, that far from redressing past errors, what was in fact created was a 'group of correspondents who conformed to the great conspiracy, the deliberate lies and the suppression of the truth'.[142]

The government, the War Office, the newspaper owners, such as Harmsworth and Beaverbrook, and ultimately the correspondents found themselves unlikely allies. Each sought the successful prosecution of the war and saw their role as contributing to that end. While a belief in your own moral virtue does not preclude participation in what others may see as a criminal conspiracy, each of the major players acted in what they perceived as the national interest. Their patriotism rarely went unrewarded:

> By absorbing whenever possible the power of the press into the service of government, by making some of its members an integral part of the defence of the realm, and by the provision of honours and appointments to certain leading editors, and proprietors thereby giving them a vested interest in the

---

[139] Gibbs, *Realities of War*, pp. 91–4.

[140] Charles, a Court Repington, military correspondent for *The Times*, wrote an article which blamed the failures of the Spring Offensives on the lack of shells. The Harmsworth Press involved itself in a full-scale campaign aimed at Lord Kitchener and the government. It contributed to the collapse of the truce between the Conservatives and the Liberals which led to Prime Minister Asquith forming a coalition government and the creation of the Ministry of Munitions under David Lloyd George.

[141] The five knighted at the end of the war were Gibbs (representing the *Daily Telegraph* and *Daily Chronicle*), Percival Phillips (*The Daily Express* and the *Morning Post*), William Beach Thomas (*Daily Mail* and the *Daily Mirror*), H Perry Robinson (*The Times* and the *Daily News*), and Herbert Russell (*Reuters News Agency*).

[142] Farrar, *News from the Front*, p. 73.

survival of the system, the British government was thus able to exploit the enormous potential of the press for the duration of the war. In short, the British Press became the servant of official propaganda more out of willing acquiescence than as a result of Government coercion.[143]

The war correspondents, now 'attired in the King's uniform, were, to all intents and purposes, Officers of the army, conscious of their debt to it and conscious too of their duty to keep up morale and to reinforce that continuing loyalty of the people at home'.[144] Even the Official History recognized the real intent behind the official accreditation:

> The new Commander in Chief [Haig] was averse to the press representatives being 'spoon fed' and held the view that when, for military reasons, it was necessary to withhold information from the public, it could only be done with the co-operation of the correspondents.[145]

Gibbs was far less circumspect after the war than in his wartime reports when he described the belated acknowledgement of the need for press coverage from the front:

> Even the enormous, impregnable stupidity of our High Command on all matters of psychology was penetrated by a vague notion that a few 'writing fellows' might be sent out with permission to follow the armies in the field, under the strictest censorship, in order to silence the popular clamour for news.[146]

After the war, he was also prepared to openly acknowledge that he believed the army made this concession firm in the belief that some stirring nationalistic reports might stimulate recruiting. Significantly, he added that the reports were expected to emphasize the 'glorious side of war as it could be seen from base...without of course, any allusion to dead or dying men, to the ghastly failures of distinguished generals, or to the filth and horror of the battlefields'.[147] At the time though, Gibbs was able to balance this awareness of the army's motives and his sense of

---

[143] M Sanders & P Taylor (1982) *British Propaganda during the First World War, 1914–1918* (London: Macmillan), p. 31.
[144] L Macdonald (1983) *Somme* (London: Michael Joseph), p. 80.
[145] Edmonds, *Official History*, p. 147.
[146] Gibbs, *Realities of War*, p. 21.
[147] Gibbs, *Realities of War*, p. 21–2.

journalistic integrity by creating for himself a job description that did not demand a more critical assessment of the system he served. He argued that the function of war correspondents were as 'chroniclers of the fighting day by day, trying to get the facts as fully as possible and putting them down as clearly as they appear out of the turmoil of battle'. Their job was not one that called for prophesy or criticism.[148] After the war, he reiterated that it was not his function to argue 'why things should have happened so, nor giving reasons why they should not happen so, but describing faithfully many of the things I saw, and narrating the facts as I found them, as far as censorship would allow. After early hostile days it allowed nearly all but criticism, protest and the figures of loss'.[149]

Some historians would argue that the failure of Gibbs and his associates to criticize or protest represents the most discreditable period in the history of journalism.[150] Knightley went so far as to write that more deliberate lies were told between 1914 and 1918 than in any other period of history, and a 'large share of the blame for this must rest with the British war correspondents'.[151] Even sympathetic writers who have recognized the dilemma facing the correspondents have described the dispatches as 'ludicrous'.[152] Yet it would be instructive to know what course of action critics such as Knightley and Farrar feel men like Gibbs might have pursued, assuming that they even perceived the need for such action. The majority of correspondents were from England and were all middle-aged men born and raised in the second half of the Victorian Age. They believed that they were contributing to the war effort during what appeared a battle for national survival. They were not, as Knightley would wish to see them, in helicopters in Vietnam or embedded with armoured columns in Iraq reporting to an audience well used to openly questioning their government's actions.

Given his relatively consistent defence of censorship during wartime, first delivered in *At War with the Cross and Crescent*, there is a strong case to be made that Gibbs did not compromise his integrity while reporting on the Western Front. He saw the need for wartime censorship,

---

[148] Gibbs, *The Battles of the* Somme, p. 18.

[149] Gibbs, *Realities of War*, p. ix.

[150] Knightley, *The First Casualty*, and A Ponsonby (1928) *Falsehood in Wartime* (London: George Allen and Unwin).

[151] Knightley, *The First Casualty*, p. 81.

[152] M Hudson and J Stainer (1998) *War and the Media* (New York: New York University Press).

outlined what he could and could not report on and proceeded according-ly.[153] Even had the High Command permitted criticisms and references to casualty figures, there was a further impediment, which Gibbs felt was per-haps greater than official controls.[154] As Gibbs stated, the correspondents

> had no other desire than to record the truth as fully as possible without handing information to the enemy and to describe the life and actions of our fighting men so that the nation, and the world should understand their valour, their suffering and their achievement. We identified ourselves abso-lutely with the armies in the field...There was no need of censorship of our dispatches. We were our own censors.[155]

The correspondents thus became part of the war effort, not impartial observers. They came to identify with the soldiers they lived with, and having been witness to their daily valour and suffering, they sought to celebrate it and legitimize it.

Charles E Montague, a journalist turned censor, passed a critical, though balanced eye over the work of the journalists in his book *Disenchantment*. Though he spoke generally, he might as well have been describing Gibbs when he wrote:

> And, almost without exception, they were good men...The general level of personal and professional honour, of courage, public spirit, and serious enterprise, was high. No average Staff Officer could talk with the average British correspondent without feeling that this was a sound human being and had a better mind than his own...When once known, the war corre-spondents were trusted and liked—by the Staff. [156]

But as Gibbs would later come to understand, Montague saw this friendship as precluding an ability to objectively assess the competency of the military's direction of the war. For they were familiar with

> the Staff world, [and knew] its joys and sorrows, not...the combatant world. The Staff were both their friend and their censor. How could they show it up when it failed?...When autumn twilight came down on the haggard trench

---

[153] Gibbs, *The Battles of the Somme*, p. 18.

[154] Gibbs would have known that the casualties were enormous without being able to quantify them.

[155] Gibbs, *Adventures in Journalism*, p. 248.

[156] CE Montague (1922) *Disenchantment* (London: Chatto & Windus), p. 96.

world of which they had caught a quiet noon day glimpse, they would be speeding west in Vauxhall cars to lighted chateaux gleaming white among scatheless woods. Their staple emotions before a battle were of necessity akin to those of the Staff, the racehorse owner or trainer exalted with brilliant hopes thrilled by the glorious uncertainty of the game, the fascinating nicety of every preparation, and feeling the presence of horrible fatigues and the nearness of multitudinous death chiefly as a dim sombre background that added importance to the rousing scene, and not as things that need seriously cloud the spirit or qualify delight in a plan.[157]

It was not necessarily a view widely shared by wartime audiences. At least one front-line soldier believed that amongst combatants at least there was considerable respect for the correspondents. Lieutenant Richard Dixon of the 251 Siege Battery, 53 Brigade Royal Guards Artillery, wrote that 'for war correspondents like Philip Gibbs we had a great respect, for in his reports he displayed an understanding of the front line soldier who carried the burden of the war, and moreover he went where the fighting was rough and tough'.[158]

Though it is dangerous to draw a generalization from one opinion, it raises an interesting parallel with the popular view of the war as uniquely terrible or incompetently conducted. Badsey argued that it is now generally accepted that 'the highly critical perspective of a British cultural and social elite (including the more famous of the trench poets) during and after the war was not necessarily shared by the majority of participants'.[159] It is an argument supported by other historians, most notably Todman[160] and Gregory.[161] It is possible that at least some of the criticism of the press is likewise the result of a general revulsion of war expressed by an articulate minority rather than representing a more widely held opinion.

Gibbs would have enjoyed being identified as someone present where the fighting was toughest. He noted that it was not always the outwardly courageous men who withstood the stress of warfare. It was the cockney who at times seemed most resilient to breakdown. For he had always

---

[157] Montague, *Disenchantment*, pp. 96–7.

[158] Imperial War Museum 2001 92/36/1.

[159] S Badsey (2005) 'The Missing Western Front: British Politics, Strategy and Propaganda in 1918'. In M Connelly & D Welch (eds) *War and the Media* (London: IB Tauris), p. 48.

[160] D Todman (2005) *The Great War: Myth and Memory* (London: Continuum).

[161] A Gregory (2008) *The Last Great War: British Society and the First World War* (Cambridge: Cambridge University Press).

'trained himself in the control of his nerves, on buses which lurch around corners, in the traffic which bears down on him, in a thousand and one situations which demand control in a nervy man'. Instead it was the 'solid fellow', unused to nerves, who suffered the most.[162] In one single admission 20 years before, never repeated in any of his autobiographical writing, Gibbs described himself as a 'Cockney born and bred'.[163] Gibbs uses this nomenclature in a generic sense to denote a working-class Londoner rather than the traditional requirement that one must be born within earshot of Bow Bells. His exploration of the reasons for the survival of 'nervy' Londoners may well have been a personal search by Gibbs to find the source of his own capacity to endure. It would have made sense to him in 1920 to link himself with men who survived the war, and in doing so endured beyond the breaking point of their ostensibly tougher, more masculine counterparts.

These arguments concerning his complicity in a propaganda war, however, were all in the future when Gibbs and the other correspondents were met by the commander-in-chief Sir John French at his headquarters in a chateau near St Omer in June 1915. French, resplendent in riding boots and spurs, welcomed them with the hope that he could trust their honour and loyalty. Recalling the meeting in 1920, Gibbs had wondered 'whether there were any light of genius in him—any inspiration, any force which would break the awful strength of the enemy against us, any cunning in modern warfare'. Unsurprisingly, given French's subsequent failure and removal, Gibbs 'thought not'.[164] Reflecting on this period as an outlaw almost 10 years and a knighthood later, Gibbs felt that he was 'hardly justified in evading military law...By some frightful indiscretion (which I did not commit) I or any other of those correspondents might have endangered the position of our troops'.[165] In 1917, some years before the wider public came to a more realistic understanding of what had transpired at Mons, Neuve Chapelle, Loos, the Somme, and Passchendaele, he remembered this period as one of 'great and wonderful days'.[166]

[162] Gibbs, *Realities of War*, p. 48.
[163] Correspondence with Mrs Suverkrop, 22 June 1901. *Philip Gibbs Letters, Special Collections Research Center, Syracuse University Libraries.*
[164] Gibbs, *Realities of War*, p. 39.
[165] Gibbs, *Adventures in Journalism*, p. 244.
[166] Gibbs, *The Battles of the Somme*, p. 1.

CHAPTER 4

Official War Correspondent: 1915–1918

Like the troops themselves, the correspondents settled into a daily pattern which brought some order to the chaos. Initially, they lived in a chateau in the village of Tatinghem near GHQ at St Omer. The correspondents moved quarters occasionally to be better placed to report on an offensive. According to Gibbs, the descriptor 'chateau' was used only as 'a courtesy'.[1] On the morning of battle, they would divide up the front line and then draw lots to see which portion they would cover. Travelling their separate ways in cars, beginning often before dawn, they would make their way to a vantage point to witness the preliminary bombardment. Following the shelling, they would then walk over the captured ground; interview the walking wounded and prisoners of war; and get lost amidst the movement of artillery, reinforcements, ambulances, and the general minutiae of modern war. In doing so, the five English and two American correspondents gained a 'personal view of all this activity of strife, and from many men in its whirlpool details of their own adventure and of general progress or disaster on one sector of the battle front'.[2]

Gibbs was adept at conveying details steeped in personal experience and emotion, but it was the next step where many of the shortcomings of the war correspondents were cruelly exposed. Moving first to Divisional and then to Corps Headquarters, the correspondents saw the reports come in

---

[1] P Gibbs (1936) *Realities of War* (London: Hutchinson & Co Ltd), p. 23.
[2] Gibbs, *Realities of War*, p. 35.

© The Editor(s) (if applicable) and The Author(s) 2016
M.C. Kerby, *Sir Philip Gibbs and English Journalism in War and Peace*,
DOI 10.1057/978-1-137-57301-8_4

by telephone, aircraft, or pigeon. It was at this level where their ability to integrate the myriad details and personal impressions into a coherent critique of the progress of an offensive was clearly absent. A century later, the same challenge confronted embedded reporters in Iraq during the Second Gulf War. They found, as Gibbs and his companions discovered, that they were often presenting 'a small slice of reality and that reality did not always reflect the bigger picture'.[3]

From Headquarters, the correspondents, 'tired, hungry, nerve-racked, splashed to the eyes in mud, or covered in a mask of dust', returned to their quarters. Here they met as a group and shared their experiences, 'each reserving for himself his own adventures, impressions and emotions'.[4] The actual writing of an article was always a pressured affair, with impatient dispatch riders and censors circling the correspondents, who battled fatigue and their own strained nerves for up to five months without a break during major offensives. Gibbs wrote 'instinctively, blindly, feverishly', all the while railing at the injustice of a public who 'cursed us because we did not tell more, or sneered at us because they thought we were "spoon fed" by GHQ—who never gave us any detailed news and who were far from our way of life'.[5]

Each correspondent had a censor attached to him, 'a kind of jailer and spy, eating, sleeping, walking, and driving'.[6] Gibbs characterized many of the censors as 'gentlemen and broadminded men of the world'. In time, he came to see them as loyal friends and allies. He believed that they too recognized the absurdity of the regulations, and he often found them flexible in the interpretation of the rules and at times prepared to actively oppose the more ridiculous ones. It would appear that, at least in this instance, if the correspondents were absorbed into the war effort, the censors were likewise absorbed into the world of the correspondents. One even confided to Gibbs, and another to Beach Thomas, that the Chief of Intelligence had given him written instructions to waste the correspondents' time.[7] Most likely, this was General Macdonagh, under whose authority there was a 'narrow view of our liberties in narration and description. Hardly a

---

[3] S Fahmy and T Johnson (2007) 'Embedded Versus Unilateral Perspectives on Iraq War', *Newspaper Research Journal*, vol. 28, no. 3, Summer, p. 102.

[4] Gibbs, *Realities of War*, p. 35.

[5] Gibbs, *Realities of War*, pp. 37–8.

[6] P Gibbs (1923) *Adventures in Journalism* (London: Harper and Brothers Publishers), p. 251.

[7] Gibbs, *Realities of War*, p. 26.

week passed without some vexatious rule to cramp our style'.[8] Gibbs felt
that his successor, General Charteris, was more broad-minded, although
others went further even than Macdonagh dared. Lieutenant Colonel
James Edmonds, who later wrote the British Official History, was one of a
number of staff officers at GHQ who amused themselves by intentionally
passing false information to the correspondents as a test of their credulity.[9]
Gibbs was well aware of how tenuous their position was in these early
months, for though they possessed 'a doubtful respectability', they were
like 'a woman of easy virtue who has been made respectable by marriage,
but is expected to break out into open sin at the slightest opportunity'.[10]

The correspondents, therefore, were in a constant battle to balance their
desire to support the war effort and act within the parameters laid down by
the government and the military while simultaneously maintaining some
degree of personal and professional integrity. This tension is apparent in
Gibbs' first autobiography written shortly after the war when he claimed
that the newspaper proprietors and editors subordinated 'everything to a
genuine and patriotic desire to play the game, to support the army, and to
avoid any criticism or controversy which might hamper the military chiefs
or demoralize the nation'. Yet without a sense of any inherent contradiction, Gibbs believed that the correspondents, who wrote the proprietors'
stories, and in doing so became household names, had no ambition other
than to tell the truth without aiding the enemy.[11] In time, Gibbs felt that
the army came to understand 'that we were loyal...and had its ideals, its
interests, and its hopes at heart'. Such a statement of allegiance is indicative of how open Gibbs was concerning his commitment to the national
war effort and the implied recognition that his role as a journalist was
always subordinate to the requirements of the military.[12]

Regardless of one's stance concerning the veracity of the correspondent's reports, it was without doubt a stressful and demanding role. Basil
Clarke, one of Gibbs' fellow war correspondents, was aware of the restless

[8] Gibbs, *Adventures in Journalism*, p. 249.
[9] Letter from Edmonds to Charles Bean 16 October 1928, File of Correspondence with
JE Edmonds 1927–1939, Papers of Charles Bean, Australian War Memorial, Canberra. In
S Badsey (2005) 'The Missing Western Front: British Politics, Strategy and Propaganda in
1918'. In M Connelly and D Welch (eds) *War and the Media* (London: IB Tauris), p. 47.
[10] Gibbs, *Realities of War*, p. 37.
[11] Gibbs, *Adventures in Journalism*, pp. 247–8.
[12] Gibbs, *Adventures in Journalism*, pp. 247–8.

energy which allowed Gibbs to maintain both an enviable work regime in wartime and a prolific literary output in peacetime:

> His broad brow, his pale, finely-chiselled face, thin, sensitive lips, and big clear eyes, show something of the thinker, idealist, and poet that he is by nature. But his spare frame and indolent pose as he reclines—one might almost say, collapses—in an easy-chair belie the fierce unquenchable energy that is his. Few men there are who can idle so unsatisfactorily as he. The cigarette in the fingers of his slim left hand is sending upwards a thin blue line. Through eyes half closed he watches its un-waving course dreamily, apparently the most thorough and most complete of idlers. But it is only for a moment. He moves, I see him turn to catch my eye, and I know full well that it is to challenge me to a game of chess—"a la mort," as we used to say. Over the game he will struggle and wriggle to gain the mastery, finding some outlet in so doing for the restless mental energy that consumes him. But for that game I know he would go to his room and work. It is a kindness to make him play. A man of great sympathy is Gibbs; a man in whom the soul-wound caused by war and war's horror and war's suffering is ever fresh and raw. Such a war as this weighs heavy on a mind like that.[13]

The Battle of Loos which began with a four-day bombardment on 21 September 1915 was the first major offensive fought under the gaze of accredited war correspondents. Joffre's plan for an autumn offensive called for convergent thrusts from Artois and Champagne against the Noyon salient and its communications. The British participation, vigorously opposed by Sir John French and Sir Douglas Haig, was an attack north of Lens in an area completely unsuitable for offensive operations. The front-line troops, however, had an 'exhilarating breath of confidence in the result' of this Franco-British offensive which, they believed, would shatter the German Front.[14] Haig, who as the commander of the First Army would have to carry out the British part in the larger Artois offensive, was well aware of the lack of heavy artillery available to him, though in time he came to see the possibility of a strategic victory. In hindsight, however, there is ample justification for Simkins' view that 1915 was a year of illusions.[15] In spite of his own misgivings, French acceded to pressure from Generals Joffre and Foch, who had Lord Kitchener as their

[13] www.greatwardifferent.com/Great_War/Reporter_on_Reporters/Reporters_01.htm. Date retrieved, 1 February 2013.

[14] B Liddell Hart (1992) *History of the First World War* (London: Papermac), p. 193.

[15] P Simkin (1991) *World War 1: The Western Front* (Surrey: Bramley Books), p. 55.

unlikely ally, and committed forces which inevitably proved unequal to the Herculean task required of them.[16] The paucity of British artillery, the failure of the poison gas which was intended to compensate for it, alterations in the French plan, the misuse of the reserves, and the overall failure either to choose an appropriate place for an attack or to provide the means to execute it led to what was a total failure from beginning to end. Over 60,000 British troops became casualties in what was merely a precursor to greater sacrifice on the Somme the following year. It would cost Sir John French his job.

Gibbs watched the preliminary bombardment from a black slag heap beyond Noeux-les-Mines and then later at the Loos Redoubt. Shortly after the War, Gibbs recalled that despite the prospect of greater access to the Front, there was little to be seen of the offensive through the 'banks of smoke...stabbed and torn by the incessant flashing of shells...there was no movement of men to be seen, no slaughter, no heroic episode. There was nothing but the tumult of noise [and] an impenetrable veil which hid all human drama'.[17] Gibbs may well have known that the attack, launched on 25 September, stalled because his dispatch written the following day ended with the less than celebratory observation that 'of the results nothing can yet be said until the Commander in Chief lifts the veil which hides them all'. In the same dispatch, he wrote that the British troops had fought 'with the spirit of men who knew their Empire's life depends upon them, and gave their own lives with a noble generosity'.[18] In his post-war book *Realities of War*, he was less confused, particularly in his assessment of the subsidiary attacks either side of the main assault:

> From the point of view of high generalship those holding attacks had served their purpose pretty well. From the point of view of mothers' sons they had been a bloody shambles without any gain. The point of view depends on the angle of vision.[19]

---

[16] Liddell Hart speculated that Kitchener may have supported the French desire for an offensive in part to pave the way for his appointment as the supreme commander of the Entente forces (Liddell Hart, *History of the First World War*, p. 197). In fairness to Kitchener, he was also faced with the reverses at Gallipoli, in Italy and Russia. The French attacks would cost them 144,000 casualties against 85,000 German.

[17] Gibbs, *Realities of War*, p. 157.

[18] *Daily Chronicle*, 29 September 1915.

[19] Gibbs, *Realities of War*, p. 159.

During the battle, Gibbs had 40 pages of manuscript deleted by General Macdonagh, the then Chief of Intelligence. Though he was less critical of censorship during the War, once he was no longer bound by it, he acknowledged that it sought not to conceal 'the truth from the enemy, but from the nation, in defence of the British High Command and its tragic blundering'. What Macdonagh rejected was never recorded, but it almost certainly was not as damning as Gibbs' post-war assessment of the battle as 'a tragic slaughter' and a 'reckless and useless waste of life' which was in part caused by 'abominable staff-work'.[20] Nevertheless, the headline under which his article appeared in the *New York Times* on 29 September read 'How British Won Loos'. For several days, Gibbs endeavoured to get closer to the actual fighting but could only see 'the swirl and flurry of gun-fire and the smoke of shells mixing with wet mist, and the backwash of wounded and prisoners, and the traffic of guns, and wagons, and supporting troops'. It was, as Gibbs admitted at the end of the War, a ghastly failure. Thirty years after the battle he wrote that even had it been perfectly directed, it could not have achieved much at that stage of the War.[21] In 1917, by which time the carnage of the Somme had dwarfed the losses at Loos, Gibbs' strongest memory of this battle was 'the revelation of the astounding courage of those men of the London, the Scottish and the Guards Divisions who proved the mettle of the New Armies...and went into battle with a high spirited valour which could not have been surpassed by the old Regulars'.[22] The sense of hopelessness that followed the failure at Loos and the winter of 1915 bore heavily on the men who had survived what Gibbs described in 1920 as the 'immense martyrdom of boys'.[23] Though he was a man who titled his final war memoir *Realities of War*, Gibbs was still able to argue that the Germans suffered worse during this winter in the trenches because they lacked the English sense of humour.[24]

Gibbs was prepared to cast a more critical eye over events, but invariably he did so in his books rather than his dispatches, which by necessity appeared well after the events they described. In 1917, in a book detailing his experiences on the Somme during middle to late 1916, he

---

[20] Gibbs, *Adventures in Journalism*, pp. 249–50.
[21] Gibbs, *Realities of War*, p. 190; P Gibbs (1946) *The Pageant of the Years* (London: Heinemann), p. 174.
[22] P Gibbs (1916) *The Battles of the Somme* (London: William Heinemann), p. 9.
[23] Gibbs, *Realities of War*, pp. 190–1.
[24] Gibbs, *Realities of War*, p. 193.

acknowledged that at both Neuve Chapelle and Loos, attacks were made that had little chance of success due to insufficient men, guns, or shells. Yet such a criticism, which would have scandalized his readership in 1915, is easily overlooked or dismissed as irrelevant in a book concerning a much larger offensive which began 17 months after the attack at Neuve Chapelle and 9 months after Loos. Shortly after Loos, but before Haig's promotion, Gibbs did have an opportunity to speak freely when Lloyd George invited him to breakfast in Downing Street. Despite being a Cabinet Minister, the future prime minister admitted that the military kept the government ignorant of the reality of what was happening in France and Belgium. Gibbs recalled that his description of conditions at the Front left Lloyd George visibly 'distressed'.[25] The meeting, however, had a quite different effect on Gibbs. With an appealing honesty, he admitted to leaving Downing Street with a 'glow of personal vanity', firm in the belief that it was impossible to resist the flattery of having one's views valued by a man holding the fate of the world in his hands.[26]

Other events away from France also attracted his not altogether impartial attention. The Easter Rebellion in Dublin in late March and early April 1916 by Irish nationalists was, in his view, not only an act of treachery to the English people 'but treachery to civilisation itself, to our French allies, to the whole code of honour'.[27] There could be no excuse, in Gibbs' view, for such a stab in the back.[28] Not even in the 'tragic heritage of Irish history, nor our own stupidities in dealing with a temperamental people' could Gibbs find a justification.[29] He could only comfort himself with the thought that it was condemned and resented by the majority of Irish. The subsequent execution of the ringleaders was, in Gibbs' view, justified, though he felt that mercy may have proven a wiser course. Yet the strange ambivalence evident in his opinion of the suffragettes is also apparent in his description of the rebels who thought they had done a 'mad, bad thing', were men of 'lofty ideals, patriots and visionaries, though grievously misguided by fanaticism'.[30] Speaking generally of the Irish question, however, Gibbs admitted to leaning 'a little to the Irish side'.[31]

[25] Gibbs, *The Pageant of the Years*, p. 174.

[26] *Harpers Monthly Magazine*, September 1921, p. 424.

[27] P Gibbs (1921) *More that Must be Told* (London: Harper & Brothers Publishers), p. 104.

[28] Gibbs, *More that Must be Told*, p. 77.

[29] Gibbs, *More that Must be Told*, p. 104.

[30] Gibbs, *More that Must be Told*, p. 106.

[31] Gibbs, *More that Must be Told*, p.133.

While the rebellion was being played out to its inevitably tragic conclusion, there were other changes in France which had a more immediate effect on the lives of the correspondents. They met with Sir Douglas Haig, the new commander-in-chief, in April 1916, at his Headquarters in a chateau near Montreuil. The shift in the official attitude to the war correspondents was evidenced by the manner in which they were greeted and given the opportunity to air their grievances. Less than a year before, in May 1915, Haig, the then commander of the First Army, sought to have correspondents banned from the Front entirely. Gibbs found Haig to be sympathetic yet totally ignorant of the role of the press. In truth, he had only accepted journalists with 'distaste and reluctance'.[32] During the meeting, Haig ventured the view that the correspondents 'wanted to get hold of little stories of heroism, and so forth, and to write them up in a bright way to make good reading for Mary Ann in the kitchen and the man in the street'.[33] Gibbs and the other correspondents took exception to this characterization of their role, but it appears that it was only Gibbs who had the courage to speak. He recalled seizing the opportunity to push for a relaxation of the censorship and a greater freedom to mention the name of military units involved in a reported action. By the end of the war, Gibbs felt that he 'had no complaint against the censorship, and wrote all that was good to write of the actions day by day, though I had to leave out something of the underlying horror of them all, in spite of my continual emphasis, by temperament and conviction, on the tragedy of all this sacrifice of youth'. He even went so far as to describe official censorship as a 'broad-minded policy' which permitted the reporting of any fact which did not aid the enemy. The only real limitation was, in Gibbs' view, the skill of the correspondent. Yet, though he denied that there was even a single word 'of conscious falsehood' in his dispatches, there were omissions.[34] In 1917, he felt compelled to spare the feelings of relatives of the fighting men. This concession jars with other claims Gibbs made to having written of the true horror of war as an antidote to militarism and his commitment to carrying the news to the Home Front.

There were also more personal reasons for the increasing deification of the men of the 'New Army'. They warmed the correspondents in a way the regular army found impossible, welcoming them into their world rather

[32] L MacDonald (1983) *Somme* (London: Michael Joseph), p. 79.
[33] Gibbs, *Realities of War*, p. 40.
[34] Gibbs, *Realities of War*, p. 41.

than seeing them as a threat to it. It is not difficult to understand why a man of non-military bearing, but of military age, might have enjoyed a sense of camaraderie with these men. Gibbs would have seen in their response to the call of Empire the glories of Victorian England and by extension he could revel in his own participation in a noble cause. He had seen them for the first time in July 1915 as they marched passed his billet to the Front:

> For as long as history lasts the imagination of our people will strive to con-jure up the vision of those boys who, in the year 1915, went out to Flanders, not as conscript soldiers, but as volunteers, for the old country's sake, to take their risks and 'do their bit' in the world's bloodiest war.[35]

Descriptions such as this were consistent thematically with his report-ing even prior to official accreditation. As early as the middle of 1915, before the New Armies had arrived on the Continent in any number, a reviewer of *The Soul of the War* noted that Gibbs was 'least interesting when he writes of our men; we have heard before all he has to say, and he insists too much on the adventure [*sic*] spirit in which the British soldier has gone to this war'.[36] In time, he would come to identify so closely with the British soldiers that he adopted their biases and their hatreds. This is particularly evident in his post-war book *Realities of War*, but by the time it was re-released for the second and penultimate time, the passions of the war years had receded, and he came to recognize that he may have gone further than he had intended. In the Preface to the 1929 edition (retained, with the addition of a third preface, in the 1936 edition), Gibbs feared that his criticism of the staff was too harsh and that he should not have 'steeped my pen in so much acid'. However, he chose not to alter these passages in later editions because it was the truth as he saw it, and crucially, it 'reflected the temper of the front line men with whom was all my sympathy and hero worship'.[37] Yet he still could not bring himself to reject the world of the regular officer, for he too was steeped in the past:

> I should hate to attack the regular officer. His caste belonged to the best of our blood. He was the heir to fine old traditions of courage and leadership in battle...So I salute in spirit those battalion officers of the Old Army who

---

[35] Gibbs, *Realities of War*, p. 76.
[36] *Times Literary Supplement*, 17 June 1915.
[37] Gibbs, *Realities of War*, p. xi.

fulfilled their heritage until it was overwhelmed by new forces, and I find extenuating circumstances even in remembrance of the high stupidities, the narrow imagination, the deep impregnable, intolerant ignorance of Staff College men, who, with their red tape and their general orders, were the inquisitors and torturers of the New Armies.[38]

For Gibbs though, it was never just about concrete issues such as class or rank. Always ready to highlight national character and the 'spirit' of a people, Gibbs believed that to the French soldier 'patriotism is a religion' and he 'has the name of France on his lips at the moment of peril'. In contrast, Gibbs did not find an overt patriotism among the New Army:

Yet the love of the Old Country was deep down in the roots of their hearts, and, as with a boy who came from the village where I lived for a time, the name of some such place held all the meaning of life to many of them. The simple minds of country boys clung fast to that, went back in walking dreams to dwell in a cottage parlour where their parents sat, and an old clock ticked, and a dog slept with its head on its paws. The smell of the fields and the barns, the friendship of familiar trees, the heritage that was in their blood from old yeoman ancestry, touched them with the spirit of England, and it was because of that they fought.[39]

Likewise, the men from London were animated by a love of homeland in a manner which tells us more about Gibbs' romanticized memories of childhood than it does of the soldiers he describes:

It was the spirit of the Old City, and the pride of it, which helped him to suffer, and in his day dreams was the clanging of buses from Charing Cross to the bank, the lights of the Embankment reflected in the dark river, the backyard where he had kept his bicycle, or the suburban garden where he had watered his mother's plants…His heart ached for it sometimes, when as sentry he stared across the parapet to the barbed wire in No Man's Land.[40]

On the evening of 30 June 1916, General Charteris visited the correspondents in their house in Amiens. In a clear sign that the days of outlaw correspondents roaming France and Belgium looking for a battle to report on were well and truly over, he not only revealed that an offensive would

---

[38] Gibbs, *Realities of War*, p. 73.
[39] Gibbs, *Realities of War*, p. 81.
[40] Gibbs, *Realities of War*, p. 82.

commence the following day but also suggested that they view the opening moments from high ground near the Albert-Bapaume road. Charteris also arranged for the correspondents to use official wires during the first day to ensure that their dispatches would make it into the following day's papers. This was in marked contrast to the Loos debacle when reports were published four days after their dispatch. However, what no one had foreseen was the situation in which the early dispatches heralding a victory reached the papers long before even the army was fully aware of the enormity of the disaster. It was a situation with the potential to embarrass both the correspondents and the military. In addition, there was the impact on Home Front morale by what Martin Bell, a modern war correspondent, described as 'premature exhilaration'.[41]

The Battle of the Somme has long been seared into the public consciousness as the epitome of military futility and needless sacrifice. The planning failures prior to 1 July 1916 remain an indictment of those entrusted with the human wealth of the Empire. Conceived as a joint Anglo-French offensive, the Somme area was chosen not for its strategic or tactical possibilities, but merely because it marked the juncture of the French and British armies. In any case, the French contribution shrank due to the carnage at Verdun, though Haig did not see fit to adjust his aims as a result. What ensued was a plan which lacked achievable objectives, in which the 'technical means were inadequate, and the methods inappropriate, to meet the peculiar set of tactical conditions then prevailing on the Somme where the Germans held most of the advantages'.[42] By June 1916, the BEF numbered well over a million troops, enough to create 58 Divisions organized into four armies. These armies contained the 'flower of British and Imperial manhood' which for the first time in history were drawn from all levels of society.[43] Of the 247 infantry battalions either selected for the initial attack or held in immediate reserve, over half were new army units. As Liddell Hart observed, the battle would prove to be 'both the glory and graveyard of "Kitchener's Army"'.[44]

In 1924, Gibbs, inspired by both the glory and the graveyard, stated that these men 'were in living splendour the priceless treasure of the British

[41] Martin Bell (1995) *In Harm's Way* (London: Penguin), p. 236.
[42] Simkins, *World War 1*, p. 111.
[43] Simkins, *World War 1*, p. 105.
[44] Liddell Hart, *History of the First World War*, p. 231.

folk—and they were squandered, wasted and destroyed'.[45] Perhaps in defence of his early characterization of the battle as a victory, in retrospect, Gibbs believed that the first day of the Somme provided the illusion of victory, and it was only after a few days that awful rumours of major reverses near Gommecourt, Thiepval, and Serre reached the correspondents. At the time though, to Gibbs' inexperienced eye, it looked like victory. Yet as he later admitted, the war correspondents were still hampered by their lack of experience in 'balancing the Profit and Loss'.[46] Although this was undoubtedly true, Gibbs' reports from the Somme, like those written by the other correspondents, were obviously profoundly inaccurate:

> The attack which was launched today against the German lines on a 20 mile front began well. It is not yet a victory, for victory comes at the end of a battle, and this is only the beginning. But our troops, fighting with splendid valour, have swept across the enemy's front trenches along a great part of the line of attack...And so, after the first day of battle, we may say: It is, on balance, a good day for England and France. It is a day of promise in this war, in which the blood of brave men is poured out upon the sodden fields of Europe.[47]

Gibbs and the other correspondents watched the opening of the battle on 1 July 1916 opposite Fricourt. Witnessing the intensity of the final bombardment which he described as a 'hurricane of fire', Gibbs pitied the Germans forced to endure it.[48] Yet even a man of his compassion was 'filled by a strange and awful exultation because this was the work of our guns, and because it was England's day'.[49] Again though, it was not a style of warfare which could be witnessed and understood by a single individual, even had the military done all in their power to permit it. Gibbs noted that 'behind the veil of smoke which hides our men there were many different actions taking place, and the messages that come back... give but glimpses of the progress of our men and their hard fighting'.[50] It is actually not surprising that Gibbs would consistently record the destructive power of the artillery. British optimism concerning a decisive

---

[45] Gibbs (1924) *Ten Years After* (London: Hutchinson and Co), p. 30.
[46] Gibbs, *Realities of War*, pp. 327–8.
[47] *Daily Chronicle*, 2 July 1916.
[48] *Daily Chronicle*, 3 July 1916.
[49] *Daily Chronicle*, 3 July 1916.
[50] *Daily Chronicle*, 3 July 1916.

breakthrough was based on the premise that the bombardment would obliterate the enemy defences. In reality, the artillery bombardment did not come close to achieving this improbable aim due to deficiencies in both number and ratio of heavy guns, their uniform placement on the Front, thus dispersing their fire, obsolete weapons, poor-quality shells, the strength of the German defences and the stubbornness and skill of their soldiers. Gibbs was probably both awed by the destruction and influenced by the general confidence that the bombardment would open the way for the infantry assault. In his book *The Battle of the Somme*, Gibbs included a chapter titled 'The Work of the Guns' in which he ascribed to them all of the successes of the offensive. He then added an impassioned call on the patriotism of the munitions workers to maintain the supply of shells.

William Beach Thomas, one of the other correspondents, recalled in his memoirs that the information supplied by the military was either wrong or misleading. In concert with the other correspondents, he sent off a short cable message announcing the success of the opening phase of the offensive. Although Beach Thomas later conceded that neither the correspondents nor the military were immediately aware of the extent of the losses, he was 'thoroughly and deeply ashamed' of what he had written.[51] In contrast, Gibbs was adamant that he wrote 'the plain unvarnished truth' and remained confident that in time 'no man or women would dare to speak again of war's glory and of the splendour of war, or any of the old lying phrases which hide the dreadful truth'.[52] It is worth remembering that these words were written in 1917 and do not form part of a post-war reassessment. He could not go further, even had he wanted to, but writing after the war, he acknowledged that the disaster on the left (north) of the line had caused a visible hesitancy and uncertainty in the High Command that was known to the correspondents.[53]

---

[51] W Beach Thomas (1925) *A Traveller in News* (London: Chapman and Hall), p. 109. Although the avowed purpose of Beach Thomas' *A Traveller in News* was to provide a sketch of Lord Harmsworth, it is also reasonably strong on autobiographical detail. Despite the jarring honesty evident in his admission of shame, Beach Thomas' description of his time on the Western Front and his views on censorship are remarkably matter of fact. Whereas the war informed all of Gibbs' subsequent work, for Beach Thomas, a far less prolific writer of wartime memoirs, his wartime experiences take a more natural place in a chronological ordering of his life.

[52] Gibbs, *The Battles of the Somme*, p. 114; 130.

[53] Gibbs, *Realities of War*, p. 339.

Even though he was repelled by the horror on the Somme, Gibbs was still able to refer to British soldiers advancing with 'a spirit of marvellous self-sacrifice' animated with something 'supernatural' as they faced 'hellish fires'.[54] Though he reported on the heavy losses, he inevitably tempered it with a celebration of courage 'which could not reach greater heights than these men showed'.[55] They were 'forgetful of self and faced the cruellest fire with a high and noble courage' as they 'go forward to the highest terrors with such singing hearts'.[56] Noble courage or not, for a limited breach in the German lines on the right (south) 5.6 km wide and 1.6 km deep, the British Army lost 57,470 officers and men, of whom 19,240 were killed. Thirty-two battalions lost over 500 men, or over 50 % of their battle strength.

On the second day, Gibbs felt that he was more able to 'get a clear idea of the fighting' and reported 'success to our arms'.[57] The third day of battle saw Gibbs at Fricourt in 'the heart of these battlefields', and the scene there was 'wonderful'. He had 'never watched before such a complete and close picture of war in its infernal grandeur'.[58] His excitement is clearly evident when he wrote that there 'was a strange exultation in one's senses at the consciousness of this mass of artillery supporting our men. Those were our guns. Ours!'[59] An attack at Gommecourt on the same day was a failure, but Gibbs assured his readers that it had drawn on the enemy's reserves, and 'great honour is due to the valour of those men of ours who fought as heroes in one of the most glorious acts of self-sacrifice ever made by British troops'.[60]

Though it would in time evolve, Gibbs' language when reporting on the Somme was ideologically consistent with his description of the *Titanic* disaster written four years before. Tragedy was softened, explained, and given value by courage and sacrifice. As he became more aware of the full extent of the losses, however, almost imperceptibly he began to use the language of attrition which had come into vogue around the time of Loos. This alteration in tone actually reflected a shift in Haig's thinking. As July wore on and hopes for the great breakthrough receded, Haig began to

[54] Gibbs, *The Battles of the Somme*, pp. 59–60.
[55] Gibbs, *The Battles of the Somme*, p. 61.
[56] Gibbs, *The Battles of the Somme*, p. 63; 71.
[57] *Daily Chronicle*, 4 July 1916.
[58] *Daily Chronicle*, 5 July, 1916.
[59] *Daily Chronicle*, 5 July, 1916.
[60] *Daily Chronicle*, 5 July, 1916.

view the offensive as a preparatory phase which would precede the decisive blow. Whether Gibbs consciously altered his tone or it reflected the information he was being fed is open to question. At the very least, it is clear that Gibbs remained a servant of the military, acting as mouthpiece rather than critic. There were times, however, when he recalled that it became 'intolerable and agonising, and when I, at least, desired peace at almost any price, peace by negotiation, by compromise, that the river of blood might cease to flow'.[61]

On 3 July, he reported continued fighting around La Boisselle and admitted that 'he could see nothing of the men in that smoke and flame, but I could see men going up towards it, in a quiet, leisurely way as though strolling on a summer morning in peaceful fields'.[62] After the war, Gibbs recalled visiting Fricourt and Montauban on the same day and being painfully aware that it was not a victory 'but only a breach in the German bastion, and that on the left, Gommecourt way, there had been a black tragedy'.[63] The next day Gibbs' dispatch made depressingly familiar reading. Echoing his Balkan experience, he claimed that 'it is behind the lines on the outskirts of the battlefields that one sees most of the activity of war' because up where 'fighting was in progress not many men were visible'. Instead, behind the actual front line is where he finds 'historic pictures of the campaign full of life and colour'.[64] Gibbs also mentioned the burial of those killed in the advance, which perhaps indicated a growing awareness of the 'heavy losses' and a tentative attempt to provide some balance to his dispatches.[65] Always susceptible to mood, and perhaps weighed down by his knowledge that all was not well, when Gibbs witnessed a storm on the afternoon of 4 July he felt the 'gloom and terror of it close around me'.[66]

It is clear that the control of the correspondents went further than just what they wrote. It was also a question of what they were shown and who they were able to interview. On 6 July, Gibbs and Beach Thomas were taken to La Chaussee, the divisional billets of the 21st Division which had succeeded at Fricourt. Perry Robinson and John Irvine interviewed troops involved in the fighting around Montauban, another relatively successful action. When actually able to view the fighting, as on 8 July, Gibbs was

---

[61] Gibbs, *Realities of War*, p. 34.
[62] *Daily Chronicle*, 5 July 1916.
[63] Gibbs, *Realities of War*, p. 330.
[64] *Daily Chronicle*, 6 July 1916.
[65] *Daily Chronicle*, 7 July 1916.
[66] Gibbs, *The Battles of the Somme*, p. 58.

able to see 'something of the battle' but conceded that he had 'no accurate idea of what was really happening beyond our guns...or whether our men are doing well or badly'.[67]

On 10 July, Gibbs revealed that the constant exposure to death and destruction had hardened him in a way peacetime journalism had never quite managed to do. He did not 'gloat over the sufferings of our enemy, though we must make them suffer, and go on suffering, that they may yield. It is the curse of war, the black horror which not even the heights of human courage may redeem, nor all the splendour of youth eager for self-sacrifice'.[68] Yet even when he should have been able to cast a more critical eye over strategy, Gibbs still wrote of the Battle as a success:

> The cost has been great, but the enemy's losses and the present position in which he finds himself prove the success of our main attack. For the first time since the beginning of the war the initiative has passed to us, and the German Headquarters Staff is hard pushed for reserves.[69]

His reference to the German reserves was in all likelihood information passed to the correspondents by the army. This speculation is supported by his constant references to German prisoners as looking 'beaten and broken', morale having been smashed and enemy troops having 'escaped' to the Allied lines to surrender.[70] Gibbs called upon anecdotal evidence in the form of letters gathered from German trenches as proof that the German Home Front was crumbling, a development which would, in Gibbs' view, encourage them to 'realize soon that war does not pay, and...haul down the flag with its skull and cross-bones'.[71] In contrast, the British wounded 'seemed to have no sense of pain, and not one man groaned, in spite of broken arms and head wounds and bayonet thrusts... straggling columns, limping and holding on the comrades, hobbling with sticks, peering through blood stained rags, tired and worn and weak, but the spirit in them was marvellous'.[72] Yet at the end of the battle, Gibbs added a note of caution which was not entirely consistent with his earlier dispatches. It suggests that he was increasingly less credulous, and gradually,

---

[67] *Daily Chronicle*, 8 July 1916; *Daily Chronicle*, 11 July 1916.
[68] Gibbs, *The Battles of the Somme*, p. 95.
[69] Gibbs, *The Battles of the Somme*, p. 96.
[70] Gibbs, *The Battles of the Somme*, p. 94; 83.
[71] Gibbs, *The Battles of the Somme*, p. 109.
[72] Gibbs, *The Battles of the Somme*, p. 125.

almost imperceptibly, becoming aware that victory was not imminent. Just as equally, it showed that he was helping prepare the nation for even further sacrifice:

> It is only the beginning. People at home must not think that the German army has lost its power of defence and that the great rout is at hand. They are drawing back their guns, but saving most of them. They are retreating, but will stand again, and dig new trenches and defend other villages. There will be greater and fiercer and more desperate fighting before the end comes, and God alone knows when that will be.[73]

Though Gibbs opened himself up to criticism for his failure to record, or perhaps to be fully aware of the losses, his emotional response to the courage of his countrymen is understandable. Liddell Hart, not noted for any disinclination to criticize military ineptitude, offered a similar view of the quality of the attacking force:

> Yet although a military failure, July 1st was an epic of heroism, and better still, the proof of the moral quality of the new armies of Britain…All along the attacking lines these quondam civilians bore a percentage of losses such as no professional army of past wars had ever been deemed capable of suffering—without being broken as an effective instrument. And they carried on the struggle, equally bitter, for another five months.[74]

The absence, however, of criticism of the High Command in Gibbs' dispatches stands in marked contrast to some of his post-war writing. In 1924, Gibbs described the battle as 'sheer slaughter' in which the soldiers were victims of 'atrocious staff work, incompetent generalship, ruthless disregard of human life, repeated and dreadful blundering'. Yet even with this knowledge and by then free to write as he wished, Gibbs felt compelled to defend the officer class, and perhaps by extension, his failure to criticize them during the war. For they 'cannot be blamed. They were amateurs doing their best in an unknown type of war'. His conclusion that they had to learn by their mistakes which 'perhaps…were not worse than those of the enemy's High Command' though self-serving was not without some truth.[75]

---

[73] Gibbs, *The Battles of the Somme*, p. 303.
[74] Liddell Hart, *History of the First World War*, p. 243.
[75] Gibbs, *Ten Years After*, p. 31.

Gibbs' observations were not just confined to his newspapers. In 1917, Darling & Sons published a 37-page booklet titled *The Germans on the Somme* based on Gibbs' articles which were then appearing in the *Daily Chronicle* and *Daily Telegraph*, as well as in papers across the Empire and the USA. Gibbs believed that this narrative, based on the British Army's view of the German experience supplemented by captured letters and diaries, was not 'coloured by imagination or bias'. Gibbs' account was coloured only by the 'red vision of great bloodshed, for the story of the Somme battles on the German side is ghastly and frightful'.[76] Given the focus on the Germans, the shortcomings evident in his assessments are clearer than in his newspaper accounts. To justify the slaughter, Gibbs felt compelled to show that the Germans were suffering and were unable to 'check our men, or stop their progress'. Though he noted that the Germans were 'hard to beat, grim and resolute' his argument that they fought 'with the courage of despair' showed that Gibbs was well aware of the propaganda value of his reports.[77] Implicit in these reports is the underlying argument that the Somme was a victory because it had contributed to the wearing down of German strength, an attrition which would in time lead to victory.

In late January 1917, George Bernard Shaw arrived at the Front at the invitation of Douglas Haig, possibly at Gibbs' own suggestion. He had mentioned Shaw's name in a 'moment of wild inspiration' when approached by General Charteris for suggestions as to which famous writer might be invited to tour the Front and then write a series of articles for use as propaganda. Though Gibbs may well have included this in his memoirs to emphasize his growing reputation on both sides of the Channel, an approach from the Chief of Intelligence on an issue of propaganda says a good deal about how the army viewed the correspondents. To Gibbs' surprise, given Shaw's reputation as a polemicist, the great writer arrived in France on 28 January and met Gibbs at St Eloi and eventually lunched with Haig himself at Montreuil before returning home on 5 February.[78]

---

[76] Philip Gibbs (1917) *The Germans on the Somme* (London: Darling and Son Ltd), pp. 3–4.

[77] Gibbs, *The Germans on the Somme*, p. 10.

[78] In a 1914 pamphlet titled *Common Sense*, he had written 'the heroic remedy for this tragic misunderstanding is that both armies should shoot their officers and go home to gather in their harvests in the villages and make a revolution in the towns'. http://www.theguardian.com/world/2008/nov/11/ed-morel-anti-war-movement, accessed 11 December 2015. Nevertheless Shaw believed that the war had to be pursued to the end.

Gibbs found him to be a man of 'genius, charm of personality, and high distinction', but also one 'who could not deny his instinctive urge to shock the conventional and rigid minds by remarks which seemed like blasphemy to their humourless way of thinking'.[79] When asked by a general in the presence of junior officers (who subsequently failed to control their mirth) when he thought the war would end, Shaw replied 'Well general, we are all anxious for an early and dishonourable peace'. Even such an irreverent figure as Shaw was criticized, however, for the 'rather odd thing' of being 'taken in by this bit of Haigery'.[80]

Shrewder than Gibbs, Shaw was well aware of the reasons for his invitation and was equally aware of why he was still prepared to make the journey. In a letter to HG Wells on 11 January, Shaw admitted that the temptation to accept was very strong as 'pure mischief is always fascinating'. Being of a less trusting nature than Gibbs, he asked Wells whether 'they demand any pledges from you as to what you shall say or not say, and also whether the fact of having been at the Front marks you out for special censorship even in respect of books. If that is the case I won't go'.[81] Gibbs recalled Shaw commenting on wartime censorship in an entirely different tone. The great playwright believed that there was no need of censorship, for in wartime 'we must be our own censors'.[82] On returning home, Shaw wrote three articles titled 'Joyriding at the Front', which Gibbs believed were far too flippant and in poor taste. Importantly, he believed that from a propaganda point of view, they were 'utterly useless'.[83] Other writers would also make the journey, with JM Barrie, Arthur Conan Doyle, and John Masefield, all spending a few days with the correspondents. Masefield had by this time written his book *Gallipoli*, which Gibbs described as 'beautiful' and had planned to write a corresponding work on the Battle of the Somme. According to Gibbs, Masefield abandoned this plan when Gibbs published his dispatches in book form in early 1917, thus depriving English literature of a 'deathless work'.[84]

[79] Gibbs, *The Pageant of the Years*, p. 196.

[80] J O'Donovan (1983) *Bernard Shaw* (Dublin: Gill & Macmillan), p. 126.

[81] DH Laurence (1985) *Bernard Shaw Collected Letters 1911–1925* (London: Max Reinhardt), pp. 448–9.

[82] *Lethbridge Daily Herald*, 30 June 1923.

[83] Gibbs, *The Pageant of the Years*, p. 197.

[84] Gibbs, *The Pageant of the Years*, p. 197. Though denied access to official records, Masefield did publish *The Old Front Line* (1917), a description of the geography of the battlefield, and two years later *The Battle of the Somme* (1919).

In order to shorten their line and free up valuable reserves of man-power, the Germans began their withdrawal to the Hindenburg Line in February 1917. Although Gibbs recognized the sound strategic reasons underpinning the surrender of ground, he nevertheless found in it a post facto justification for the casualties on the Somme the previous year. He described it as a retreat compelled by the 'smashing of his divisions by incessant gun-fire and infantry assaults'.[85] As such, it is not surprising that his dispatches in February and March reflected an excitement borne out of the illusion that the end of the war beckoned. In the third week of February, he observed the Germans yielding 'to our pressure, the ceaseless pressure of men and guns, by escaping to a new line of defence along the Bapaume Ridge', a development which revealed 'a new phase of weakness in their defensive conditions'.[86] Ten days later, though repeating that it was a strategic retreat, Gibbs argued that it was forced upon a German military which feared 'that our fighting power in the spring might break his armies if they stayed on their old line'.[87] The excitement for Gibbs of being above ground and part of an advancing army continued through the next month with the occupation of Bapaume being 'one of the great days of the war'.[88] The next day, Gibbs described the whole German line south of Arras as 'one vast fortress, built by the labour of millions of men, dug and tunnelled and cemented and timbered, with thousands of machine gun redoubts, with an immense maze of trenches, protected by forests of barbed wire' just slipping away 'as though by landslide'.[89] In one report alone, Gibbs emphasized the changed circumstances by using the words retired, retreat, fled, gone, crept, hurrying and, most tellingly, pursuit.[90]

No doubt chastened by the premature elation in the dispatches report-ing on the Somme in the previous year, a note of caution crept into Gibbs' dispatches at the beginning of April. With the approach of the Battle of Arras, Gibbs again warned his readers that greater sacrifice was needed:

All this is an interlude between greater and grimmer things. We have not yet come to the period of real open warfare, but have only passed over a wide belt of No Man's Land: and the fantasy of cavalry skirmishes and wandering

[85] P Gibbs (1918) *From Bapaume to Passchendaele* (London: Heinemann), p. 3.
[86] *Daily Chronicle*, 18 February 1917.
[87] *Daily Chronicle*, 28 February 1917.
[88] *Daily Chronicle*, 17 March 1917.
[89] *Daily Chronicle*, 19 March 1917.
[90] *Daily Chronicle*, 20 March 1917.

Germans and civilians greeting us with outstretched hands from ruined villages will soon be closed by the wires and walls of the Hindenburg line, where once again the old fortress and siege warfare will begin, unless we have the luck to turn it or break through before the Siegfried divisions have finished their fortifications.[91]

A week later, he shared with his readers the hope that this 'titanic conflict' might 'be the beginning of the last great battles of the war'.[92] As he had done at Loos in 1915 and on the Somme in 1916, Gibbs witnessed the preliminary bombardment prior to the battle. It was a bitterly cold night with rain and sleet, but he recalled being 'awed by the hellish vision I watched'.[93]

It was a beautiful and devilish thing, and the beauty of it and not the evil of it put a spell upon one's senses. All our batteries, too many to count, were firing and thousands of gun flashes were winking and blinking from the hollows and hiding places, and all their shells were rushing through the sky as though flocks of great birds were in flight, and all were bursting over German positions with long flames which rent the darkness and waved sword blades of quivering light along the ridge.[94]

On the second day of the battle, Gibbs visited the ground east of Arras, the same ground where, with his love of history and literature, he noted that D'Artagnan and the Musketeers had fought the Spaniards. He visited the tunnels that had protected the troops and it made a 'vivid impression on my mind so that I remember it as though it were yesterday, though another war has happened since then'.[95] A couple of days later he stood under a hill at Monchy and witnessed a cavalry charge which, when recalled in 1946, appeared 'magnificent but it was not war—in a war of machine guns, aeroplanes and artillery...The charge was an heroic adventure but very foolish'.[96] In his dispatch, however, there were echoes of his description of the *Titanic* disaster. He described the cavalry as having behaved

[91] *Daily Chronicle*, 3 April 1917.
[92] *Daily Chronicle*, 10 April 1917.
[93] Gibbs, *The Pageant of the Years*, p. 198.
[94] *Daily Chronicle*, 10 April 1917.
[95] Gibbs, *The Pageant of the Years*, pp. 199–200.
[96] Gibbs, *The Pageant of the Years*, pp. 200–1.

'with the greatest acts of sacrifice to the ideals of duty', and thus, as it had been in the Atlantic in 1912, Death was compelled to give way to Glory.[97]

Gibbs still hinted that the German Army might be on the point of collapse by noting that the prisoners taken in the first week of the battle, 'Prussians, Bavarians, Hamburgers, have lost all spirit for this fighting, hate it, loathe it as a devilish fate from which they have luckily escaped at last with life'.[98] In contrast, soldiers from Nova Scotia, who were 'dragging one foot after another in sheer exhaustion' and were 'spent and done', had eyes that 'were steel blue and struck fire like steel when they told me of the good victory they had shared in'. Yet Gibbs was a shrewder man than the one who reported on the Somme in 1916, for he finished the day's dispatch with a conditional assessment:

> Our men have still most bloody fighting before them. The enemy is still in great strength. We shall have to mourn most tragic and fearful losses. But the tide of battle seems to be setting in our favour, and beating back against the walls of the German armies, who must hear the approach of it with forebodings, because the barriers they built have broken and there are no impregnable ramparts behind.[99]

The following day, Haig ordered an end to the offensive, which after early gains had ground to a halt at the cost of 150,000 British casualties. Farrar argued that the war correspondents had by this time become a valuable asset to the military. He was equally correct in observing that they had demonstrated their full support for the military with which they shared a common goal. Where Farrar overstepped the mark was in his claim that they 'had turned a blind eye to the true reality of war'.[100] In his collection of dispatches covering this period titled *From Bapaume to Passchendaele*, admittedly not published until the start of 1918, Gibbs was remarkably forthright in describing the true reality of war in a manner which should have satisfied even critics such as Farrar. For he had watched 'the tide of wounded flowing back, so many blind men, so many cripples, so many gassed and stricken men'. Even after three years of war, Gibbs was staggered by the 'vastness and the unceasing drift of this wreckage

---

[97] *Daily Chronicle*, 13 April 1917.

[98] *Daily Chronicle*, 16 April 1917.

[99] *Daily Chronicle*, 16 April 1917.

[100] M Farrar (1998) *News from the Front: War Correspondents on the Western Front* (Phoenix Mill, Gloucestershire: Sutton Publishing), p. 146.

of war'.[101] His description of German corpses after the retreat to the Hindenburg Line also left little to the imagination of the human cost for both sides:

> From the mud, arms stretched out like those of men who had been drowned in bogs. Boots and legs were uncovered in the muck heaps and faces with eyeless sockets on which flies settled, clay coloured faces with broken jaws, or without noses or scalps, stared up at the sky or lay half buried in the mud. I fell once and clutched a bit of earth and found that I had grasped a German hand.[102]

What Gibbs does not do is criticize the higher direction of the war. In this instance, Farrar does not explicitly demand this of the correspondents, but it is really this failure which underpins most of his criticism of their dispatches.

Prior to the opening of the Battle of Messines, which Gibbs considered a 'model battle' and an overwhelming defeat for the enemy, the correspondents witnessed something that they could not have possibly envisaged even months before.[103] General Harington, who with General Plumer was responsible for the organization of the surprise attack on Messines Ridge, briefed the correspondents about the forthcoming attack with complete candour. Farrar saw it as a reward for their loyalty and by implication the abrogation of their journalistic responsibilities. Yet as evidence of how differently the correspondents viewed this development, Beach Thomas saw it as the complete surrender of the army and War Office to the press. In fact, their candour left him 'aghast' for by now the correspondents, having been joined by American, French, and Italians, were 'almost a mob'.[104] Nevertheless, there were still limitations. When he asked the Chief of Intelligence what he could write about the Battle, Beach Thomas was nonplussed to receive the reply 'Say what you like. But don't mention any places or people'. As Beach Thomas remarked in his autobiography, 'it did not occur to him that one's style was a little cramped by such a prohibition, and I did not ask him what he thought was left of a battle after

---

[101] Gibbs, *From Bapaume*, p. 2.

[102] Gibbs, *From Bapaume*, p. 3.

[103] Gibbs, *The Pageant of the Years*, p. 202. The objective was Messines Ridge which afforded the Germans a clear view of the surrounding area. Its capture was seen as vital to the success of the planned offensive near Ypres.

[104] Beach Thomas, *A Traveller in News*, p. 120.

place and people were subtracted'.[105] He added that 'beyond all dispute the cardinal sin of a reporter is inaccuracy…I have never received opposite advice. The first exception is recorded against the Intelligence branch of the army'.[106]

On 7 June 1917, Gibbs witnessed the opening of the Battle heralded by the explosion of 19 mines buried under the German front line. Requiring 2 years of preparation and a million pounds of explosives, the resulting upheaval killed 10,000 German soldiers. The explosions, which could be heard in England, drew on a dwindling supply of adjectives available to the correspondents after they had exhausted so many during the Battle of the Somme:

> It is my duty to write the facts of it, and to give the picture of it. That is not easy to a man, after seeing the bombardments of many battles, has seen now the appalling vision of massed gunfire enormously greater in its intensity than any of those, whose eyes are still dazed by a sky of earthquakes shaking the hill sides, when suddenly, as a signal, the ground opened and mountains and fire rose into the clouds. There are no words which will help the imagination here. Neither by colour nor language nor sound could mortal man reproduce the picture and the terror and the tumult of this scene.[107]

Three decades later, Gibbs still recalled the 'tall pillars of earth and flame…as though hell had been opened up'.[108] Within three hours, the whole ridge had been secured, lending some credence to Gibbs' description of it as a 'great victory' and one in which he had 'never seen the spirit of victory so real and so visible among great bodies of British troops since the war began'.[109] As to the possibility of the war ending, he left it to a German prisoner to observe that 'the attack ought to end the war'. Yet having raised the issue amidst a glowing report of victory, he cautioned his readers 'not to base too much optimistic belief on such words by German prisoners'.[110]

While celebrating victory on the ground, Gibbs did not forget his countrymen serving in the Royal Flying Corps. Gibbs' reference to the joy of

[105] Beach Thomas, *A Traveller in News*, p. 122.
[106] Beach Thomas, *A Traveller in News*, p. 148.
[107] *Daily Chronicle*, 8 June 1917.
[108] Gibbs, *The Pageant of the Years*, p. 202.
[109] *Daily Chronicle*, 8 June 1917; *Daily Chronicle*, 9 June 1917.
[110] *Daily Chronicle*, 9 June 1917.

battle and his use of the metaphor of the hunt might have been forgiven had he not resorted to the word 'smite' with its overt biblical connotation:

> They flew as men inspired by passion and a fierce joy of battle. They were hunters seeking their prey. They were Berserkers of the air, determined to kill though they should be killed, to scatter death among the enemy, to destroy him in the air and on the earth, to smite him in his body and in his works and in his soul by the terror of him. This may seem language of exaggeration, the silly fantasy of a writing man careless of the exact truth. It is less than the truth, and the sober facts are wild things.[111]

Defeats, such as the one suffered at Lombartzyde in July 1917, were presented as though British heroism was an end in itself, one which almost transcended victory or defeat. In Gibbs' view, it was a tragic event 'great in spiritual value and heroic memory'. He even observed that it was 'wonderful to think that after 3 years of war the spirit of our men should still be so high and proud that they will stand to certain death like this'.[112] It was a pattern to be repeated regularly as the Third Battle of Ypres later ground to a bloody stalemate in the mud and blood of Flanders. For it was the same spirit which had inspired men to obey the 'women and children first' order as the end of the *Titanic* neared, and three years of war had not completely stripped Gibbs of his romanticized view of a loyalty unbroken by the fear of death.

In his report on the opening day of the Third Battle of Ypres, Gibbs availed himself of the opportunity to boast about how effective the self-censorship had actually become. The build-up, evident to the correspondents, was not even 'hinted at' in their dispatches, although he added that other people were not so discreet.[113] Although he does not explicitly make the link, he may well be referring to the disastrous Nivelle offensive, 'much advertised in advance, openly talked about for months in French restaurants and estaminets, and perfectly well known to the enemy'.[114] Such a claim revealed how free the correspondents were of any sense that their silence was anything but honourable.

Though this first dispatch was still optimistic, his dispatches, and those of his fellow correspondents, were markedly different from those written

---

[111] *Daily Chronicle*, 9 June 1917.
[112] *Daily Chronicle*, 14 July 1917.
[113] *Daily Chronicle*, 1 August 1917.
[114] Gibbs, *The Pageant of the Years*, p. 205.

during the Somme only just over 12 months before. Thirty years later, Gibbs was still astonished that the censors passed them.[115] Even Farrar, a strident critic of the correspondents, found the truthfulness of the dispatches 'shocking' in their descriptions of the helplessness of the soldiers and the futility of pursuing the offensive in worsening weather over almost impossible terrain. Neville Lytton, Head of Censorship at GHQ, was also aware of the change in the tone of the dispatches, a fact often overlooked amidst the accusations that the correspondents lied or censored themselves into irrelevancy:

> During the Flanders offensive they spoke of the angelic patience of the men and of their great sufferings; they did not actually say that the task was impossible, but they gave clearly the impression that to fight the whole German army, on that narrow strip of land between the Belgian inundations (on the north) and the industrial valley of the Lys (on the south) in torrents of rain, was almost hopeless.[116]

This new freedom was reflected in the constant references to the terrain and the weather. On 1 August, Gibbs referred to the swamps in the north around *Dixmude* and the low flats around Ypres as being so 'full of peril for attacking troops that optimism itself might be frightened and downcast'.[117] Gibbs' reports for 2, 4, and 6 August all opened with references to the appalling weather. Observations such as these would never have been permitted in earlier reports. Two weeks later in his description of attacks launched near Langemarck, Gibbs struggled to describe the scale of what he was witnessing. He conceded that 'these words of mine convey nothing to people who read them. How could they when for 3 years we have been talking in superlatives without exaggerating the facts, but without understanding them, as minds are numbed by colossal figures'.[118] In October, he wrote that the 'theme' of the battle was the appalling condition of the ground and of the weather, and that success was due to 'sheer courage', and where there was failure 'it was because

---

[115] Gibbs, *The Pageant of the Years*, p. 207.

[116] N Lytton (1920) *The Press and the General Staff* (London: W Collins & Sons & Co), p. 114.

[117] *Daily Chronicle*, 1 August 1917. Although written on the 31 July, it was, of course, not published until the following day.

[118] *Daily Chronicle*, 17 August 1917.

courage itself was of no avail against the power of nature'.[119] After the war, Haig reputedly commented that Gibbs' dispatches had exaggerated the conditions.[120] Gibbs rejected the charge of inaccuracy, as he did most others, yet at the same time would have seen this as a vindication of the veracity of his reports.

Summing up 1917 as a year of unending battle, Gibbs made an effort to correct the deification of the British soldiers to which he had contributed:

> Through all these battles our men were magnificent—not demi-gods, nor saints with a passion for martyrdom, nor heroes of melodrama facing death with breezy nonchalance while they read sweet letters from blue eyed girls, but grim in attack and stubborn in defence, getting on with the job—a damned ugly job—as far as the spirit could pull the body and control the nerves.[121]

Towards the end of 1917, Gibbs returned home on leave, having spent time in hospital in Amiens in October with trench fever. On 27 December 1917, he gave a speech about the fighting in Flanders at a private dinner organized by his editor Robert Donald and attended by Prime Minister Lloyd George, Lieutenant General JC Smuts, and representatives of over a dozen newspapers. Held at the Savoy Hotel, the text of the introductory speeches and Gibbs' address were published in a commemorative booklet.[122] Each speaker in turn acknowledged both the burden of censorship and Gibbs' integrity and skill in offering as truthful a vision of the war as conditions permitted. In the opening address, Donald noted that after the army's initial opposition, the correspondents 'were harnessed to the wheels of war...and are now allowed to see more of the war than correspondents have in other wars—and are permitted to write less'. Lord Burnham described Gibbs as a 'real hero of the war in a war waged by heroes'. He had also done 'honour to himself, and honour to his profession [while rendering] to the State and the Nation just as good service as any other branch of the Nation in arms'. This was achieved despite 'irksome restrictions' and 'mistakes'. He went even further, however, for in his opinion Gibbs had not written 'a single line that is not literature; not a single article that is not the truth. He is a great realist and a great idealist

---

[119] *Daily Chronicle*, 10 October 1917.
[120] Gibbs, *The Pageant of the Years*, p. 207.
[121] Gibbs, *From Bapaume*, p. 18.
[122] Gibbs Family Archives.

at the same time...He has not only been a great impressionist, but he has never swerved from noble aims. He has done honour to his craft, honour to his country, honour to the matchless qualities of the men'.

Gibbs viewed the speech as an 'ordeal', but delivered it in a 'trance-like way' for 'it was not I that was making the speech. It was the voice of the boys on the Western Front that spoke through my lips'. He would have been pleased by references to his courage but opened his speech with the self-deprecatory claim that if he put a mark against every place in France where he had been frightened, 'the map would be covered in splotches from Nieuport to St Quentin'. Taking advantage of the freedom offered by the occasion, Gibbs offered details that the censor would never have allowed. He attempted to offer an approximation of the casualties suffered in Flanders and revealed that censorship had forbidden reference to German mustard gas and its terrible effect upon the wounded. Nevertheless, the tone is not entirely dissimilar to his dispatches. Outside Arras, he witnessed 3000 wounded men queuing outside a dressing station:

> Blind boys came groping their way, men with their faces smashed and their heads all bloody—a tragic and unforgettable sight...the strange miracle is that these men of ours chaff each other, and find any old joke in any old place. That side must not be left out. It is allowed by the Censor. But, as one of these men said to me, 'Don't make us too bloody cheerful'. They do not like us to write about their cheerfulness unless we write also about the misery, and the agony, and the terror they have endured.

Gibbs also addressed the issue of censorship by criticizing the continued refusal to allow the naming of specific divisions as it put 'out the flame of enthusiasm which would be lighted in the counties, and it is always a great disappointment to the soldiers'. However, he went even further, perhaps further than he ever was prepared to again in assessing the impact on the sensibilities of correspondents exposed to these horrors over long periods of time. In his awareness of the repetition of experience which he referred to as a formula, Gibbs gave an insight into the challenge of making daily reports interesting for a war-weary public by outlining a 'normal' day in the life of a correspondent. There is also a sense that Gibbs had not only been overwhelmed by the carnage but was battling with a sense of the futility of the war and his role in it. In all of his published works, there is no other comparable discussion of the futility of reporting on yet another battle. Ever ready to discuss the futility of war, it was rare to see Gibbs touch on the futility of being a correspondent.

Gibbs began the narrative with a car journey to a village where 'there is no village, or to some heap of ruins like Ypres'. Then in increasing levels of horror, he recounted the various signposts that indicated the transition from the relative safety of the rear areas to the battlefield:

First we walk past dead horses, and their stench rises and fills the air about us. Then we walk past dead men—old dead and new dead; then we walk through the heavy batteries which are being shelled by the enemy, so that the gunners are working with death searching for them. And then we walk further to the field batteries some miles forward, where the shell fire is heavier and the gunners are being killed and wounded.

Significantly, Gibbs then talked of his fear, for it does his critics well to remember that he spent longer on the Western Front than any other correspondent. Though his life was safer and more comfortable than that endured by a front-line soldier, the stress and strain of constant exposure to battle cannot be underestimated. He finished his description with images of the confusion and flotsam of battle:

And then, if our courage takes us further, we reach the support troops going up to the front lines along tracks taped out by German shells. Beyond this we can see very little in weather like this but smoke and bursting shells and mist. Presently, out of the mist come the first men back. They are the walking wounded. They have a long way to walk—sometimes five or six miles over dreadful ground, and it is a Via Dolorosa; the scene burns itself into one's heart and brain. They come limping down their tracks until they drop, and sometimes until they die. One can do nothing for them—these poor, bloody men, these blind men, these cripples.[123]

Gibbs recalled that it left the prime minister in tears. Lloyd George described his reaction the following day to CP Scott, the editor of the *Manchester Guardian*:

I am in a very pacifist temper. I listened last night...to the most impressive and moving description of what the war in the West really means...Even an audience of hardened politicians and journalists was strongly affected.

[123] *Harpers Monthly Magazine*, September 1921, p. 425.

The thing is horrible and beyond human nature to bear...I fear I can't go
on with this bloody business: I would rather resign.[124]

Nevertheless, Lloyd George would not remember the most famous
of the war correspondents affectionately. Possibly out of spite for Gibbs'
later opposition to his Irish policy, Lloyd George claimed in his autobiography that Gibbs' sense of public duty had not prevented his 'suppressing every check or repulse, and exaggerating with unbridled extravagance
every trifling advance purchased at a terrible cost'.[125] Though Gibbs felt
it very unjust of Lloyd George 'of all men' to make such an accusation,
he believed that his anguish at the carnage in Flanders showed the little Welshman in 'all his humanity [with] a sensitive heart and mind, not
smothered by power and politics'.[126] Gibbs' use of the phrase 'of all men'
probably reflected his belief that Lloyd George was sincere in his distress
and should have been a witness to Gibbs' honesty rather than his accuser.
Less kindly observers would also be aware that for all his qualities, Lloyd
George was not a paragon of virtue where the truth was concerned. There
was much truth in Taylor's assertion that Lloyd George was the 'most
inspired and creative British statesman of the twentieth century', but he
was equally on the mark in adding that he 'was devious and unscrupu-
lous in his methods'.[127] Regardless, Gibbs would have recalled that during his speech in 1917, Lloyd George acknowledged that he considered
it his duty to read his dispatches, as well as conceding that 'many incidents' were brought to his attention by a correspondent who had shown
'courage in describing what he has seen without fear or favour'. In 1935,
while serving on the Royal Commission into the Arms Trade, Gibbs and
Lloyd George spoke light heartedly of the passage in the latter's book and
parted amicably in a manner the ex-prime minister described as 'the peace
of Passchendaele'.[128]

---

[124] CP Scott (1970) *The Political Diaries of CP Scott*, 1911-1928 (London: Collins),
p. 324.

[125] D Lloyd George (1934) *War Memoirs of David Lloyd George* Vol. IV. (London: Ivor
Nicholson & Watson), p. 2230. In 1935 while serving on the Royal Commission into the
Arms Trade, Gibbs and Lloyd George spoke light heartedly of the passage, and parted ami-
cably in a manner the ex-Prime Minister described as 'the peace of Passchendaele' (Gibbs,
Ordeal in England, pp. 93–4).

[126] Gibbs, *The Pageant of the Years*, p. 208.

[127] Taylor, *English History*, p. 192.

[128] P Gibbs (1938) *Ordeal in England* (London: William Heinemann), pp. 93–4.

Whether Gibbs took heart from being able to report directly to the prime minister is unknown, though in 1921 he described the fighting in Flanders as a shambles and a waste of human life.[129] Even given the greater freedom in reporting permitted by 1917, he was still quite open about the limitations of his dispatches. In his book *From Bapaume to Passchendaele* (1918), he acknowledged again the absence of criticism, judgement, and a detailed summation of the success or failure of the fighting in Ypres. This was because it 'was not within my liberty or duty as a correspondent'.[130] Around the same time, Gibbs recalled Lord Milner, who he incorrectly places at the Foreign Office, seeking his views on the possibility of a negotiated peace. Though Gibbs was, as always, 'weak on dates', it is not entirely inconceivable that the second most powerful figure in the War Cabinet, behind the prime minister himself, might have sought out the opinion of a correspondent.[131] He may have done so at the instigation of Lloyd George himself after Gibbs' speech, he may have been giving voice to his own dissatisfaction concerning the conduct of the war, or he may have been guilty of making a passing observation. If it is indeed true that such an approach was made, it is a sad indictment of the lack of rapport between the civilian government and the army then engaged in the greatest war in history. It would also suggest that the correspondents were seen, at least in this instance, as reliable witnesses. Having given what he believed was a balanced report, Gibbs wrote that he was asked the same question later again in France by an unnamed British general. In any event, Gibbs felt that such efforts were futile because the 'military caste and the Junkers, and the German Foreign Office, and Big Industry, would have seen to it that no such ideas would prevail…the Germans have no genius for revolution, and prefer obedience, and order, and authority, even if it leads to their doom, as now it has'.[132]

In the author's note in *Open Warfare: The Way to Victory*, which covers the final year of the war, Gibbs again assured his readers that he had written the truth 'simply and with sincerity'.[133] The truth which he offered them in early 1918 was not comforting. Beginning in early 1918, the newspapers published articles which were written with the express

[129] *Harpers Monthly Magazine*, September 1921, p. 425.

[130] Gibbs, *From Bapaume*, p. 21.

[131] P Gibbs (1949) *Crowded Company* (London: Allan Wingate), p. 19.

[132] Gibbs, *The Pageant of the Years*, p. 211.

[133] P Gibbs (1919) *Open Warfare: The Way to Victory* (London: Heinemann), Author's Preface.

intention of preparing the Home Front for the coming German offensive. On 31 January 1918, Gibbs wrote that 'all along the lines our men are ready and waiting' while on 9 February, he wrote that it was 'as though Nature herself were in suspense waiting and watching and listening for the beginning of that conflict of men which is expected before the year grows much older'. On the day this report was published, Gibbs visited his brother Arthur who was commanding a battery of field guns opposite St Quentin. He recalled not daring to tell his 'kid brother' the date of the coming attack. Arthur remembered their meeting a little differently, recalling the endless tension being exacerbated by his brother 'rolling up one day and giving out the date definitely as the twenty first'.[134] The disparity in their recall of this meeting, occurring as it did under conditions of extreme stress, might simply have been an error on the part of Philip or Arthur, or even a combination of both. Yet it also raises the intriguing possibility that Gibbs, either with intent or subconsciously, sought to justify the correspondents' preparedness to omit details in the national interest by showing that his silence extended even to his own family.

Nine days later, having feared that it would be the last time he would see his brother alive, Gibbs wrote that 'at any moment now we may see the beginning of the enemy's last and desperate effort to end the war by a decisive victory, for the offensive which he has been preparing for months is imminent'.[135] One writer for the *New York Times* was particularly generous in his praise, however, of what he saw as Gibbs' reticence to play the prophet:

> He has written while the theme and the very earth itself were hot, and he is to be envied not merely the versatility and brilliance of his pen, but the deep and broad and throbbing human sympathy which links him with the men of whom he writes, and his capacity for infecting with this quality even the stony heart of remorseless officialism...He is the last man in existence to don the mantle of prophet, and his far outlook, not to mention his bedrock honesty, would forbid him to cheer his readers with a prospect of early peace in which he cannot yet believe.[136]

---

[134] A Gibbs (1924) *Gun Fodder: The Diary of Four Years of War* (Boston: Little, Brown, & Company), p. 234.

[135] *Daily Chronicle*, 18 February 1918.

[136] *New York Times*, 24 February 1918.

Four thousand German guns opened fire on the morning of 21 March 1918, announcing an attack on a 42-mile length of front between Gouzeaucourt and Barisis. It was launched with the intent of separating the British line from their French allies, and by the end of the day the Germans had advanced four-and-a-half miles through crumbling British defences. Gibbs' dispatch opened with the bald statement that 'a German offensive against our front has begun'. He continued with the observation that 'it is impossible to say yet how far the enemy will endeavour to follow up the initial movement of his troops over any ground he may gain in the first rush…But the attack already appears to be on a formidable scale, with a vast amount of artillery and masses of men, and there is reason to believe that it is indeed the beginning of the great offensive advertised for so long a time and with such ferocious menaces by the enemy's agents in neutral countries'.[137] On the second day, with the British Army in retreat, he wrote of 'their courage and discipline under the fiercest ordeal which has ever faced British soldiers'. Near Bullecourt, he was free to describe British soldiers retiring in good order having left behind them 'masses of German dead heaped up near our wire'.[138] Nevertheless, it was clear that Gibbs was describing a German advance conducted in the face of the British soldiers' 'unconquerable spirit to death'.[139] The following day he noted that 'our armies are able to control the situation within the limits of ultimate safety, though our losses in men are inevitably severe'.[140] A few days later, on 27 March, the German advance began to lose momentum, and this is reflected in Gibbs' description of British soldiers moving up to the line:

> It is a pageant of heroic youth and our heart beats to see them. It is their bodies and their spirit which stand between us and a German victory. It is their courage which will break down the enemy's onslaught.[141]

It was also a time to reassure the Home Front, as on 31 March, when Gibbs wrote that 'we are continuing to make the enemy pay a dreadful price for any advance' and that even when an advance is made 'he is never able to break our line entirely'. When British forces are compelled to retire

[137] *Daily Chronicle*, 22 March 1918.
[138] *Daily Chronicle*, 23 March 1918.
[139] *Daily Chronicle*, 25 March 1918.
[140] *Daily Chronicle*, 26 March 1918.
[141] *Daily Chronicle*, 28 March 1918.

they do so 'in an orderly way...under cover of dauntless rearguards'.[142] The German losses, though Gibbs did not want to exaggerate them, 'have reached figures so high that the enemy command must be deeply anxious as to the morale of their men'.[143]

By 30 March 1918, the Germans had advanced to within 11 miles of Amiens where a counter-attack first slowed, then halted the advance. By 5 April 1918, the Germans had halted the Somme offensive and switched their attack to the north in Flanders. On 9 April, they began an attempt to break through to Calais and the Channel ports, an effort which began well when they punched a hole 30 miles wide and 5 miles deep. The next day Gibbs made it clear to his readers that this attack was 'a new and formidable offensive with large objectives'. He also added that it was now clear that the Germans were not going to divide their forces and attack the French but were intent on destroying the British Army in the field.[144]

Gibbs did not report on the opening of the British counter-offensive on 8 August 1918, for 'with the worst kind of luck' he was in England on sick leave, at least partly the result of sheer exhaustion and shattered nerves.[145] His place was taken by Henry Nevinson, who had been wounded while reporting on the Gallipoli campaign. Unlike most of his colleagues, Gibbs had not enjoyed extended periods away from the Front and generally had taken only seven days home leave every six months. During these weeks, he found England 'drab, weary and bored with the war'. Gibbs found the gap between the Home Front and the trenches frustrating, and it is possible that he sensed the failure of the correspondents to bridge that divide. For now, he was not just a chronicler, but a participant, because 'one had to be there to understand'. Yet Gibbs' desperation to return to France stemmed not just from his desire to be there as the end approached but was also because in spite of 'war's hell', there was 'more comradeship, a cleaner spirit, a finer morale'.[146]

In 1915, Agnes had moved to Finsbury Park from Holland Street in Kensington and had taken on war work. On a two-and-a-half acre property surrounded by slums, she ran 3-day retreats for 14- and 15-year-old Catholic 'Cockney types' from the London slums and suburbs. The retreats

---

[142] *Daily Chronicle*, 30 March 1918.
[143] *Daily Chronicle*, 1 April 1918.
[144] *Daily Chronicle*, 11 April 1918.
[145] Gibbs, *The Pageant of the Years*, p. 225; *Fort Wayne Journal Gazette*, 21 February 1921.
[146] Gibbs, *The Pageant of the Years*, pp. 226–8.

had a spiritual and social purpose and were borne of the fear that with their fathers away at the war, these children were in 'moral danger because of wartime wildness'. Gibbs was shy of the boys, but felt that Agnes, through a mix of laughter and strictness, ensured that they behaved like little gentlemen. Nevertheless, he still found them a 'damn nuisance'. In addition, the garden was scattered with shrapnel from the anti-aircraft fire aimed at German Zeppelins, not a pleasant reminder for a man home on war leave.[147] To make matters worse, a number of the priests who helped run the retreats had fallen in love with Agnes 'without evil intent...I didn't like it, though I understood, and was sorry for them'.[148]

This dissatisfaction ran even deeper as the war had not left Agnes unmarked either. Gibbs found her 'worn and thin', fatigued by the unending horror, unable to justify the suffering with the fierce hatred which sustained others. Though she drew comfort from her faith and prayed for Gibbs, she felt 'she had lost him'. He had returned changed by his experience of war and was 'no longer the delicate boy she had loved—her shy fawn'. In return, he found her 'cold, a little distant, with some invisible barrier between us'.[149] Anthony Feinstein described this kind of estrangement from peacetime life in *Journalists under Fire: The Psychological Hazards of Covering War* (2006), which was, almost unbelievably, the first research into the psychological impact of war reporting on journalists. In the course of his research, he observed that modern war journalists are acutely aware of the contrast between the intensity of their professional experiences and the apparent mundaneness of the domestic pressures of 'normal living'. Chris Hedges, former *New York Times* war correspondent, wrote in the foreword to Feinstein's book that 'once you sink into the weird subculture of war, it is hard to return home, where all seems banal and trivial'. For a gentle and refined man such as Gibbs, it was intoxicating to confront danger in a world where 'the polarities of life and death are laid bare', but it was an experience which made the return to England difficult to endure.[150] He yearned to return to the war and the essential

---

[147] In 1949, Gibbs recalled being on leave in England in September 1916 when the German airship *SL-11* was shot down by Lieutenant W Leefe Robinson, who was subsequently awarded the Victoria Cross. He incorrectly, though understandably, described it as a Zeppelin, when in fact it was actually an Army Schutte-Lanz airship.

[148] Gibbs, *The Pageant of the Years*, p. 226.

[149] Gibbs, *The Pageant of the Years*, p. 226.

[150] A Feinstein (2006) *Journalists under Fire: The Psychological Hazards of Covering War* (Baltimore: The Johns Hopkins University Press), p. x.

paradox of the war correspondent—war is the catalyst to one's creativity, not the nemesis.[151] This would not have escaped the notice of an intelligent woman such as Agnes. She was perhaps well used to a husband besotted with her and would have been hurt by his obvious desire to return to the Front.[152] One can find in Agnes' pastoral work and her rejection of the correspondents' dispatches a growing revulsion at the cost of war. Yet it can also be understood as an attempt to combat what Feinstein saw as the abrogation of her identity occasioned by the view 'that equates war with meaning and relegates everything outside of war to the boring and mundane'.[153]

Covering a war he might otherwise have participated in as a combatant, Gibbs dealt with pressures even more confronting than a modern journalist covering a war in Africa, possibly of little consequence to his or her own people. Whatever professional detachment behind which a journalist might shield himself (or herself, a development Gibbs could never have envisaged), a total war involving friends and family raised the issue of a participation that stopped short of a direct involvement in combat. For Gibbs, it was never merely a question of whether he worked as a correspondent or returned home to more genteel journalistic pursuits. His country was at war and he needed to confront not just the worth of reporting, but of the alternatives, one of which would have been enlistment:

> Sometimes I felt ashamed of myself. I felt that I was wasting my time writing instead of fighting, but I comforted myself with the thought—perhaps it was a little dishonest that I was telling the British people what the soldier was doing, the kind of life he was leading in frightful places where it seemed no man could live, and that perhaps the truth might be passed down in history as a warning to the generations to follow.[154]

Gibbs' uneasy justification of his privileged position as a spectator rather than a direct participant provided a poignant insight into his sensi-

---

[151] Feinstein, *Journalists under Fire*, p. 23.

[152] Feinstein found that half of the war journalists he studied were either single or divorced as against one-third for domestic journalists. Though these figures can in part be explained by changing attitudes to divorce, they underline the difficulty of a transition from a war zone to the comfort and safety of the Home Front, particularly for a highly strung man such as Gibbs.

[153] Feinstein, *Journalists under Fire*, p. 35.

[154] Gibbs, *The Pageant of the Years*, pp. 225–8.

tivity to being dismissed as a mere propagandist. Such a claim questioned not only his authenticity as a journalist, but more wounding, it questioned his authenticity as a man. He was of military age, wore a uniform, but was not a soldier. He witnessed the conflict at first hand, marvelled at the courage of the soldiers, agonized for them, but he was not one of them. His sustained efforts to report the war drove him to the edge of a complete breakdown. For if the casualty figures from the First World War teach anything, it is that once you were in the range of the guns, you were at risk. Unlike most of the soldiers he yearned to identify with, Gibbs could remove himself from this danger without fear of censure let alone imprisonment or the firing squad.

Seven years after Agnes' death, Gibbs admitted that by this time she too had come to believe that the correspondents were complicit in a national tragedy. It represents possibly the only time that Gibbs acknowledged openly that his dispatches, and those of his colleagues, were flawed in more than just the details:

> She hated the despatches of war correspondents always holding out hope which was never fulfilled, always describing the heroic valour of boys who, of course, were sentenced to death. In the end she hated mine, for the same reasons, and I didn't blame her, because that was the truth. She hated the calm way in which many people—her own friends, the priests and the women—took the monstrous casualties of the Somme and Flanders as a matter of course, as though boys were only born to be killed for King and Country, as though they ought to like being killed. She wanted it to end, somehow and anyhow, and there seemed no end.[155]

Gibbs returned to the Front in the third week of August and felt that that the advancing troops were 'buoyed up with the enormous hope of getting on with this business quickly'. The Germans no longer 'have even a dim hope of victory...All they hope for now is to defend themselves long enough to gain peace by negotiation'.[156] He saw in the German prisoners, as he often had before, the proof that the end was near. For the next three months he accompanied the advance across 'old battlefields and beyond them into country we had never held, and into cities long in German hands'.[157] The liberation of Lille, which 'I am glad that I lived to see',

---

[155] Gibbs, *The Pageant of the Years*, p. 226.
[156] *Daily Chronicle*, 28 August 1918.
[157] Gibbs, *The Pageant of the Years*, p. 229.

remained a 'vivid and precious memory' even 30 years later.[158] In Bruges, Gibbs found Agnes' sister Beryl at the convent of St Andre and quickly was surrounded by a swarm of nuns 'like black and white birds fluttering out of an aviary'.[159]

In October, Gibbs resigned from the *Daily Chronicle* on an issue that was effectively about political censorship and the freedom of the press. Though the paper supported the left wing of the Liberal Party, it had attracted the ire of Prime Minister Lloyd George. He had formed a group including Sir Henry Dalziel and bought the *Daily Chronicle*, prompting the resignation of its editor Robert Donald. Out of loyalty to his former boss, Gibbs signed a contract with the *Daily Telegraph*, although his dispatches continued to appear in both papers. After the Armistice, he transferred back to the *Daily Chronicle* until the Lloyd George policy of reprisals in Ireland prompted a second resignation. Gibbs would maintain a love–hate relationship with the Welsh politician spread over many decades, going so far as to remark in an article that he hated him for his talk of the 'knockout blow', for arranging a peace which appeared to guarantee another war and for handing Ireland over to a Prussian style militarism. Yet in the same article, Gibbs wrote that in analysing this attitude, he, like most of Lloyd George's political opponents, found 'not hatred, but admiration strangely mingled with regret, affection twisted by anger and annoyance, amusement causing laughter with a groan in it'.[160]

In December 1917, Gibbs wrote that it was his great hope that he would have the 'supreme luck of writing the last message which shall tell the English people that Tommy Atkins is out of the trenches, and that we have peace with honour'.[161] On 11 November 1918, Gibbs was on his way to Mons where for the English the war had begun. It was here that he heard that it was all over and could make good on that wish. The following night he wrote his last dispatch from a war zone 'which now was silent...with the beautiful silence of the nights of peace...as though God gave a benediction to the wounded soul of the world'.[162] Fittingly, his final words were for the soldiers who he had grown to love and whose deeds he had lionized with an emotion that continues to attract the ire of modern

---

[158] *Daily Chronicle*, 18 October 1918; Gibbs, *The Pageant of the Years*, p. 231.

[159] Gibbs, *The Pageant of the Years*, p. 232.

[160] *Harpers Monthly Magazine*, September 1921, p. 423.

[161] Gibbs, *From Bapaume*, Author's Note.

[162] *Daily Chronicle*, 12 November 1918.

critics. Yet without doubt, his war dispatches 'constitute one of the classic chronicles of World War One'.[163] In the tumult and confusion of that first evening of peace, Gibbs congratulated the officers 'who went over the top at dawn and led their men gallantly, hiding any fear of death they had, and who in dirty ditches and dug outs, in mud and swamps, in fields under fire, in ruins that were death traps, in all the filth and misery of this war held fast to the pride of manhood'. For the sake of Britain, they had sacrificed their lives 'and all that life means to youth, as a free, cheap gift'. As was the case in his description of the *Titanic* disaster, there was a jarring note of class consciousness in the contrasting manner in which the enlisted men had 'been patient and long suffering and full of grim and silent courage, not swanking about the things you have done, not caring a jot for glory, not getting much, but now you have done your job, and it is well done'.[164]

Gibbs accompanied a troop of the Dragoon Guards as they crossed the Belgian frontier into Germany on 4 December 1918. He found that the German people reconciled to defeat, relieved that the agony had ended without humiliation. They had chosen, in his view, to place their faith in English fair play and President Wilson and his Fourteen Points. It was a faith which was soon shown to be misplaced. In Wilson, Gibbs believed that never in history 'had one man been regarded by countless millions with such reverence and such faith as the arbiter of destiny'.[165] Gibbs was amongst the millions of Londoners who crowded the streets to get a look at this 'Messiah in a top hat'. He recalled weeping and, with a jarring note of bitterness, added that here was the man 'who was going to make the good peace. His name would live for ever as the architect of the League of Nations which would ensure us against future wars. Wilson was going to turn back the old pages of history written in blood and on a new leaf write the beginning of a new chapter which would change human history'.[166]

Although Gibbs would later come to see the war as the greatest experience of his life, the change it wrought on his belief system was not immediately obvious. What it did alter in an overt manner was his sense of self. The responsibility of being one of five official war correspondents and the demands subsequently placed on his hitherto unrealized reserves of cour-

[163] M Hoehn (ed) (1947) 'Sir Philip Gibbs' *Catholic Authors 1930-1947* (Newark: St Mary's Abbey), p. 265.
[164] Gibbs, *Open Warfare*, pp. 551–2.
[165] P Gibbs (1931) *Since Then* (London: William Heinemann), p. 24.
[166] Gibbs, *The Pageant of the Years*, pp. 243–4.

age and endurance gave the sensitive and fragile Gibbs the opportunity to live up to his ideals of service and duty. The little boy who shook with fear at facing the fast bowling of his cousins on Sunday outings would later shake with excitement while rescuing wounded soldiers under fire in Belgium in 1914. War gave him the chance to participate, rather than being forever 'the onlooker, the recorder'.[167] The promotion of world peace became a crusade for Gibbs in the same way that other Victorians campaigned for better living and working conditions or for better hospitals. Both war and peace thus afforded Gibbs countless opportunities to become the embodiment of those values he cherished, rather than merely reporting on their presence, or otherwise, in the actions of others.

---

[167] Arthur Gibbs, *Gun Fodder*, p. vi.

CHAPTER 5

Adventures in Journalism: 1918–1939

The war ended so abruptly in November 1918 that the victorious powers found themselves with little idea of how to translate their military success into a sustainable peace. Four months passed before serious negotiations began. This lack of purpose and the conflicting desires of the peacemakers meant that it was not until 1925 that there was a general détente and a relaxation of tension.[1] So high were Gibbs' hopes for a legitimate peace that his disappointment was inevitably going to be commensurately keenly felt. In 1931, Gibbs noted that even in these early days of peace 'idealism was passing' and it was clear that it was 'the beginning of bitterness and vengeance'.[2] The terms imposed by the Allies were so harsh that Gibbs believed that the Germans 'would never fulfil or forgive them'.[3] Gibbs saw Clemenceau, who thought of France first and last, seeking to secure her borders against German militarism. He saw his old sparring partner Lloyd George risking his 'soul in the election' by pandering to calls of 'make them pay'. All the other 'plenipotentiaries' were likewise able to think only of 'their national interests and aspirations, and last of the ideal justice which eludes the grasp of human nature'.[4]

---

[1] G Craig (1966) *Europe since 1815* (New York: Holt, Rinehart & Winston), p. 538.
[2] P Gibbs (1931) *Since Then* (London: William Heinemann), p. 32.
[3] Gibbs, *Since Then*, p. 42.
[4] Gibbs, *Since Then*, p. 41.

© The Editor(s) (if applicable) and The Author(s) 2016   141
M.C. Kerby, *Sir Philip Gibbs and English Journalism in War and Peace*,
DOI 10.1057/978-1-137-57301-8_5

In Gibbs' view, it was only Wilson who was free from claims which trespassed on the national frontiers of other people, 'but he did not think clearly or quietly. He lost his grip on this complicated problem'.[5]

Yet for all that the peacemakers did their best, honestly and honourably [but] they were not big enough...for the task that gave them the chance of drawing the human tribes closer and banishing war between them, and raising them up to a higher vision of civilisation in which nations once at enmity might co-operate in human progress, with liberty for the individual and a greater share of the world's gifts for people still in misery. They thought of divisions rather than unity. They were old fashioned, traditional, limited. They dared no great spiritual adventure for the sake of peace. They had no touch of magnificence. They made a peace lower than the best instincts of European intelligence, though higher than the worst.[6]

Gibbs was less forgiving in 1946 when he wrote of 'dragon's teeth being strewn about the map of Europe' by a 'badly made peace' and a 'betrayal of the League'.[7]

For Gibbs, these immediate post-war years brought with them little personal happiness. Despite possessing a world view firmly grounded in the Victorian values of service in a cause greater than the self and a general optimism in the progress of humanity, four years of almost constant exposure to death and destruction had not left him untouched. Indeed, his good friend GK Chesterton was disappointed with the change in the tone of Gibbs' dispatches as the end of the war approached. Gibbs had not hidden 'my loathing of it and my despair [because] of this unending agony and sacrifice of young life on both sides of the line, which I could not reconcile with the teaching of Christ'.[8] Though never a pacifist, Gibbs was by nature a sensitive and compassionate man. He could not openly reject the war and his role in it and could only seek meaning and purpose where others, his brother Arthur for one, found only futility and death. In retrospect, Gibbs believed that it had been a deep and abiding conviction that:

We who had survived and had seen those things had a sacred duty to do in this world. Such a war must never happen again, we thought, and it was for

[5] Gibbs, *Since Then*, p. 44.
[6] Gibbs, *Since Then*, pp. 44–5.
[7] P Gibbs (1946) *The Pageant of the Years* (London: Heinemann), pp. 254–5.
[8] P Gibbs (1949) *Crowded Company* (London: Allan Wingate), p. 88.

us to prevent it so that the next generation of youth would be saved from its agonies and sacrifice. I dedicated myself to peace, and made a vow in my heart that I would work for it above all other motives and interests...Out of this dreadful history of which we had been the chroniclers we must try to find a different way of life for the common man who had been its victim and hero. In any case, our mission, surely, was to remind people everywhere, not let them ever forget, the armies of the dead—the young dead—not let the younger crowd believe that war had any glamour or romance.[9]

Gibbs was no longer able to shield himself from the horror of death and mutilation with abstract notions of glory. Nothing less than an enduring and sustainable peace could, in Gibbs' view, justify the suffering and the pain. It was a watershed moment, not so much an epiphany but a dawning realization that glory had indeed been compelled to give way to death. This change in Gibbs' understanding of the war and what it had meant required an alteration in language and the adoption of what Hynes saw as an alternate rhetoric. Many writers, though how fully they represented broader society is in dispute, adopted just such a rhetoric in the mid- to late 1920s. It might be best described as a 'soldier's style'. It was 'stripped' of 'abstract values' and instead was 'plain, descriptive [and] emptied of value statements'.[10] Gibbs sought to emulate these writers, a shift which required more than an alteration in language; it required a change in tone:

Gibbs was neither an Owen nor a Hemingway, but he had come to something like their sense of what was real in the world of war: the end of the war had freed him to write like a soldier, in the language of fact...The implications of this change are considerable: war for Gibbs was no longer a struggle toward victory, but a cruel thing done to young men.[11]

It was a rhetoric adopted by writers such as Wilfred Owen, Siegfried Sassoon, and Robert Graves that offered an emasculated and passive anti-hero as a replacement for the heroic pre-war model. It was not as widespread a view as postulated by Paul Fussell in *The Great War and Modern Memory*, having been subject to revision by authors such as Rosa Maria Bracco, Jay Winter, and Dan Todman who argued that traditional

---

[9] Gibbs, *The Pageant of the Years*, pp. 242–3.
[10] S Hynes (1991) *A War Imagined: The First World War and English Culture* (New York, Atheneum), p. 114.
[11] Hynes, *A War Imagined*, p. 285.

representations not only survived but also continued to thrive after the war. Likewise, Hynes noted that:

> It is not true, as is sometimes assumed, that a general wartime enthusiasm for war and its values was overturned and replaced at the war's end by a total disillusionment that informs and defines English culture of the twenties. Rather, both existed throughout the decade.[12]

Indeed, Gibbs himself never dispensed with his sentimental and romanticized view of the common soldier no matter how much he gave himself over to the 'waste and pity' style which Winter dismissed as 'both untrue to the events of the war and a profoundly inaccurate account of the mentality of the trench soldiers'.[13] It is perhaps more accurately understood as a cultural rather than an historical view; as Barnett argued, the war 'crippled Britain psychologically, and in no other way'.[14] This was something, however, of which Gibbs was well aware, for when he came to write about the Somme in *Realities of War*, he titled it 'Psychology on the Somme':

> Modern civilization was wrecked on those fire blasted fields, though they led to what we called victory. More died there than the flower of our youth and German manhood. The old order of the world died there, because many men who came alive out of that conflict were changed, and vowed not to tolerate a system of thought which had led up to such a monstrous massacre of human beings who prayed to the same God, loved the same joys of life, and had no hatred of one another except as it had been lighted and inflamed by their governors, their philosophers and their newspapers.[15]

Yet for all his efforts to adapt to a changing interpretation of the war, Gibbs remained trapped between the traditional rhetoric and the soldier's style which were 'mutually exclusive, mutually contradictory'.[16] Though he gave himself over more fully to the new rhetoric in the 1920s, he remained with a foot in both camps, an adherent to two ideologies which were 'separate and mistrustful of each other', one a conservative culture with traditional values and the other a 'counter culture', which

[12] Hynes, *A War Imagined*, p. 283.

[13] Winter, J. (1988) *The Experience of World War One* (London: Macmillan).

[14] C Barnett (1970) 'A Military Historian's View of the Great War Literature'. *Transactions of the Royal Society of Literature* 36, p. 18.

[15] P Gibbs (1936) *Realities of War* (London: Hutchinson and Co Ltd.), p. 399.

[16] Hynes, *A War Imagined*, p. 283.

rejected the war and the 'empty principles' for which it was fought.[17] He could never quite discard the ideals which he had espoused in hundreds of dispatches, no matter how passionately he adopted the beliefs of this counterculture which were, in effect, a collective understanding of the war which dominates our modern understanding of the conflict.[18] It was, in short, the belief that an idealistic generation had been betrayed and then destroyed on the Somme and elsewhere by the ineptitude and lies of their elders.[19]

Though Gibbs argued that this alteration did not contradict any of his earlier dispatches, the decision to title the narrative of his wartime experiences *Realities of War* would indicate that Gibbs knew that it was, at least from a personal viewpoint, a revisionist history. Although Gibbs did not authorize the choice of title in its American publication, the decision to rename it *Now It Can Be Told* would indicate that at the very least his American publisher was aware of the change in language and tone. In a review in the *New York Times*, the English journalist, novelist, and fellow adherent of liberalism, Cecil Roberts, trumpeted the book as 'an uncensored chronicle', one which 'has a frankness, a truth and stern reality never before shown in all the literature of war'.[20] Gibbs openly acknowledged that he was now adopting the point of view of the soldiers, hating the staff officers with 'their rows of decorations' awarded for 'initialling requisitions for pink, blue, green and yellow forms', hating those people 'who had not seen because they could not understand', but most of all, accepting that the great theme of the war was 'not victory, not defeat, but simply loss'. At times, the war had appeared little more than 'a long struggle with no visible end'.[21]

This sense of speaking with an authority conferred by his participation rather than in the more passive role of witness is evident in Gibbs' description of General Headquarters, though he presents it through the eyes of an unknown officer. It existed in a 'rose coloured' world 'remote from the ugly things of war. They had heard of trenches…but as the West End hears of the East End—a nasty place where common people lived'. He saw the staff officers in Montreuil displaying 'careless hearted courage

---

[17] Hynes, *A War Imagined*, p. 283.

[18] Hynes described it as the myth of the war, which he argued was distinct from a lie or fabrication and was really a set of attitudes about what the war was and what it meant.

[19] Hynes, *A War Imagined*, p. xii.

[20] *New York Times*, 14 March 1920.

[21] Gibbs, *Realities of War*, p. 52.

when British soldiers were being blown to bits, gassed, blinded, maimed and shell shocked'.[22] Gibbs' identification with those 'who were to die' allowed him to find 'reason in their hatred of the staff', an attitude which became 'intense to the point of fury'.[23]

The elements of this new discourse, as Gibbs revealed them in *Realities of War*, were present almost in their entirety in his description of the hospital at Corbie; it was one of the 'butcher shops…where there was a great carving of human flesh which was of our boyhood, while the old men directed their sacrifice, and the profiteers grew rich, and the fires of hate were stoked up at patriotic banquets and in editorial chairs'. It was just this type of 'imagining' of the War which Hynes saw as creating a 'set of abrupt disjunctions' or a gulf 'between generations, between fighting soldiers and those who controlled their lives, between the present and the past'.[24] For Gibbs, this break with the past was irreversible for there was 'no resemblance between this Europe after the war and that Europe before the war'. Gibbs also anticipated another element of this imagining of the war by arguing that the conflict had made a return to the pre-war status quo impossible. Modern civilization had been 'wrecked' and those who had survived 'were changed and vowed not to tolerate a system of thought which had led to such a monstrous massacre of human beings who prayed to the same God'. Gibbs saw in the post-war years the promise of 'a new era in the world's history', but he saw just as clearly the looming battle between the forces of reaction on the one hand and the forces of revolution on the other. He may have distanced himself ideologically from Carlyle, but he would have remembered the Scotsman's vision of a society imploding into butchery and anarchy:

> For good or ill, I know not which, the ideas germinated in trenches and dugouts…will prevail over the Old Order…If the new ideas are thwarted by reactionary rulers endeavouring to jerk the world back to its old fashioned discipline…there will be anarchy…If by fear, or by wisdom, the new ideas are allowed to gain their ground gradually, a revolution will be accomplished without anarchy.[25]

---

[22] Gibbs, *Realities of War*, p. 43.
[23] Gibbs, *Realities of War*, p. 53.
[24] Hynes, *A War Imagined*, p. 52.
[25] Gibbs, *Realities of War*, pp. 456–57.

Though he never ceased to lionize the efforts of the front-line soldiers, he began increasingly to see them as victims, the 'flower of our youth cast into that furnace'.[26] The Germans ceased to be the servants of Prussian militarism, but fellow sufferers caught in a 'devil's trap from which there was no escape'.[27] Gibbs' attempt to distance himself from the old rhetoric is clearly evident in his description of two British soldiers executed for cowardice, a topic he would never have been permitted to discuss in a wartime report. In his recording of one of the doomed men's final day, there is pity and compassion without hint of judgement. Another forbidden topic, shell shock, was also one of the 'realities' he could now broach. He could not bring himself to look at the afflicted soldiers, but nevertheless wished that they 'might be seen by bloody minded men and women who, far behind the lines, still spoke of war lightly, as a kind of sport, or heroic game'.[28] Though he might have found himself unable to look at shell-shocked soldiers, he was prepared to work for their rights to a modern and effective treatment. For many years, Gibbs was a vice president of the Ex-Services Welfare Society which had been founded in 1919. It was an organization that was an implacable opponent of the government's treatment of those 'afflicted' by the mental scars of war. In an article he wrote in 1927, he 'extolled' the work of the Society to the extent that the Ministry of Pensions 'took exception'.[29] Gibbs was even moved to describe French prostitutes giving their 'base counterfeit of love in return for a few francs'. Though he could not quite refrain from passing a gentle moral admonishment, he offered some comfort to his readers by adding that God understood human weakness.[30]

Though some reviewers criticized Gibbs' growing bitterness, his version of the war as outlined in 1920 was generally accepted as accurate, consistent as it was with a growing re-evaluation of the conflict. Gibbs was knighted in the same year *Realities of War* was published, and though it was in recognition of his war service, it would not have harmed his standing that he had the good fortune to discard the rhetoric of wartime in step with popular taste. Though Gibbs' work as a war correspondent still attracts criticism from contemporary scholars, it is interesting that he is

[26] Gibbs, *Realities of War*, p. 324.
[27] Gibbs, *Realities of War*, p. 195.
[28] Gibbs, *Realities of War*, p. 49.
[29] P Barham (2007) *Forgotten Lunatics of the Great War* (London: Yale University Press), p. 414.
[30] Gibbs, *Realities of War*, p. 181.

rarely, if ever, linked with the 'soldiers' view of the war' which he helped to popularize and which is still widely regarded as the 'truth'.

Despite this self-appointed crusade and the sincerity with which he pursued it, almost inevitably, it did not offer Gibbs the same singularity of purpose as his wartime service. Like many returning soldiers, he found it difficult to adjust to the slower pace of peacetime life in a world which seemed bereft of the camaraderie of the trenches. Gibbs felt that the coming of peace was 'as great a strain to the civilized mind as the outbreak of war...The sudden relaxation left them limp, purposeless, and unstrung. A sense of the ghastly futility of the horrible massacre in Europe overwhelmed multitudes of men and women who had exerted the last vibration of spiritual energy for the sake of victory'.[31] He saw no 'peace as yet in the souls of men' and even in England he found in his friends and 'to tell the truth, in one's own heart, a melancholy and disillusionment not easy of cure'.[32] He felt that:

> We are all victims of the war now. We know its brutality, its tragedy, its waste. Some of us are filled with disillusion and despair because of the degradation that has followed war and the unfulfilment of passionate hopes for the progress of humanity after the frightful conflict. The very name of the last war sickens many minds who cannot bear the reminder of its blood and sacrifice, and who see nothing but mockery in its results.[33]

Unable to move beyond his wartime experiences and overwhelmed by the sense of tragic waste, Gibbs exhibited signs of what a modern audience would recognize as post-traumatic stress or what might also be characterized as survivors' guilt. Some sufferers seek solace in helping others, as Gibbs would attempt to do by promoting peace and supporting the League of Nations. The dire financial difficulties endured by thousands of his fellow survivors, many of whom had suffered far more than him, exacerbated these feelings of guilt:

> I was obsessed with its horror, and felt guilty of having a car, of living in comfort in this good house and lovely garden when so many men who had been the heroes of the war were trudging about the streets looking for

---

[31] P Gibbs (1923) *Adventures in Journalism* (London: Harper & Brothers Publishers), p. 273.

[32] *New York Times*, 18 January 1920.

[33] P Gibbs, 'The Cemeteries of the Salient' *The Ypres Times*, April 1923, p. 198.

jobs. I agonized foolishly—what could I do about it?...over the state of the world, the interminable delays and disappointment of the League, the ghastly happenings in Russia, the misery of Germany and Austria in time of inflation, the economic madness of tariffs and exchange barriers throughout Europe, the Black and Tan brutality in Ireland. I was in search of peace when there was no peace.[34]

At least one friend was anxious for Gibbs' health, fearing that he was on the verge of collapse when he returned to England after the war.[35] His nerves, already stretched by the years of war, were not helped when he injured his arm a few days after the Armistice when a military lorry collided with the vehicle he was travelling in. Gibbs' sense of 'disconnectedness' which he had first felt on leave in England was not atypical, for it had been so vast an enterprise that the 'years after the war seemed discontinuous from the years before' ensuring that the generation who had experienced it 'looked back at their own parts as one might look across a great chasm to a remote, peaceable place on the other side'.[36] By the time Gibbs travelled to the USA in 1919, he was described in the press as 'war weary' with his 'face white, shrunken and haggard'.[37] For Agnes, her unhappiness was also exacerbated by ill health and her own revulsion at the wartime slaughter to which she felt the war correspondents had contributed. There is also some evidence of what might now be termed a midlife crisis. To her, the English country life and her role as hostess were foolish and futile.[38] Her grandson Martin described this dissatisfaction as a 'hanker[ing] to escape from the housewife's role and follow a career'.[39] An intelligent and gifted woman, Agnes was able to pursue university studies and though poor eyesight thwarted her medical ambitions, she graduated with a Bachelor of Science in Geology in 1932 at the age of 57. Her daughter-in-law Maisie Martin (1897–1986), who married Tony in

[34] Gibbs, *The Pageant of the Years*, p. 265.

[35] Cecil Roberts in the *New York Times*, 14 March 1920.

[36] Hynes, *A War Imagined*, p. 245.

[37] *Bridgeport Standard Telegram*, 14 February 1919; *Chillicothe Constitution*, 4 October 1919.

[38] Gibbs, *The Pageant of the Years*, p. 265.

[39] M Gibbs (2000) *Seven Generations—Our Gibbs Ancestors* (London: Martin Gibbs), p. 26.

September 1928, remembered her as a 'severe woman' although she knew Agnes during a period of illness and 'spiritual unhappiness'.[40]

Both Philip and Agnes sought a peace in their surroundings that it appears they were unable to find in each other. They moved from their old Georgian house in Finsbury Park to a bungalow at Dorking in Surrey in 1922 where they had a couple of acres surrounded by meadows and trees. Always the romantic when writing of the English countryside, particularly if it had a connection with Agnes, Gibbs described Dorking in 1946 as having been a place where 'nightingales still sing in the holly trees, rabbits still scuttle in the meadows, the cuckoo calls in the great park of Peper Harrow, as it did to Saxon ears before the Doomsday Book was written. The cattle browse on the short turf of the heath where a Roman legion pitched its camp'.[41] Forced out by the encroachment of a housing estate, they moved again two years later in 1924, this time to just outside the village of Puttenham to a house called 'Overponds'. It also became one of the rural idylls that Gibbs so loved.

Though there were still moments of joy, there was a continuing unease that was exacerbated by Agnes' ill health which in time required two operations. There were, however, the material compensations of peace. Soon after he arrived at Puttenham, two men from Harrods arrived 'with a van, and inside it was a miracle'. Through the aid of the wireless, 'a polished box with wires and interior mechanism of a mysterious kind', over the coming years Gibbs would hear 'words of tragic and tremendous history'.[42] AJP Taylor would later describe this 'miracle' as the symbol of the interwar period.[43] Other technologies would intrude on Gibbs' world. He purchased an Iris Landaulette, 'an extremely boring and pedestrian motorcar' in the eyes of his son Tony, then an Austin Twenty, a Buick, and finally a 45-horsepower Daimler which Agnes learned to drive after they had employed a few young men from the village as chauffeurs.[44] Though he had a guilty feeling that no writing man should own a car and he became restless if he spent over an hour travelling in one, in 1949, he remembered 'the loveliness of old towns and villages through which we motored and the endless beauty of England'. Even the convenience of car

[40] Gibbs, *Seven Generations*, p. 26; Gibbs, *The Pageant of the Years*, p. 17.
[41] Gibbs, *The Pageant of the Years*, pp. 264–65.
[42] Gibbs, *Crowded Company*, p. 154.
[43] AJP Taylor (1965) *English History 1914–1945* (Oxford: The Clarendon Press), p. 307.
[44] A Gibbs (1974) *A Passion for Cars* (Newton Abbot: David & Charles), p. 5.

ownership was recalled by Gibbs only in the context of an English countryside 'away from its industrial ugliness'.[45] There were also 'golden days' when Gibbs, his brother Cosmo, and his son Tony all sat on the terrace working on their next project.

Working again as a freelance journalist, Gibbs spent the years between late 1918 and 1923 as a 'wanderer' in Europe, Asia Minor, and the USA. He assumed the mantle of a 'student of psychology...trying to see beneath the surface of social and political life to the deeper currents of thought and emotion and natural law set in motion by the enormous tragedy through which so many nations had passed'.[46] Later, he would describe this period of wandering as having taken him 'further afield year after year in search of something which I never found. I went in search of peace'.[47]

Despite calling on the world's leaders to move beyond their wartime hatreds, he was himself unable, or unwilling, to make a clear ideological or professional break with the trauma of the Western Front. His postwar writing and his lectures are steeped in the horror of war and perhaps indicate a sense of his own complicity as a correspondent, a development hinted at in at least one piece of his personal correspondence. In the second week of May 1919, Gibbs finalized arrangements with his literary agent for the production of a book which he intended to call *The Scottish Troops—Heroic Episodes of the Great War*. Within a week, he reneged on the deal, and his explanation suggests that at one level Gibbs might have been aware of shortcomings in his dispatches which he would never have explicitly acknowledged:

> The truth is, that apart altogether from time, when I sat down to write about the heroic deeds of the Scots I felt that in a psychological way I simply could not do it. The only thing I want to write now about the war is absolute realism, giving the plain unvarnished truth of its misery and abomination, as well as its heroism. A romantic narrative of the Scots in action, such as would be necessary for a school book, would not only be very false in its picture, but would, I know, damage my reputation in the larger sense. It would be nothing but a pot-boiler at its best, and I think the time has come when I ought to give up writing pot-boilers.[48]

[45] Gibbs, *Crowded Company*, p. 155.
[46] Gibbs, *Adventures in Journalism*, p. 279.
[47] Gibbs, *The Pageant of the Years*, p. 241.
[48] Letter to Curtis Brown 21 May 1919. *Philip Gibbs Letters, Special Collections Research Center, Syracuse University Libraries.*

In the years prior to the First World War, Gibbs' political and social commentaries had concentrated almost exclusively on domestic social issues, a preoccupation which reflected the wider liberal trend of being semi-indifferent to foreign policy, while still being 'internationally minded' and ardently believing 'in concord between nations'.[49] Issues that attracted Gibbs' notice were gender, *The New Man* (1913), marriage, *The Eighth Year* (1913), and humanitarian issues abroad, *The Tragedy of Portugal* (1914). After the First World War, there was a steady stream of political commentaries on the European political situation—*The Hope of Europe* (1921, published in the USA as *More That Must Be Told*), *Ten Years After* (1924), *Since Then* (1931), *European Journey* (1934), and *Across the Frontiers* (1938). Each possessed varying degrees of autobiography and a repetition or reworking of material used elsewhere.

Though there is a clear interrelationship between Gibbs' imaginative works of fiction and his work as a reporter, his novels also fall into two relatively distinct categories, those written before and those written after the war. Novels such as *The Street of Adventure* (1909), a thinly veiled fictionalized account of the ill-fated liberal newspaper the *Tribune*, and *Intellectual Mansions, SW* (1910), based on the suffragette movement, were responses to specific historical events which he covered as a reporter. Equally true of these pre-1914 novels is that they possess a stronger narrative structure and are less driven by Gibbs' political agenda than his later efforts. *The Street of Adventure*, his most successful novel, is a highly readable and warmly human novel, and even *Intellectual Mansions, SW* is less overtly political than later books which were all informed by his exposure to war.

Gibbs travelled extensively during the interwar period and pursued a writing formula his son Tony referred to as 'a particularly successful racket'.[50] Travelling for pleasure, often in the company of family or friends, he would send back articles for publication in the press. On his return to England, he would then produce a political travel book, give lectures, and then finally write one or two novels on the same theme. Examples abound of Gibbs using his experiences as a journalist as the

---

[49] I Willis (1972) *England's Holy War A Study of English Liberal Idealism during the Great War* (London: Garland Publishing Inc), p. 5. Gibbs was not guilty of the attached claim that the pre-war liberal did not question overmuch whether such a concord existed. He was aware of talk of war, but placed undue emphasis on 'the man in the streets' aversion to war rather than the world of international politics.

[50] A Gibbs (1970) *In My Own Good Time* (Boston: Gambit Incorporated), p. 49.

basis for his fiction: *Back to Life* (1920) about the difficulty experienced by ex-soldiers adjusting to peacetime; *The Middle of the Road* (1923), unemployment, Ireland, and the state of continental Europe, particularly Russia; *Blood Relatives* (1935), Anglo-German relations from 1912 to 1935; *Broken Pledges* (1939), the lead-up to the Second World War; *The Amazing Summer* (1941), the Battle of France; *Thine Enemy* (1950), Germany in the immediate aftermath of the Second World War; and *The Cloud above the Green* (1952), the threat of Communism. Though they provide a rich source of evidence concerning his opinion of events and his hopes for the future, they also became forums for extended political discussions where narrative is clearly secondary to proselytizing. One obituary included the rather frank admission that 'their survival as literature is undeserved but the future social historian seeking to know how average men and women behaved during the inter war period may well turn to the novels of Philip Gibbs and, discounting sentimental gloss, find trustworthy guidance'.[51]

Interestingly, he saw something of this same quality in the writing of two other authors he knew and admired. George Bernard Shaw, who he met in France in early 1917, wrote plays in which 'there is no sweetness or warmth...His characters are not fully human [but] appear on the stage as types and exponents of one side or another in his argument on life'.[52] Though as a satirist Gibbs believed that Shaw was without a rival, it is interesting that he either chose not to comment on the similarity in style or even more remarkably, that he was not consciously aware of it. John Galsworthy, whose book *The Forsyth Saga* was a 'work of genius', also used characterization as a didactic tool, with Gibb's noting that 'from the point of view of art that is their weakness'.[53] Though some of Gibbs' novels such as *The Street of Adventure* and *The Middle of the Road*, and others such as *Intellectual Mansions, SW* were courageous in their preparedness to comment on divisive issues, there is an element of the production line about some of them, inspired perhaps more by crippling taxation than by a burning desire to tell a particular story.

Yet for all his desire to be an advocate of peace, a desire which had motivated the dismissal of his own work as 'potboilers', even in a broader sense Gibbs did not fit easily into this post-war world. Between 1914 and

[51] *Guardian*, 12 March 1962.
[52] P Gibbs (1957) *Life's Adventure* (London: Angus and Robertson), p. 14.
[53] Gibbs, *Life's Adventure*, p. 16.

1929, the traditional liberals lost almost everything they most valued in political life, a loss even more traumatic for men such as Gibbs for whom the ideology of liberalism transcended mere politics and assumed the qualities of a faith.[54] It was an alienation recognized by at least one of his contemporaries. His friend and fellow journalist Mary Hamilton, who for a time had been married to his cousin Charles, noted that:

> The war had lifted him into a best seller: it provided him with the kind of situations really suited to his somewhat naïve outlook and great descriptive, journalistic, gifts; into the post war reaction, he did not fit. Miserable when not writing, he wrote; but the notes of the contemporary scale were not right for his tunes...Not until mounting apprehension in Europe gave him, once again, the chance of setting slightly drawn characters against large events, and writing novels that are, really, imaginative reportage, expressed through typical figures, did Philip make a comeback.[55]

Gibbs was just as equally ill at ease with the social changes wrought by the war as he was with the political ramifications. The 'new rich' now occupied the homes of 'the ancient order' and had not yet learnt 'those traditions of kindness, of generosity, and of noble manners which made the old gentry pleasant people, whatever faults they had'.[56] The 'smart set' dressed 'loudly and talk loudly, in a nasal way. They sprawl in the presence of their women folk. Their idea of gallantry is horse play with pretty girls'.[57] The 'nation was in a mood to dance',[58] and Gibbs noted that for 'hour after hour' the youth of England 'gyrate with the grotesque movements of the modern dance, cheek to cheek with their little ladies... It is a ritual which they perform earnestly as part of their new duties in life, but as far as I have observed them, they do not get any real pleasure out of the exercise'.[59] In one of his novels, written 30 years later, he still could not hide his dislike for the racial origins of jazz or for the

[54] M Bentley (1977) *The Liberal Mind 1914–1929* (London: Cambridge University Press), p. 1.

[55] M Hamilton (1944) *Remembering My Good Friends* (London: Jonathon Cape), p. 144.

[56] P Gibbs (1921) *More That Must Be Told* (London: Harper and Brothers Publishers), p. 219.

[57] Gibbs, *More That Must Be Told*, p. 219.

[58] J Nicolson (2009) *The Great Silence: Britain from the shadow of the First World War to the Dawn of the Jazz Age* (New York: Grove Press), p. 159.

[59] Gibbs, *More That Must Be Told*, p. 220.

nightclubs and cabarets which 'sprang up like toadstools in all the capitals of Europe':

> After a while there was something ghastly in it or at least unsatisfying, one boredom after another, and always the thump, thump of a jazz band like the beating of a tom-tom in the jungle, and always the saxophone bleating and gibbering and cackling like a mad monkey.[60]

Gibbs was not alone in his condemnation of this new craze. Nicholson observed a 'mixed reaction' to jazz, especially among the upper class. *The Daily Mail* was anything but mixed, however, in its description of the 'jungle elements of the dances and of the primitive rituals of negro orgies'.[61] Though Gibbs did not overtly acknowledge the growing promiscuity which spread across all levels of society in the years following the war,[62] often during this period of disenchantment Gibbs used jazz as a metaphor for all that was being destroyed in the England he loved. Unsurprisingly, Gibbs reserved his most biting critique for the women who 'paint their lips, wear hideous little frocks and openwork stockings'. Though in the 'larger moralities' Gibbs did not find them 'outrageous', they were nevertheless 'self-possessed, bad mannered, vulgar young people, supremely indifferent to public opinion, pleased to shock the sensibilities of old fashioned folk'. It was not just their manners, however, which Gibbs found wanting, for they 'had not yet acquired the refinements of wealth…Their faces, their voices, their manners betray a lowly origin, for heredity still has something to say'. Though they 'make so much noise and take up so much room', they had not yet found a place in English life.[63] Perhaps more accurately, Gibbs could not find them a place in his construct of English life, for they clearly had not had the opportunity, as those on the *Titanic* were afforded, of assuming the qualities of the upper class during moments of extreme peril.

Though no doubt sincere in his search for peace, Gibbs pursued an itinerary that ensured he continued to be a chronicler of death and destruction. He travelled to Berlin shortly after the Armistice, and though he witnessed some communist agitation and a general shabbiness, he did not

[60] P Gibbs (1951) *The Spoils of Time* (London: Hutchinson), p. 183.
[61] Nicolson, *The Great Silence*, pp. 157–8.
[62] Nicolson, *The Great Silence*, p. 160.
[63] Gibbs, *More That Must Be Told*, p. 220.

feel that it was a city 'stricken by defeat'.[64] In Vienna, Gibbs witnessed the 'tragic plight of the city' facing a winter without sufficient fuel or food, while in Hungary he found 'bitterness beyond words'.[65] In Vienna, Gibbs met Eglantyne Jebb, the founder of the Save the Children Fund. Forty years later in a pamphlet celebrating the anniversary of the Fund's foundation, Gibbs wrote that even then he was aware that he was in the presence of a saint, 'a woman with a white flame in her soul, inspired by a spiritual vision'.[66] It is unsurprising that Gibbs was prepared to anoint Jebb a saint, given that she had shared with him her belief that the hatreds of the world could be broken down by appealing to the love of children.

In an undated letter found amongst his personal papers, probably from the same period, Gibbs recalled this first meeting with Jebb in Vienna. Though he made the rather innocuous observation that the children protected by the Fund were the 'promise of the future,' after two world wars, and having been the chronicler of so much death, he was determined to go further. Gibbs wanted, needed, to separate the children from the agony they would inherit:

> They are the innocent ones. They have no hand in the hatreds, the ill will, the cruelties, the injustices of this world. They come to it clean, their spirit is unsmirched. They have a right to happiness, and to all loveliness and beauty. It is our fault—the fault of all evil doers if all this is spoilt, and if later on, they find the fairy tale is untrue and that life is a grim and terrible thing. So let us keep them happy and laughing as long as possible and bring laughter and joy to children everywhere charity can reach.[67]

Though he remained a committed supporter of the League of Nations, Gibbs heard of the intrigues and cynicism of the peacemakers with a growing apprehension. He travelled to Geneva on a number of occasions during the 1920s and remained an unrepentant advocate of the League even after the Second World War. He saw in it the 'hopes and efforts' of 'millions of common folk and liberal minded men and women' who 'wanted a world at peace and sure of peace'. Its failure did not dissuade Gibbs from this view, for he felt that the ideal itself was sound, but it was betrayed by the sceptics, the critics, and the reactionaries who 'believed only in

[64] Gibbs, *The Pageant of the Years*, p. 246.
[65] Gibbs, *The Pageant of the Years*, pp. 248, 250.
[66] Pamphlet, courtesy Gibbs Family Archives.
[67] Undated letter, courtesy Gibbs Family Archives.

force, naked and unashamed'.[68] He was present on 10 September 1926 when Germany was admitted to the League, and always vulnerable to the emotion of the moment, he stood and cheered 'with tears in my heart if not in my eyes'.[69] Years after this moment of hope, he delivered a stinging rebuke to those he believed had betrayed the League:

> The leaders of Europe, the politicians, the diplomatists, the propagandists, the jingoes, and the corrupt, let down the decent minded common folk everywhere in all countries, not only by a badly made peace, but worse still, afterwards, by their betrayal of the League. If they had made a better peace, if they had been sincere in their lip service to the League, the Second World War would not have happened. They missed one of the great opportunities in history, in a time of deep human emotion, caused by the long agony of war and by the sense of relief when peace came, to rise above national egotism and narrow patriotism.[70]

In early 1919, Gibbs made the first of four lecture tours of the USA, having been first offered the opportunity by American agent JB Baxter in 1916. Despite his own lingering concerns about his ability as a public speaker, Gibbs would make subsequent tours in 1920, 1921, and 1941. When he arrived in New York on 11 February 1919, he was met at the docks by his brother Cosmo Hamilton who was then in 'the heyday of fame and fortune'.[71] To his surprise, Gibbs discovered that he was actually also quite famous by virtue of the fact that his wartime articles had been published in the *New York Times* and syndicated throughout the USA. For example, in 1918, the *New York Times* reported that Gibbs' dispatches were being used in schools and public libraries for those wishing 'for stories of courage and heroism'.[72] Later that same year in a letter to the editor, a reader described the dispatches as 'great literature' and 'some of the most remarkable writing of the epoch'.[73] It was a theme picked up by the reviewer of the *New York Times* who in his description of *From Bapaume to Passchendaele* argued that Gibbs' dispatches were probably

---

[68] Gibbs, *The Pageant of the Years*, p. 359.
[69] Gibbs, *The Pageant of the Years*, p. 363.
[70] Gibbs, *The Pageant of the Years*, p. 255.
[71] Gibbs, *The Pageant of the Years*, p. 269.
[72] *New York Times*, 26 May, 1918.
[73] *New York Times*, 24 November, 1918.

the only ones which were literature as well as war correspondence.[74] Four months later, another reader described him as the most 'moving of the war correspondents because he dwelt on the human side of the great conflict as well as the inhuman'.[75]

Gibbs' fame brought him considerable pleasure 'for there is no reward in the world so good to a man who for years has been an obscure writer, as to realize at last that his words have been read and remembered with emotion, by millions of fellow mortals'.[76] There were also more practical benefits. His articles were syndicated in American newspapers, and such was their success that by 1923 articles drawn directly from his autobiography *Adventures in Journalism* were appearing across the country. His short stories were published in *Cosmopolitan* while his observations of American life found a ready market in *Harpers Monthly Magazine*. The deal with *Cosmopolitan* was so profitable that it not only allowed Gibbs to butter his bread but even provided 'a little jam'.[77]

An old colleague on the *Daily Chronicle*, Frank Dilnot[78] wrote an article introducing him to American audiences. To him, Gibbs was the greatest of the war correspondents. He was equally enthused about Gibbs' skill as a public speaker:

> He is fortunate, however, in possessing a voice which gives more than a hint of himself. It is deep and melodious in inflection, which admirably serves his wit and feeling…There is a touch of studiousness in him until he forgets himself in his narrations, and a touch of colour comes into his pale cheeks and the torch flames out in his eyes…He talks as he writes, with a fluidity of phrase and with the slow readiness of the natural orator…He tells stories admirably, and a glint of humour breaks through the most moving of his speeches.[79]

Despite such a ringing endorsement, Gibbs' first lecture at Carnegie Hall terrified him more than the war. The very size of New York, the numerous telephone calls, and the introductions and crowded receptions

---

[74] *New York Times*, 18 August, 1918.
[75] *New York Times*, 15 December, 1918.
[76] Gibbs, *Adventures in Journalism*, p. 343.
[77] Gibbs, *Pageant of the Years*, p. 347.
[78] At the time, Dilnot was President of the Association of Foreign Correspondents in America. He had worked on the *Daily Chronicle* investigating social and economic conditions in England as well as being an experienced political journalist and editor.
[79] *New York Times*, 23 February 1919.

left him 'dazed and bewildered'.[80] His reputation was such that the first lecture sold out within four hours. Though almost immobilized with fright, he found that first audience numbering 10,000 'immensely kind, extraordinarily generous and long suffering...Some spirit of friendship and good will reached up to me and gave me courage'.[81] He took this opportunity, the first time he had ever spoken to an audience of any size, to dedicate his pen 'to furthering friendship between America and England' because he believed that the war would have been a futile exercise if these two countries 'did not seal in bonds of friendship the sacrifice made together in the trenches'.[82] The background to the first tour was dominated by the clash between those Americans who supported President Wilson and the League of Nations and those who opposed any further involvement in European affairs. For his part, Gibbs believed that the League was 'the only hope of stricken humanity' and without American involvement it would be a 'mockery'.[83]

He found New York 'vital and dynamic' and the people 'conscious of their own power and with a dramatic instinct able to impress the multitudes with the glory and splendour of their achievement'.[84] As a supporter of women's suffrage and a man given to idealizing women, it is interesting that he believed American women had 'made themselves the better halves of men and the men know it and are deferential to the opinions and desires of their women folk'.[85] He felt that it was natural that these women would have a wider knowledge of literature and ideas because their husbands were busy at work, while they kept 'themselves as beautiful as God made them...decorating their homes; increasing their housekeeping expenses, and reading prodigiously'.[86] By keeping up to date with 'the world's lighter thought' and skimming 'the surface of the deeper knowledge', these women were able to provide 'sparkling' dinner table conversation. Dangers lurked for the man too tired to offer his wife the minimum

---

[80] Gibbs, *The Pageant of the Years*, p. 268.

[81] Gibbs, *Adventures in Journalism*, p. 346. The *New York Times* put the number at 3700 (21 February 1919). The largest hall, named the Isaac Stern Auditorium in 1996, seats 2800 on five levels. In fairness to Gibbs, a nervous public speaker, it probably looked like 10,000 at the time, particularly given that 300 sat on the stage and scores more were standing.

[82] *New York Times*, 21 February 1919.

[83] *New York Times*, 25 June 1919.

[84] *Harpers Monthly Magazine*, August 1919, p. 326.

[85] *Harpers Monthly Magazine*, September 1919, p. 461.

[86] *Harpers Monthly Magazine*, September 1919, pp. 461-2.

of 'comradeship' for Gibbs believed that American women sought divorce quicker than their European counterparts. In New York society, there was no 'stoning sisterhood to fling mud and missiles at those who have already paid for errors by many tears'. For these women, however, 'their furs and diamonds were no medicine for the bitterness of their souls, nor for the hunger in their hearts'. Middle-class women, however, possessed too much common sense to be worried by such 'emotional distress'.[87]

On 20 October 1919, in between his first and second tour of the USA, Gibbs scored what was probably the greatest journalistic coup of his career. He was sent to Rome none too hopefully by the news editor of the *Daily Chronicle* in quest of the first ever interview with a Pope. A cardinal to whom he made his petition laughed good-naturedly at such a request, yet the astonished Gibbs received an invitation for a private audience with Pope Benedict XV just three days later. Gibbs devoted over one-third of his article to detailing his experiences prior to the moment when he was confronted by 'a simple figure dressed in white, not so tall as I expected, and with a scholar's look, a little austere at the first glance'.[88] In a 20-minute conversation, conducted in French, Gibbs found the Pope to be a genial man who seemed as interested in Gibbs' view of the post-war world as he was in stating his own. The Pope appeared particularly concerned with the plight of the working class and referred to the encyclicals on labour written by Pope Leo XIII. Benedict believed that 'if men behave justly and with real Christian charity toward each other, many of the troubles of the world will be removed; but without justice and charity there will be no social progress'.[89] Linking mainstream Christianity and progress would have appealed enormously to Gibbs. For as one author noted of Dickens (and it was just as true for his disciple Gibbs), though his traditional Christianity gave shape to his own vision, it was actually 'something quite different from an orthodox theology or codified ritual practice. It is a religious impulse that tries to distil the humanistic spirit of Christianity and breathe it into the yearning of the fiction for a more humane world'.[90]

---

[87] *Harpers Monthly Magazine*, September 1919, p. 465.
[88] *New York Times*, 21 October 1919.
[89] *New York Times*, 21 October 1919.
[90] J Gold (1972) *Charles Dickens: Radical Moralist* (Minneapolis: University of Minnesota Press), p. 276.

The Pope also outlined some of the humanitarian work of the Vatican during the war, conceding that it was little when compared to the extent of the suffering. The interview ended after precisely 20 minutes, and one suspects that it was only then that Gibbs became aware that the occasion was always going to overshadow anything that the Pope would actually say to a journalist. He justified the absence of headline-making statements by arguing that 'there is nothing sensational to say: and he spoke about the problems of the time simply and frankly, without oratorical effect or high flown phrases, but with keen common sense'. A quarter of a century later, Gibbs also conceded that for all the attention the interview received 'its warning and its wisdom were utterly ignored, and those people of power who may have read it did exactly the contrary of the Pope's emotional and noble pleading'.[91] The text of the interview does not warrant Gibbs' hyperbole, for it remains a disappointing document possessing neither passion nor gravity. Gibbs was always deeply affected by historical pageantry and ritual, and one suspects that he was moved far more by these secular considerations than by any sense of religious belief. It is difficult to divest oneself of the view that Gibbs saw in the Pope's support for social progress little more than the statement of a simple political manifesto entirely compatible with his own brand of liberalism. If ever Gibbs was going to make a statement concerning religious belief generally and his own faith specifically, this was the moment. In its own way, it conforms to the pattern of Gibbs' silences often speaking far more stridently than his written words.

Other more earthly honours came Gibbs way the following year. In company with three other correspondents, Gibbs was knighted in April 1920, the same year in which he was made a Chevalier of the Legion of Honour. After discussing with Beach Thomas the possibility of refusing the honour, to the anger of some of his colleagues he accepted. In 1957, Gibbs recalled that Hamilton Fyfe hated him for accepting the knighthood and even his old comrade Tomlinson never quite forgave him. Though not explicitly identifying Fyfe, in 1923, Gibbs wrote that one colleague in particular felt it a statement of 'allegiance to (the) part authors of the war, traitors to the men who died, perpetrators of hate, architects of an infamous peace, and profiteers of their nation's ruin'.[92] When Fyfe wrote his own memoirs, he countered by suggesting that

[91] Gibbs, *The Pageant of the Years*, p. 260.
[92] Gibbs, *Life's Adventures*, p. 30.

any resentment was 'imagined' by Gibbs, adding unconvincingly that such a response on his part would have been 'absurd'. He added that it was Gibbs' right to 'alter his mind when the offer was made'. Yet in Fyfe's discussion of his own motives for refusing the honour when Harmsworth offered to arrange it, there is a thinly disguised criticism of Gibbs, the only correspondent to write extensively about the war after 1918. Fyfe believed that 'for any man whose eyes were open to the shame and stupidity of that order to adorn himself in this way would be not only meaningless but infamous. I had no right to judge those who still found no fault with the system they saw in operation. But I could not reconcile condemning that system with acceptance of its bribes'.[93] In fairness to Gibbs, as a bribe it was worthless given that it was awarded after the war when censorship had been lifted.

How seriously Gibbs countenanced a refusal, or even what had motivated this reluctance beyond a sense that others may have deserved it more, is unknown. Beach Thomas does not mention the episode, or the knighthood, in his memoirs, while Gibbs does not linger over his reasoning in his autobiographical writing. Having done his duty as he saw it and perhaps to his private joy with considerable courage, there was no shame in Gibbs accepting such an honour. Yet this half-hearted reluctance and the semi-humorous suggestion that the only difference the knighthood made to his life was the slight increase in his tradesmen's bills might suggest some moral unease on Gibbs' part.[94] More in keeping with his nature was his emotion at being rewarded by his King:

> So one fine morning, when a military investiture was in progress, I went up to Buckingham Palace, knelt before the King in the courtyard there...I should be wholly insincere if I pretended that at that moment I did not feel the stir of the old romantic sentiment with which I had been steeped as a boy, and a sense of pride that I had 'won my spurs' in service for England's sake. Yet as I walked home with my box of trinkets and that King's touch on my shoulder, I thought of the youth who had served England with greater gallantry, through hardship and suffering to sudden death or to the inevitable forgetfulness of a poverty stricken peace.[95]

[93] www.greatwardifferent.com/Great_War/Hamilton_Fyfe/Seven_Selves_01.htm, accessed 22 June, 2013.
[94] Gibbs, *Adventures in Journalism*, p. 277.
[95] Gibbs, *Adventures in Journalism*, p. 277.

In 1920, Heinemann published *Back to Life*, which was, in his view, the 'best thing I have ever written'.[96] In an echo of his own sense of alienation from those who had not shared the incommunicable experience of war, he described returning soldiers as morbid, neurotic, and listless. He felt that it was a 'bad novel from the point of view of art, but I tried to get the truth into it'.[97] At the same time, he became editor of *Review of Reviews*, a short and unhappy sojourn ended when it was sold almost without warning, though Gibbs had spent much of his time in charge in the USA on a lecture tour. His cousin Mary Hamilton, who he had hired to work with him, recalled that it was the only time in a friendship spanning many years that she had seen him 'really angry'.[98]

In the spring of 1921, Gibbs, with his son Tony for company, travelled to Southern Europe with the intention of reporting on escalating tension between Greece and Turkey. Travelling between Brindisi and Constantinople on the *Gratz*, a 7000-ton steamship, he contrasted the 'sea of enchantment' with his fellow passengers, who were a motley collection of merchants and travelling salesmen. Not a man skilled at criticism, Gibbs described them as 'an unattractive crowd'. After passing through the Corinth Canal, the ship docked at Athens where Gibbs was disappointed to be denied the opportunity to disembark despite possessing a visa from the Greek Consulate in London. He had to content himself with viewing the Parthenon through binoculars from the deck of the ship which nevertheless still provided him with a thrill of emotion. Leaving Athens, the *Gratz* steamed into the Aegean Sea, past Gallipoli where the 'flower of Australian and New Zealand youth had fallen' and then to Constantinople.[99] His first view of the city impressed him enormously, particularly the domes of San Sophia, which 'lay like rose coloured clouds above the cypress trees', and the Grand Mosque with 'minarets' 'white and slender, cut[ting] the blue sky like lances'.[100] It was everything that the romantic Gibbs could have hoped for on his first visit to the Near East.

In Constantinople, he found Percival Phillips, one of his colleagues from the Western Front, ensconced with numerous English and American

[96] Letter to Curtis Brown, 13 January 1920. *Philip Gibbs Letters, Special Collections Research Center, Syracuse University Libraries*.

[97] Letter to Christie Murray, 10 Nov 1925. *Philip Gibbs Letters, Special Collections Research Center, Syracuse University Libraries*.

[98] Hamilton, *Remembering My Good Friends*, p. 144.

[99] Gibbs, *Adventures in Journalism*, p. 290.

[100] Gibbs, *Adventures in Journalism*, p. 291.

correspondents awaiting the outbreak of war. It was a conflict which Gibbs believed had seen the raising of 'the old flag of Islam' and the 'stirring up [of] fanaticism through the whole Mohammedan world'.[101] Gibbs feared, not unreasonably given the events of August 1914, that this 'drama' might result in another European war and 'set the whole East aflame'.[102] The drama which Gibbs witnessed was the result of the collapse of the Ottoman Turkish Empire which had initiated an internal political revolution. This pitted Sultan Mohammed VI, who had accepted the Treaty of Sevres offered by the Allies in August 1920, against the nationalist supporters of Mustapha Kemal, the hero of Gallipoli and soon to be father of the modern Turkish nation.

From the smoking room of the Pera Hotel which looked out onto the Grand Rue, Gibbs observed the local population, as was his reporting style. He saw a 'ceaseless procession of Turks, Greeks, Armenians, Israelites, French and Italian officers, Persians, Arabs, Negroes, Gypsies, American "drummers", British soldiers and Russian refugees—the queerest High Street in the world, the meeting place between the East and the West'.[103] From Constantinople, Gibbs travelled to Smyrna on a British ship on which he felt a 'thrill of patriotic pleasure' to get porridge for breakfast with ham, eggs, and buttered toast.[104] Here on the ship, he also learnt from other passengers of Turkish atrocities, particularly the Armenian genocide. It shocked him to the extent that he believed that 'under the stars in the Aegean Sea' he had learnt 'more than I know about the infernal history of mankind'. Though like Shakespeare's Macbeth, Gibbs had 'supped full of horrors' these 'were stories of the East, unknown and unrecorded, as primitive in their horror as when Assyrians fought Egyptians, or the Israelites were put to the sword in the time of Judas Maccabaeus'.[105] Gibbs sided with the Greeks, for despite seeing shortcomings in their behaviour he may well have been seduced by an inability to distinguish between the place of ancient Greece as a cradle of civilization and the contemporary actions of her politicians. Interestingly, this was the same quality that Gibbs saw in President Wilson's attitude. For he might just have easily been describing himself when he speculated that the American

---

[101] Gibbs, *The Pageant of the Years*, p. 291.
[102] Gibbs, *Adventures in Journalism*, p. 292.
[103] Gibbs, *Adventures in Journalism*, p. 294.
[104] Gibbs, *Adventures in Journalism*, p. 306.
[105] Gibbs, *Adventures in Journalism*, p. 309.

President had been swayed by 'the glory of their past' which had 'stirred his mind with a vague benevolence towards their present hopes'.[106] While the impact of his romanticized view of Greek history is purely speculative, Gibbs' opposition to the Turks was not. He felt that it was time that the Turks were 'thrust out of Europe and that their blight over subject peoples—Armenian, Jew, Arab, Greek and Bulgarian—should be lifted at last'. For wherever 'the Crescent has gone, their progress had ceased under a frozen and rigid faith'.[107] During another European sojourn, Gibbs would later visit refugee camps near Phaleron and Piraeus where some of the one-and-a-half million Greeks removed from Turkish territory awaited resettlement. He found them 'beggared, homeless, hungry and diseased' but they were 'of the old Greek stock...Out of their blood and genius had come the fine flower of civilisation in the dawn of history'. Gibbs believed that their survival showed that 'it is hard to kill the spirit of a brave people'.[108]

By early 1921, when he began his third tour of the USA in as many years, Gibbs was so familiar that one newspaper contracted to print his articles could trumpet that he was the 'most popular Englishman that has ever talked to the American public and written for the American Press'.[109] Another joined in the homage by arguing that he was 'not a propagandist for any country' but rather was a 'propagandist only for the truth'.[110] One newspaper, however, viewed Gibbs as nothing less than part of an orchestrated campaign to create a favourable environment in which England could pressure the American Government to cancel her war debts. In an article titled 'English Propaganda', he was mockingly referred to as the 'accurate journalist' who had been so 'brilliant a propagandist war correspondent that he waited until after the war to write his book *Now It Can Be Told* and who was subsequently made Sir Philip by King George'. In particular, Gibbs' performance when invited to speak before the House Committee on Naval Affairs attracted the ire of the editor who referred to it being delivered to a 'matinee audience'.[111] Gibbs was certain, however, that he spoke on behalf of Great Britain's desire for Anglo-American friendship and peace. In a broad-ranging discussion on British Foreign

---

[106] Gibbs, *Since Then*, p. 95.
[107] Gibbs, *Since Then*, p. 95.
[108] Gibbs, *Since Then*, p. 115.
[109] *Salt Lake Tribune*, 28 October, 1921.
[110] *Wichita Daily Times*, 26 March, 1921.
[111] *Capital Times*, 11 February, 1921.

Policy, Ireland, and the state of Europe, Gibbs spoke well enough to be congratulated by the members of the British Embassy and the Naval Attaché who had all attended to hear his evidence. Nevertheless, Gibbs found the lecture circuit exhausting, and when offered the opportunity of a fourth tour in the late 1920s, he declined with the curt observation that 'nothing except extreme destitution would persuade me to make another lecture tour. I found it killing work and I am a rotten lecturer'.[112]

This third lecture tour was dominated by the question of Ireland. Shortly before it commenced, Gibbs resigned from the *Daily Chronicle* because of its support of Lloyd George's use of the 'Black and Tans'. They were special members of the Royal Irish Constabulary who were recruited by the British in 1920 and were named for their uniform of dark green caps and khaki tunics and trousers. They were active in suppressing Irish national unrest between March 1920 and January 1922 during which time they were provoked into violent reprisals by terrorist acts. Their methods generated considerable opposition in Britain and the USA. In Taylor's view, the Black and Tans became an 'autonomous terror squad', staffed by men with 'a taste for fighting and brutality'.[113] In Gibbs' view, it was a policy of meeting terror with counterterror.[114] For a second time, Gibbs chose unemployment on a question of principle, although the prospect of work as a freelance in this period was not as fraught as it had been before the war. Despite his opposition to Britain's Irish policy, many of his lectures were disrupted by riots and jeering by Irish Americans who assumed that he condoned his government's actions. When able to speak, Gibbs pleaded for greater American involvement in world affairs and generally found support for American and British cooperation.

As for his old antagonist Lloyd George, Gibbs still believed that he was by instinct 'always on the side of humanity and good will, though in many of his acts he compromises with the spirit of harsh reaction, makes friends too readily with the mammon of Unrighteousness, sells some quality of his soul for political power, the safety of his office, and the advantage of immediate triumph'.[115] Lloyd George returned fire in his *War Memoirs*, questioning Gibbs' integrity by disputing the accuracy of his war

---

[112] Letter to JB Pond, 23 May 1928. *Philip Gibbs Letters, Special Collections Research Center, Syracuse University Libraries.*

[113] AJP Taylor (1965) *English History 1914–1945* (Oxford: The Clarendon Press), p. 155.

[114] Gibbs, *More That Must Be Told*, p. 262.

[115] *Harpers Monthly Magazine*, September 1921, p. 425.

dispatches. Given his earlier meetings with Gibbs, it was a spiteful act which did not reflect well on this brilliant, though morally erratic politician.

As a Catholic and a liberal, Gibbs was more than just an interested observer of the increasingly violent developments in Ireland. He believed that peace with Ireland was essential to the liberties of the English people, not merely for practical reasons but as a means of regaining 'her moral character...for her own soul's sake'.[116] Gibbs saw the continuing violence as an indictment of British politicians who had 'betrayed the honour and good name of England'.[117] In doing so, they had damaged the nation's reputation to the point that it would need 'the saving grace of time to wash it clean again in times of noble leadership'.[118] In abandoning the ideal of self-determination even then being trumpeted at Versailles, Gibbs believed that the English government had adopted 'Prussian methods' and the 'old primitive law of an eye for an eye...without any reference at all to other laws of a more recent and more civilized kind'.[119] Yet he could not absolve the Irish of 'evil acts and obstinate stupidities' for there were limits 'even to the claims of Liberty'. Gibbs saw no grinding tyranny by which 'terrible deeds [might be] ennobled'. Despite many 'beautiful qualities of Irish character', he also saw an 'unforgiving, ungenerous nature', one which 'answers fair play by ill will...nourishing grievances for their own sake'.[120] Most damning of all for a man possessed of a gentle nature, he found in the Irish an 'unexpected cruelty'.[121]

Interestingly, given his own experience of censorship, Gibbs deplored the effect of the government's control of many newspapers and the 'timidity or incredulity or dishonesty of others'.[122] The absence of a dissenting voice was exacerbated by a readership which saw all criticism of government as unpatriotic and 'all truth which disturbs the self-righteousness of the English conservative mind [as] revolutionary'.[123] He saw in those who supported the government's actions as 'John Bull' characters—unrepresentative of the people, but 'hard' in their Imperialism,

[116] Gibbs, *More That Must Be Told*, p. 260.

[117] Gibbs, *More That Must Be Told*, p. 332.

[118] Gibbs, *More That Must Be Told*, p. 333.

[119] Gibbs, *More That Must Be Told*, p. 261.

[120] Gibbs, *More That Must Be Told*, p. 335.

[121] *Harpers Monthly Magazine*, March 1921, p. 412.

[122] Gibbs, *More That Must Be Told*, p. 265.

[123] Gibbs, *More That Must Be Told*, p. 265. Gibbs noted the honourable exceptions of the *Daily News*, the *Manchester Guardian*, and the *Nation*.

narrow in their Protestantism, and firm believers in 'resolute rule with
machine guns and tanks for all rebellious people, such as native races, and
working men who want more wages'.[124] It is interesting that he would
explicitly link narrow Protestantism with the excesses of English rule in
Ireland, because in other respects he appeared reticent to view the conflict
through a religious prism. Gibbs' language was almost entirely political
in nature or based on the idiosyncrasies of national character. Where it
veered into questions of morality he did not readily link notions of right
and wrong with religious doctrine.

Gibbs did not confine his attention during this period to home-grown
tragedies. He travelled to Russia in October 1921 at the invitation of the
Imperial Famine Relief Fund (IFRF) and witnessed suffering that at times
threatened to dwarf even his experiences on the Western Front. With his
amazing capacity to be present when great events unfolded, Gibbs was in
Moscow on 17 October when Lenin outlined the New Economic laws
(NEP) which saw a rollback of communist-enforced economic changes.
Nevertheless, there was open suspicion that the famine was a Russian conspiracy to compel the Western Powers to feed her armies, though Gibbs
was very quickly able to bear witness to the human tragedy unfolding in
the East. Yet for all his empathy and compassion for those starving to
death in their hundreds of thousands, he was a shrewder man than the
one who had left for the Western Front in 1914. He knew enough to be
highly sceptical of claims and counterclaims of atrocities, for he knew from
experience the pervasiveness of propaganda in war. Though moved by the
plight of the people, Gibbs was certainly no communist apologist, for he
saw the 'red horseman looming upon the Eastern horizon'. He also saw
that until 'hope and confidence come out of the misery...it is idle to look
to an improvement in the shattered morale of those who must be saved
from the apocalyptic disaster which threatens'.[125]

The sympathy Gibbs had for the tragedy unfolding in the East was still
inevitably coloured by his distaste for any radicalization of politics. He had
not moved as far from Carlyle as he had hoped, for his abhorrence is not
just a reaction to the human toll, but a philosophical rejection of all revolutionary change. It was for Gibbs a 'horror of anarchy and executions,
revolution and counter revolution, victories and defeats by Red armies
and White armies, massacre and pillage and famine, atrocities worse than

---

[124] *Harpers Monthly Magazine*, March 1921, p. 411.
[125] *Muscatine Journal and News Tribune*, 24 September 1920.

beastlike, tragedies innumerable, plague and death, and long agony to a hundred million souls'.[126] Such fanaticism was the antitheses of Gibbs' liberalism and his spiritual-like faith in compromise and political evolution. He was not, however, completely averse to a little anti-red propaganda when the opportunity arose, as he showed during his speaking tours of the USA. He warned America as it retreated into isolationism at the end of the war that the red horseman 'would bolshevize the world. As he rides, he brings nearer to America the fifth scourge. He can be checkmated best by helping those nearest him unhorse this enemy of the civilisation we know today'.[127]

Despite his resignation, the *Daily Chronicle* agreed to publish a number of articles, but only after his return in order to avoid difficulties with the Russians. Accompanied by Leonard Spray, who was a correspondent in Berlin, he travelled via the German capital through East Prussia and into Riga in Latvia. From there, they accepted a lift on a train with the American Relief Administration (ARA), which took them safely to Moscow, then Petrograd, and then finally to the Volga which was then in the grip of famine. Always sensitive to the plight of women, Gibbs was deeply moved by the Russian women he saw in Petrograd, who were thinly clad in the icy conditions and clearly suffering from starvation. He recalled that the obvious tragedy of their circumstances made him 'shiver in [his] soul'. There was worse to come. In a morgue, he saw 'a pile of dead bodies, men, women and children flung one on top of the other like rubbish for the refuse heap. Hands and legs obtruded from the mass of corruption'.[128] The hospitals were little better; 'patients, stricken with typhus, dysentery, and all kinds of diseases, lay together in unventilated wards. Many of the beds had been burnt for fuel, and most of the inmates lay on bare boards'. One family Gibbs saw left an indelible mark on his mind. Travelling to the Volga, he entered a dwelling where 'the father and mother were lying on the floor...and were almost too weak to rise. Some young children were on a bed above the stove, dying of hunger. A boy of eighteen lay back in a wooden settle against the window sill in a kind of coma'.[129]

The famine, the combined result of war, drought, and government incompetence, killed 5 million people and sparked an international relief

---

[126] Gibbs, *Since Then*, p. 46.
[127] Gibbs, *Since Then*, p. 46.
[128] *Lethbridge Daily Herald*, 11 August 1923.
[129] Gibbs, *The Pageant of the Years*, pp. 327, 329.

effort that would eventually feed over double that number. Gibbs saw the work of the ARA and the IFRF as 'nobly done in the spirit of Christianity kept alight in a dark and cruel world, which is the jungle of Europe'.[130] The impact of death on a scale that in pre-holocaust days would have seemed unbelievable to an English reporter brought out in Gibbs a hitherto hidden belief in a vengeful God:

> Every civilized soul must seek the truth [of the famine], for if some millions of the human family are just allowed to starve to death without governments or peoples of other countries showing great concern or making an effort at rescue, the vengeance of the gods men worship or reject will strike at them.[131]

After his return from Russia, Gibbs found himself introduced to the Soviet Ambassador, who promptly claimed to have a dossier on him. It pleased Gibbs to be blacklisted by the Russians, as it later pleased him to receive similar treatment from the Germans. Such a response implied that his work was important and that he was not merely a chronicler but a participant in these mighty events. It also allowed him scope to attempt to use his fame and reputation to influence government policy. Using his friendship with the American Ambassador in London, Gibbs presented an economic plan at a dinner party attended by, among others, the German Ambassador. Gibbs also sent the 'Memorandum on the Reconstruction of Russia' to his editor who in late March 1922 passed it to Sir Edward Grigg, Lloyd George's private secretary. Buoyed by a positive reaction from some American financiers, Gibbs also sent it to President Hoover and the American Ambassador. Central to Gibbs' thesis was his conviction that the demobilization of the Red Army, or at the very least its considerable reduction, was essential to any European peace. Seeing in the Russian need for economic aid, an opportunity to impose this reduction, he urged the governments of the four great powers to deal with the Soviet Government as a united bloc rather than risk being played off against each other. The plan would have seen France, Germany, England, and the USA fund the reconstruction of Russia, thereby stimulating their production, in return for peace guarantees.

---

[130] Gibbs, *Adventures in Journalism*, p. 340.
[131] *Indianapolis Star*, 8 December 1921.

The Memorandum shows an evolution in Gibbs' thinking. He offers a pragmatic, almost cynical plan to those unlikely to be moved by altruism in order to achieve humanitarian goals. For as much as he discussed, the demobilization of the Red Army, a more definite acknowledgement of pre-war debts, freedom of international trade for private citizens, and a wider application of the new laws regarding the rights of private property, Gibbs' real concern was with 'the lives of many millions of starving people in the famine areas', and those not faced with starvation who are nevertheless 'hungry, diseased and devitalized'. Gibbs believed that the idea was passed on to Lloyd George who had 'it up his sleeve' when he attended a world economic conference in Genoa in April 1922.[132] Whether Lloyd George would have seriously entertained such a proposal is unclear, even had the conference not been a dismal failure. Gibbs' faith in the influence he could exert through personal contacts, and of his own ability to help shape world affairs, is almost embarrassingly naive,[133] yet it is indicative of both a sincere desire for peace and a more personal search for participation and self-worth.

Though it is tempting to see Gibbs as merely a well-intentioned peace activist, he was also a professional writer who made his living selling not only newspaper articles but also books. His experiences in this 'vast country of interminable distances with many races, half civilized and half savage, slightly westernized and deeply oriental' became the basis for his very successful novel *The Middle of the Road*.[134] In it, Gibbs portrays post-war England, rent with division and seething with potential violence, dominated by a clash looming between an increasingly threatened upper-class intent on the maintenance of its hereditary privileges and a disenchanted working class agitating for a fairer division of the nation's wealth. His main protagonist, Bertram Pollard, is a returned officer struggling to adjust to peace and 'the worrying business of life after war, with its enormous disappointments' which had 'loosened his hold on old beliefs [and] old loyalties of tradition'.[135] Pollard's wife and her upper-class family and friends, threatened by post-war change, agitated for the violent suppression of dissent, both in Ireland and at home. Branded a class traitor by his in-laws,

---

[132] Gibbs, *The Pageant of the Years*, p. 336.
[133] He shared this belief with his son Tony who attempted his own peace deal in 1940.
[134] Gibbs, *Since Then*, p. 48.
[135] P Gibbs (1923) *The Middle of the Road* (London: Hutchinson and Co), pp. 8; 11.

Pollard finds work as a journalist travelling through France and Germany, and finally to the famine in Russia.

It is not difficult to see Gibbs' own experiences finding expression in his fiction, but equally it is clear that his writing had increasingly become a vehicle for a discussion of his political convictions. One of Pollard's sisters marries a Prussian officer, while another marries an Irish rebel who is later executed for murder. His brother is killed while serving with the Black and Tans and after a series of chaste romances, one of which is ended by the death from typhus of a beautiful and heroic Russian, the denouement sees him reunited with his wayward but reformed wife. As one modern reviewer noted, 'if a good novelist is one who describes human relationships with subtlety, Gibbs is not a good novelist'.[136] Yet as the same reviewer conceded, he was an excellent reporter and this is reflected in the wealth of detail concerning the state of post-war Europe. Another reviewer writing in the year of its release was less forgiving of its obvious journalistic origins. He dismissed it as little more than 'several hundred Sunday special feature stories digested into fictional form', which though harsh, was, by Gibbs' own admission, not too far from the truth.[137] More profoundly, however, its grimness reflected Gibbs' own state of mind during this period of unhappiness and disenchantment.

Less than a year after the *Nation* published this dismissive review of *The Middle of the Road*, one of its writers described Gibbs as 'a magnificent journalist'. In a review of Gibbs' first autobiography, *Adventures in Journalism*, the writer observed that Gibbs was a 'fascinating storyteller' with the 'power of communicating his thrill with a sentimental melancholy'. The reviewer also sensed something that even Gibbs may not have been able to admit with complete candour. He believed that 'one cannot help feeling that Philip Gibbs enjoyed riding in his own car up and down along the front'. In an interesting statement on the degree to which wartime censorship was by now accepted as a matter of historical fact, this most laudatory of articles credited him, without even a hint of criticism, with 'telling the British people what they were allowed to know of [the war's] glory and its horror'.[138]

---

[136] http://greatwarfiction.wordpress.com/2007/11/06/the-middeofthe road/, accessed 10 November 2008.

[137] JW Krutch, *Nation*, vol. 116, no. 3020, 23 May 1923, pp. 602–3.

[138] *Nation*, vol. 118, no. 3054, 16 January 1924, p. 67.

Gibbs did not confine his travel during this period to lectures or political reportage. Agnes loved foreign travel, and together they visited Egypt, Palestine, Germany, France, Hungary, Italy, and Switzerland. On one trip, in company with his brother Arthur and his American wife, they went by ship across the Mediterranean to Alexandria, and then on to Cairo and Palestine. Gibbs was deeply moved by his journey to the Holy Land which was 'unforgettable'.[139] In Cairo, he woke one night with an excruciating pain in his right eye, a precursor to serious eye trouble in later years. He also became a passionate painter in oils, and went on sketching holidays to France with Edgar Lander, his friend from his Fleet Street days. Each year Gibbs, Agnes, and Tony holidayed on the Côte d'Azur where his brother Arthur rented a little villa in the grounds of the Hotel Cap d'Antibes. Here, he relaxed in the company of people such as HG Wells, WJ Locke, and Baroness Orczy. In a reaction reminiscent of his frustration with those who had not seen the war, he characterized it as a world of make-believe in which there was wealth but no happiness, and the rich who passed the time gambling as little more than 'lotus eaters in a world which was slipping down the slopes of ruin'. These holidays, however, were merely brief interludes for Gibbs 'between hard spells of work and the anxious study of a world going from bad to worse, with an occasional gleam of hope and a mirage of peace ahead'.[140]

The early 1920s also marked Gibbs' first foray into the world of movies with the release of *The Street of Adventure* in 1921. Produced by the Astra Film Corporation, an American company which operated for only five or six years from 1915 onwards, it was the first of eight films to which Gibbs contributed either stories or screenplays. The extent of his contribution is almost impossible to ascertain given that the only reference he made to this part of his career concerned his second film, *Die Stadt der Versuchung* (1925) (known as *The City of Temptation* in the USA). Filmed at Starken, it was an American production with an international cast. According to Gibbs, the Turkish Embassy brought pressure to bear on the German Foreign Office because of their concern that the villain was one of their countrymen and, in the way of all Gibbs' stories, the action leads inevitably to the death of the undeserving. The film was a failure, and at least one commentator unintentionally corroborates Gibbs' description of events

---

[139] Gibbs, *The Pageant of the Years*, p. 350.
[140] Gibbs, *The Pageant of the Years*, p. 354.

in seeing in the 'ragged' 60-minute movie proof that censorship had left some of the action on a cutting room floor.[141]

Gibbs' third film *High Steppers* (1926) was based on his book *Heirs Apparent* (1924) which had been the fourth bestselling work of fiction in the USA in the year of its release. Starring Mary Astor and Delores del Rio, it follows the story of Julian Perryman who is expelled from Oxford for his 'jazz existence' and must return to the family mansion. Here, he finds his mother and sister pursuing an equally vacuous lifestyle, one unquestioned by an uninterested father immersed in his work as editor of a paper specializing in scandal. Perryman has an unrequited affection for Evelyn Iffield (del Rio), but finds true love with Audrey Nye (Mary Astor) who helped him expose a corrupt publisher whose unsuitable son was courting the intrepid hero's sister. Both the novel and the movie deal with Gibbs' view of the generation which, though too young to have fought in the war, reached what he saw as an incomplete maturity in its immediate aftermath. Though he was obsessed with keeping the sacrifice of the war years in the public consciousness and rejects what he sees as the flippancy of the jazz age, he refrains from condemning youth outright. For he finished the novel with the assertion that 'Youth's alright', which one contemporary believed was 'the sincere expression of Philip Gibbs' own perfect faith'.[142] This faith was a far cry from his claim in 1923 that 'one does not find much hope of moral progress or intellectual idealism in the younger generation. They seem to have learned nothing out of their experience of the war'.[143] It was a frame of mind observed by his American audiences, who were admittedly less directly touched by the war. In 1925, Philip Sims, a war correspondent, ventured the opinion that Gibbs' middle name was 'gloom'. Sims recounted a story from the Western Front when he pointed out a little doghouse on a canal boat and described it to Gibbs as 'pretty and artistic'. Gibbs replied 'it looks like a child's coffin to me'. In the same article, another writer described him as 'famed for his pessimistic fiction and predictions'.[144]

In 1926, *The Reckless Lady*, based on the book of the same name, was released. It was set in Monte Carlo, where the title character, divorced because of an affair with a Russian who had paid off her gambling debts,

---

[141] www.allmovie.com/work/city-of-temptation-87356, accessed 23 June 2013.
[142] G Overton (1924) *Cargoes for Crusoes* (New York: D. Appleton and Company), p. 25.
[143] *Davenport Democrat and Leader*, 25 March 1923.
[144] *Titusville Herald*, 6 July 1925.

ekes out an existence for herself and her daughter with careful gambling. Her world is threatened when the Russian returns to pursue her daughter and she loses everything in a vain attempt to win sufficient money to fund her daughter's escape. Contemplating suicide, a familiar motif in Gibbs' fiction, she is saved by the timely intervention of her ex-husband. *Out of the Ruins* (1928), *Paradise* (1929), *Darkened Rooms* (1929), and *Captured* (1933) starring Leslie Howard and Douglas Fairbanks Jr followed, but it must not have been a career tangent Gibbs saw as particularly noteworthy, for it was certainly one that he appeared content to have fade into obscurity. Nevertheless, it does not indicate any entrenched opposition to the cinema. Gibbs believed that movies had contributed to a social revolution by providing to the 'great masses' a 'larger outlook on life and some sense of the beauty and grace of life'.[145]

Gibbs returned to Europe in 1923 to find that French troops had occupied the Ruhr in response to the German failure to meet the astronomical reparations demanded of her. He had always considered the demand for reparations from Germany as absurd, a view no doubt reinforced in April 1921 when the Reparations Committee set the German liability at 132,000 million marks (£66,000 million), a figure so fantastic as to be at once profoundly ridiculous and profoundly dangerous. When, inevitably, Germany found it impossible to pay, the French Premier Raymond Poincaré, who Gibbs saw as a 'formidable and stubborn man', put the bailiffs in.[146] The occupation brought them only hatred, and when Gibbs travelled to Essen to report on the crisis, he found nothing but silence and desolation.[147] Such was the German anger at both the humiliation of the occupation and the brutality which accompanied it, Gibbs believed that it was now inevitable that Germany would fight a war of revenge. Knowing the Germans as he did, his despair was palpable in his claim that the 'German people will never rest until they have made France pay in blood and tears' and in doing so, these two antagonists would fight 'a war to the death' which would see 'European civilisation extinguished'.[148]The humiliation was compounded by the catastrophic inflation that followed during which Gibbs gave a dinner party in Berlin for eight people, and when the bill arrived it had reached some thousands of marks, the equivalent of just

---

[145] *Syracuse Herald*, 1 July 1923.
[146] Gibbs, *The Pageant of the Years*, p. 338.
[147] Gibbs, *Since Then*, p. 159.
[148] *Ogden Standard Examiner*, 29 January 1923.

over seven shillings. The German mark fell from 20,000 to the dollar in January 1923 to 100,000 in June to 5 million in August, 50 million in September, and 630,000 million in early November. At the time, Gibbs interviewed two officials of the Reichsbank and was embarrassed when they wept openly in front of him. He saw some hope in the form of the German Chancellor Gustav Stresemann, who he had first met in October 1922, and who he believed had delivered the German people from the threat of anarchy.[149] He was a politician cast very much in a role which Gibbs was ideally suited to appreciate. Gibbs believed him to be clearly middle class, with no hint of fanaticism, belonging to the dangerous place, 'the Middle of the Road'.[150]

Ten Years After is steeped in Gibbs' disenchantment, for in this overview of European affairs he is barely able to contain his anger at the failure of the peacemakers to justify the sacrifice of the war years. He characterized the years since the Armistice as a period of 'blundering, moral degradation and reaction to the lowest traditions of national politics'.[151] Though he still acknowledged German war guilt, he now saw the statesmen of Europe as complicit in the tragedy, for they had maintained, defended, and intensified the 'old regime of international rivalry with its political structure resting entirely on armed force'.[152] Not one of these leaders was 'inspired by any vision of world policy higher than material advantage or Imperial aggrandizement'. In particular, he turned his vitriol on the Treaty of Versailles, a 'peace of vengeance, and a peace of greed and a peace of hypocrisy'.[153] Yet even in his anger, Gibbs could not condemn fellow human beings outright, conceding that except in minor details, it was difficult to see how a better peace might have been made. A just peace needed a 'spiritual leader so high in virtue, so on fire with human charity, so clear and shining in vision that the people of Europe would have been caught up and carried on by his call to the New World'.[154] For a period, Wilson appeared cast in such a heroic mould, possessed as he was with a vision that was 'like a new Gospel, or the old Gospel recalled in this time

---

[149] AJP Taylor ranked him as Bismarck's equal as a German and European statesman and 'perhaps even greater'. Taylor, *Origins*, p. 79.

[150] Gibbs, *Since Then*, p. 163.

[151] Gibbs, *Ten Years After*, p. 1.

[152] Gibbs, *Ten Years After*, p. 1.

[153] Gibbs, *Ten Years After*, p. 1.

[154] Gibbs, *Ten Years After*, p. 14.

of hatred and massacre'.[155] Though Gibbs saw Wilson's failure as tragic, and ascribed it in part to his 'hard, autocratic temper', his 'vanity', and 'fatal egotism', he was still drawn to a man who clung determinedly to his ideals even as they failed. Perhaps seeing something of his own championing of liberalism, which was as dead as Wilson's Fourteen Points, Gibbs cheered a man who never 'hauled down the banner of his idealism, and torn and tattered though it was...he nailed it to the mast with his crippled hand, and never surrendered in his poor dazed soul'.[156]

Agnes' unhappiness led them back to London from 'Overponds' in 1928, and after living in various furnished flats near Sloane Square they settled in 'Little House' in D'Oyley Street. When spring and summer came, Gibbs 'yearned for the country' so they compromised, and also purchased an Elizabethan cottage at Ewhurst in Surrey called Bildens Farm. It took hold of 'one's heart' and most importantly, it had been modernized, 'but not too much'.[157] Agnes, who loved roses, planted a rose garden in the shape of an enormous fan. It was while dividing their time between Ewhurst and D'Oyley that Gibbs made what he called his beau geste on behalf of youth as part of the King George V Jubilee Trust Fund. They donated a five-and-a-half acre field and contributed £500 towards the construction of a youth hostel.[158] It was Agnes' idea, in part inspired by the young friends she had made while studying for her B.Sc. at London University. After it was opened in late May 1936, Gibbs spent a night there in the company of young travellers and was struck by 'their intelligence and their spirit, and their love of the things that matter most in life—good company, laughter, songs, the open road, the fellowship of youth, and a faith in values not based on money or power or cruelty'.[159]

In 1929, Philip and Agnes left D'Oyley Street and moved to a home in Shamley Green, and even though Agnes transformed the house and gardens they left after only two years. It came as a blow to Gibbs when Agnes decided she could not live there anymore. Though he cites two particularly blustery years and 'other reasons I have forgotten', one suspects that it was the sense of purposelessness and alienation that Gibbs had first witnessed in her while on leave in 1917.[160] They moved to Bildens

[155] Gibbs, *Ten Years After*, p. 15.
[156] Gibbs, *Ten Years After*, p. 16.
[157] Gibbs, *Crowded Company*, p. 159.
[158] Gibbs, *Crowded Company*, p. 162.
[159] Gibbs, *Crowded Company*, pp. 163–4.
[160] Gibbs, *Crowded Company*, p. 166.

Farm before returning to Shamley Green where they lived at 'Dibdene', a house near the village green. Agnes died there in October 1939 and Gibbs remained there until he died in 1962.

In the late 1920s, Gibbs rediscovered something of his optimism which had been badly shaken by the disappointments of Versailles and perhaps more personally by his strained domestic situation. In the preface to the 1929 edition of *Realities of War*, written in August of that year, he was confident enough to state that 'peace efforts have prevailed' and that 'renewed prosperity and a return to sanity' was indicative of an 'awakening wisdom'. His sense of security was probably enhanced by the birth of his first grandchild Martin in the same month, but with an unfortunate sense of timing (the Wall Street Crash occurred in October) he added that the 'crash I anticipated in Europe has not come'.[161] In *Since Then*, he was still confident enough to argue that 'the struggle for peace, which now seems assured for a fair spell of human progress, unless the world goes mad again, is one of the forward movements of humanity'.[162] The easing of political tension permitted Gibbs to fall back into the familiar Victorian optimism which had deserted him in the immediate post-war years. Yet Gibbs believed that only a few people were fully aware of 'how thin the ice was above the dark waters of anarchy, disease and despair in that time of uncertain peace'. He had seen the 'smouldering fires which flared up at times and threatened to light the torch of war again', but somehow peace was maintained by a 'thread' as people 'slowly cured of their madness, and by the leadership of the best intelligence in the world fighting desperately against the powers of darkness'.[163]

In the midst of his father's spiritual rejuvenation, Tony Gibbs published his third novel *Heyday*, six years after he had first tasted success with *Little Peter Vacuum* in 1925. When Philip read the novel, he was forced to conclude that he had exerted little influence on his son's writing style or his attitude to life. Having never assumed an authoritarian parenting style, instead having nurtured a relationship more akin to an elder and younger brother, Gibbs was more than mildly surprised at this philosophical revolt. In response, he penned a letter to Anthony in which this normally most private of men laid bare his innermost thoughts concerning human nature, the war, art, literature, and the father/son relationship. It was not only a

---

[161] Gibbs, *Realities of War*, p. xi.
[162] Gibbs, *Since Then*, p. 2.
[163] Gibbs, *Since Then*, pp. 1–2.

testament to his idealism but also the strength and depth of the relationship between the two.

Gibbs admitted to Tony that in spite of 'some shrewd knocks' he still believed in the 'heroic possibilities of human nature'. Though still capable of the hero worship that underpinned some of his early works of historical research, Gibbs conceded that he lived in a world beset with a 'scarcity of heroes'. Yet in what is perhaps a break with his own father, Gibbs noted that he also retained a simple faith in what men of his father's generation called idealism, 'although their definition of that quality was very vague and the results of it somewhat deplorable'. It is conceivable that this marks part of his own attempt to repudiate the emotional touchstones of Empire and patriotism, or at the very least distance himself ideologically from them. Yet it also shows him at his most conflicted. For he still possessed a 'sneaking respect for democracy, duty, and even now and again, for discipline', although he preferred 'liberty'. In 1946, after the death of his wife and the despair at the failure of his crusade for peace, Gibbs abandoned all of those qualities when he argued that pity was greater than all of them. It was a sad postscript to a life spent chronicling the abuses of liberty, justice, and pity.

A dozen years after the end of the First World War, it still dominated his thinking, and this letter was no exception. For to him, the war was 'an enormous tragedy which I can never forget'; but to Tony, he believed it was 'an absurdity which reveals the most incredible stupidity of my generation and makes a mockery of all its consequences which you and your generation have to endure'. The sense of having experienced things that a civilian could barely comprehend again finds voice, this time in contrasting the civilian experience of war and that of the combatant. Gibbs also takes the opportunity for another swipe at the English education system and the role it played in disseminating jingoism:

> You are old enough to remember the War as a small boy. But some of its effects upon the minds of my crowd are hidden from you. You saw the excitement and emotion of older people. At school you listened to masters talking patriotic stuff, cursing the Germans, swanking about the number of old boys who had been killed on the field of honour, urging upon you the duty of dying like little gentlemen in the same way, if it should last long enough.

His contempt for an education system which he believed perpetuated a belief in the virtue of dying like a little gentleman is indicative of the extent to which Gibbs' views on death and glory had evolved. In *The Deathless Story of the Titanic*, published two years before the outbreak of war, he had lauded those who faced death as English gentlemen. Though it was in a different context, and he did not appear to make any connection between the two experiences, Gibbs now saw a link between the Edwardian view of 'the stiff upper lip' with the very militarism which had started and then sustained the greatest war in history. He then shifted to a more personal tone, again contrasting those who had seen war in 'its infernal grandeur' with those who had remained in England:

> You had an idea, I believe, that England enjoyed the war and that it was our day out as a nation—'Heyday' as you call it in your last novel—intoxicated with war fever, flag wagging, drum beating, spy hunting, and all the rest of it. That happened, but you weren't old enough to realize that behind the mask of cheerfulness, beyond the shouting and the cheers, even in the theatres where soldiers were laughing on seven days' leave, there were infernal agonies of mind, and that England stood steady on the whole in an ordeal by fire which wasn't 'enjoyable'.[164]

Yet for all the influence exerted on his thinking and his writing by the years on the Western Front and later the horrors of famine in Russia, Martin Gibbs cannot recall a single instance when his grandfather spoke of the war, let alone the topic dominating his conversation. His memories are of a man far more interested in current affairs; for such a man, the 1930s in Europe would have provided many avenues for political discussion. In Italy, he saw in Mussolini a mysterious genius who represented the 'forcefulness, the dynamic energy, the national egotism, the ancient pride, and the present confidence of the post war generation in Italy...He has a touch of the bully when it serves the purposes of Italy among the other nations, but a subtlety of statecraft when that is the better way to secure an advantage. He is impetuous in speech, but not rash in action'.[165] As a Catholic, even if his grandson's recall of his mildness in religious matters is correct, it was not surprising that Gibbs saw the concordat with the Papacy in 1929 as one of Mussolini's greatest acts of statesmanship. It was one which was facilitated, on both sides, 'by a generous spirit of conciliation, and a desire to end an historic quarrel which prevented friendly

---

[164] Correspondence between Philip Gibbs and his son Tony, circa 1931. Courtesy Gibbs Family Archives.

[165] Gibbs, *Since Then*, pp. 122, 135.

co-operation between Church and Government'.[166] Gibbs was not blind to the possible results of Mussolini's brand of aggressive nationalism, but chose to place his faith in the Italian people 'who still believe in the kind of liberty in which Mussolini once believed, who do not worship this State he has helped to create, who will never forget or forgive those bludgeonings of liberal minded men, nor the penal laws and punishments which have imprisoned or exiled all his critics'.[167]

Any commentator on European affairs in the interwar period would naturally write extensively on Germany and Gibbs was no exception. In the years following the end of the war, the German people were 'stricken... morally as well as physically. All their old gods had fallen from the altars'.[168] Yet even in this chaos, exacerbated by the blockade, 'our great disgrace', Germany possessed an 'anti-toxin' against the 'poison of despair and rage'. The 'instinct of industry in the very blood and spirit of the people' expressed itself in a German manhood which 'braced itself to repair the ruin of war, and to forget its horrors by intensity of work'. In addition, the spirit of youth, which 'wouldn't be baulked of laughter and dancing and love...weakened the spirit of hatred and revenge. It was more powerful than machine gun fire against revolution and anarchy'.[169] Gibbs saw the burgeoning German youth movement (*Jugendbewegung*) in the vanguard of a process which 'changed the heart of Germany'. It was this 'new romanticism which acknowledged and acclaimed the defeat of the gods once set up on the altars of German nationalism—military tyranny, materialism, machine made conditions of life'. Gibbs was impressed by what he saw as a desire on the part of the young to revert to the earlier German traditions, replete with folk songs, village dances, sleeping in woods and fields, tramping through rural areas, and living a free gypsy life. Politically, he saw the Germans as having been liberated from 'their old militarism' and having acquired a 'new faith in liberty itself'. In the early 1930s, he believed that they were intent on righting the injustices of the Versailles Treaty 'by methods of conciliation and common sense without threat of force before the parliament of nations at Geneva'.[170] Gibbs' views were symptomatic of British foreign policy in the 1920s which tended to view European

---

[166] Gibbs, *Since Then*, p. 134.
[167] Gibbs, *Since Then*, p. 136.
[168] Gibbs, *Since Then*, p. 137.
[169] Gibbs, *Since Then*, pp. 21, 140.
[170] Gibbs, *Since Then*, pp. 170–1.

security as being only the concern of France and Germany. There was considerable unanimity in the view that French fears were 'imaginary' and that concessions to Germany would ease international tension.[171] Gibbs would shortly be proved horribly wrong in this assessment.

By 1931, Gibbs had also renewed his faith in the League of Nations, which had 'grown through fever stricken years and through periods of almost mortal weakness to its present strength and prestige'. He even felt confident enough to assert that the League was now 'sure of a long lease of life'.[172] Gibbs named Lord Cecil of Chelwood, Dr Benes of Czechoslovakia, Dr Fridtjof Nansen, and Aristide Briand as being among those 'who had faith, with an idealism reaching beyond their own frontiers and a gift of patience and diplomacy'.[173] The romantic in Gibbs believed that to be present in Geneva was to have one's mind altered:

> Some mental atmosphere there, a contact with former enemies and other types of intelligence, perhaps some spiritual vibrations reaching them from the outer world, broadened their vision and enabled them to see beyond their own boundaries. They learned to think internationally. They became the missionaries of the League ideal. They exerted pressure on their own governments. They refused to let the League be betrayed by the cynics. They did admirable and unknown work. They helped to save Europe from utter downfall.[174]

This celebration of the League would stand in marked contrast to his announcement in early 1939 that it lay 'stricken in the big white palace on the Lake of Geneva, which is now a mausoleum of lost hopes'. Though even then he stopped short of pronouncing it dead, he compared it to a mediaeval king 'once powerful and flattered...now lying in mortal agony...deserted by many who swore allegiance to it, mocked at by its enemies, laughed at by the wits, and forgotten by the crowd who thronged its corridors'.[175]

Through the 1930s, Gibbs experienced a disenchantment more profound as any wrought by his wartime exposure to death and destruction. He became desperate, almost fanatical in his desire for peace. His political

---

[171] Taylor, *English History*, p. 216.
[172] Gibbs, *Since Then*, p. 305.
[173] Gibbs, *Since Then*, p. 307.
[174] Gibbs, *Since Then*, p. 308.
[175] P Gibbs (1939) *Across the Frontiers* (London: The Right Book Club), p. 121.

commentary, once almost totally informed by his Victorian morality, became inconsistent and at times almost shockingly cynical. It is perhaps one of the great ironies of his life that his wartime writing was criticized as being too martial, while his peacetime commentaries appear too committed to appeasement and peace at any price. In time, he would come to see the events of this period having made a 'mockery of all that agony, and death, and valour on all fronts'.[176] Perhaps more personally, they also made a mockery of his ideals and the part he had played in interpreting the great events of the age. Increasingly, Gibbs came to realize that his belief system was now an anachronism and that the liberalism with which he ideologically bookended his life was now lost to the modern mind.

This process of disenchantment had well and truly begun by the spring and summer of 1934 when Gibbs journeyed by car through western and central Europe researching a book on political developments on the Continent.[177] In response to the success of Priestley's *English Journey*, Charles Evans of Heinemann commissioned Gibbs to write a book on his travels, which was given the rather obvious title *European Journey*. His travelling companions were Edgar Lander, who provided sketches for the American edition, and the novelist Cecil Roberts. As he never learnt to drive, in fact being something of a latter-day Luddite in his attitude to technology, Gibbs and his companions hired a car and driver in Paris. Mixed in his view of road travel, Gibbs also conceded that he was 'not air-minded, having no confidence as yet in that way of travel'.[178] His suspicions went deeper than just issues of transport, for he believed that 'we need at least a thousand years to control what knowledge we now have and to prevent it from destroying humanity itself. The machine has become a Frankenstein monster. Science has put powers into the hands of men who are still unable to control their own passions, though they may wield the thunderbolts of Jove'.[179] When he first used a telephone in 1897 he was

---

[176] Gibbs (1939) *Across the Frontiers*, p. 12.

[177] Taylor saw September 1931 and the end of the gold standard as marking a watershed of English history between the wars. The keywords of the 1920s were reconstruction, restoration, and recovery in a world where peace was regarded as the norm. In the 1930s, there was a hope that peace would work itself out (Taylor, *English History*, pp. 298–9). Furthermore, though in theory Britain was committed to the League and disarmament, in reality she had little faith in either. Though Gibbs never articulated a belief that war was inevitable, as far back as 1931 there was a growing disenchantment in his writing.

[178] P Gibbs (1934) *European Journey* (New York: The Literary Guild), p. 7.

[179] P Gibbs (1935) *England Speaks* (London: Heinemann), p. 175.

'rather scared of it'.[180] That would prove to be a consistent response to new technology.

In the course of a leisurely tour of France, Switzerland, Italy, Austria, and Germany, Gibbs' research was as idiosyncratic as his war reporting. He saw his task not 'to interview statesmen and politicians, or the new rulers of the human tribes...but to get in touch with the common folk whose lives are unrecorded and whose ideas are unexpressed'.[181] He was well suited to such an approach, for as a reviewer in *The Times* noted, Gibbs was 'a sentimental traveller with a lively sympathy for all his fellow travellers along the European highway'; yet he was also one whose 'emotional reaction... is almost too swift and intense not to have affected his judgement'.[182] Another writer in an otherwise positive review in *International Affairs* saw an endemic weakness in Gibbs' reliance on anecdotal conversations when making sweeping generalizations:

> The book is simply a rather discursive account of the author's travels and of innumerable conversations with fellow travellers...The weakness of this method lies in the difficulty of determining what is in reality the common mind and the common will when so many different points of view are reproduced verbatim. Sir Philip handles his material very skilfully, but he does not always avoid the insignificant, nor does the ease of his style always keep above the level of triviality.[183]

The journey, which one well-wisher hoped would begin with pessimism and end with optimism began in Paris 'as all good journeys do'.[184] The group then proceeded across France to Switzerland. In Geneva, Gibbs observed the construction of the new Palace of Nations and was unsettled by the cynicism of the workmen who claimed that it would serve either as a hospital for the wounded of the next war or as a barracks for the Germans when they invaded. Earlier Gibbs had felt that the League represented 'a time of conciliation' and 'common prosperity' but now he found 'no sense of peace in Europe'.[185] There was a jarring note of pessimism as

---

[180] Gibbs, *Life's Adventure*, p. 203.
[181] Gibbs, *European Journey*, p. 1.
[182] *The Times*, 16 November 1934.
[183] *International Affairs*, vol. 14, no. 3 (May-Jun. 1935), p. 432.
[184] Gibbs, *European Journey*, p. 5.
[185] Gibbs, *European Journey*, pp. 105–6.

well, a characteristic which marked an ideological break with his renewed optimism evident in his writing since the late 1920s:

> I was one of the common folk. There is nothing they can do about it. That is the tragedy of these times. Perhaps there is a greater tragedy. When Youth decides to do something about it, it seems quite likely that they will do the wrong things, in different coloured shirts, with different war cries, with new hatreds, with new intolerance towards their fellow man.[186]

In Sion, he fell desperately ill for ten days and only recommenced the journey at a slower pace once Agnes had joined them from England. With her in company for part of the remainder of the trip, Gibbs visited Italy, Germany, Austria, and Hungary. Gibbs' views of the political and economic situation in Italy were coloured by his belief that it was the loveliest country in Europe. It was also one in which 'this civilisation of ours reached its first splendour', but Italy now had 'a new renaissance, and there is a new Caesar there, leader and tyrant to his people'. Nevertheless, Gibbs saw in Mussolini 'real qualities of greatness' and chose to dwell on the improvement in living standards rather than 'certain episodes in his career, certain phases of his mind, which do not put an aureole round his head'.[187]

Gibbs' experiences in Germany, both during this trip and earlier in the year when he was in Berlin and had witnessed the celebrations marking the 14th anniversary of the opening of Hitler's political campaign, filled him with apprehension. When he returned to England to write the record of his travels, his judgement was coloured not by images of peasants singing in the fields as had been the case with his descriptions of Italy, but by the Night of the Long Knives on 30 June 1934 which had shaken Europe a few days after he left Germany. He saw it as a 'return to the darkest period of medievalism' for it did not 'come within the code of civilized people'.[188] Yet in keeping with a general inconsistency in his attitude to all things martial, the spirit of Hitler's Germany both repelled and attracted him. He found something 'awe inspiring' in the 'vitality and freshness of youth' and had felt 'the touch of a cold finger down [his] spine at such moments of ceremony—the funeral of a king or hero, the passing

[186] Gibbs, *European Journey*, p. 109.
[187] Gibbs, *European Journey*, pp. 192, 182.
[188] Gibbs, *European Journey*, p. 290.

of some spiritual force'. It was the language of Carlyle, just as surely as was his fear that the voices proclaiming a 'national loyalty to one man invested with enormous power over a great people...were perhaps calling out the destiny of Europe'.[189] Gibbs would have been familiar with Carlyle's view of the French Revolution as a warning from history of the destructive apocalypse awaiting any society which imploded. This knowledge, acquired in his formative years, would have appeared vindicated by his own experiences on the Western Front and in Russia. Gibbs' observations are therefore cloaked in an unusual pessimism partly borne of exasperation. In his eyes, everyone wanted peace, yet few possessed any faith in achieving it. Looking back on the journey, Gibbs was unable to see 'much light ahead with any promise of happiness and peace for the European peoples'.[190] To Gibbs, there was 'one hope and one hope only, in Europe today for a recovery of order and tranquillity. It is the intelligence of the common crowd'.[191] It was very Dickensian—if men behave decently, then the world will be decent.

The following year, Gibbs published *England Speaks*, which was a rather perfunctory collection of conversations with everyone from street sweepers to statesmen in which he sought to articulate a 'panorama of the English Scene'. It is an unremarkable book, although as he had done in *European Journey* in 1934, he insisted that it is only among ordinary people 'where one hears the authentic voice of England'.[192] *England Speaks* has no integrating theme, nor any sense of chronology to help place the discussions in context. Gibbs was more successful in capturing the mood of his countrymen in *Ordeal in England* published in 1938. Like so many of his works of non-fiction though, it reads as a stream of consciousness, ranging backwards and forwards over topics as disparate as the abdication crisis, militarism, rearmament, communism, and the growing road toll in England. The one constant theme was his increasingly desperate arguments in favour of peace which were based more on hope than political analysis. The book opened with the death of George V, who as monarch during the First World War was 'one king, almost alone [who] received the homage of the men who had gone through those fires'.[193] Gibbs saw

---

[189] Gibbs, *Adventures in Journalism*, p. 290.
[190] Gibbs, *European Journey*, p. 339.
[191] Gibbs, *European Journey*, p. 332.
[192] Gibbs, *England Speaks*, p. 25.
[193] P Gibbs (1938) *Ordeal in England* (London: Heinemann), p. 11.

in Edward, George's successor, a 'serious, even spiritual side', and in the subsequent coronation of his brother, a national determination to show that 'the Empire was steady and strong and powerful, and that England was still England'.[194] The book ended with the rather hopeful message to the 'younger generation whose world it will be' that the war will not happen 'if we do not wish it to happen'.[195]

Ordeal in England also covers Gibbs' experience as a member of the Royal Commission on the Manufacture of and Trade in Armaments which held its first day of hearings on 1 May 1935. When asked by the then Prime Minister Ramsay MacDonald to participate, Gibbs saw it, in his idealism and credulity, as a chance of doing something for world peace. Eventually, he came to see the Prime Minister's invitation as a 'man trap' and his participation as a 'waste of time'.[196] Between the springs of 1935 and 1936, the Commission sat for 22 public sessions, which resulted in a unanimous report recommending greater government control of the armaments industry, though it stopped short of calling for a nationalization of the industry. Gibbs believed that the report was buried because it fell 'with a thud between two political stools'.[197] Its failure was hardly a shock given that in March 1935 a Defence White Paper was published, one which effectively acknowledged that the British government 'had ceased to rely on collective security and was now going to rely on the older security of armed force'.[198] Unwittingly, Gibbs had again found himself used by cynical people. The Commission was created by the government as 'merely a sop to the public outcry against the "evils" of the arms industry, not as yet another critic of the country's beleaguered rearmament effort'.[199] Government procrastination, a limited scope of enquiry, and the appointment of eminent people likely to have the public's respect but just as equally unlikely to make radical recommendations were indicative of a government determined to maintain its alliance with private industry.[200]

[194] Gibbs, *Ordeal in England*, pp. 28, 38.

[195] Gibbs, *Ordeal in England*, p. 423.

[196] Gibbs, *Ordeal in England*, p. 53; Gibbs, *Crowded Company*, p. 425.

[197] Gibbs, *Crowded Company*, p. 427.

[198] Taylor, *English History*, p. 376.

[199] D Anderson (1994) 'British Rearmament and the "Merchants of Death": The 1935–36 Royal Commission on the Manufacture of and Trade in Armaments'. *Journal of Contemporary History*, vol. 29, no. 1, January, p. 29.

[200] Anderson, 'British Rearmament', p. 13.

In spite of the failure of the Commission, Gibbs was proud that as a group the members of the Commission 'subordinated prejudice to pure reason, cold logic, and a judgement of which Solomon might approve'.[201] Nevertheless, in William Arnold Forster's impassioned indictment of the arms firms, which even Gibbs conceded was stronger on rhetoric than evidence, he felt transported from the Court Room of the Westminster Guildhall to Paris during the French Revolution. Forster was cast in the heroic mould of a Jacobin preaching the *Rights of Man*.[202] Though Gibbs sought to temper his own emotional and intellectual predisposition to oppose an unregulated arms trade, his nervousness, perhaps exacerbated by a sense that he was representing 'millions of men and women desperately anxious for peace in our time', led to a ferocity of questioning that surprised even himself.[203] In his verbal duel with Sir Charles Craven, the managing director of Vickers, Gibbs' 'voice became harsher than I intended, and my manner more repulsive than I had ever thought possible, and my temper less under control than it ought to have been'.[204] His questioning forced one concession, which, to his own surprise, found him in the offices of Vickers searching a mountain of correspondence. In keeping with the Commission's overall findings, his search revealed little tangible proof of illegal activity, but supported an overwhelming suspicion regarding the actions of the arms manufacturers.[205]

Witnesses who gave evidence against the arms firms were hampered by both the lack of concrete evidence and the fact that the Commission was held against the background of Mussolini's invasion of Abyssinia. Though identifying himself as a supporter of the League of Nations, even Gibbs saw the inaction over Italian aggression as proof of the League's impotency. The deteriorating international situation and the fact that the arms firms were even then responding to the Admiralty's urgent orders for more shells led Sir John Eldon Bankes, the head of the Commission, to question the efficacy of further public sittings. The members of the Commission chose to push on based on the consensus that they were dealing with general principles that should be unaffected by passing events. Yet it would not be enough, for almost inevitably the government remained unmoved

---

[201] Gibbs, *Ordeal in England*, p. 64.
[202] Gibbs, *Ordeal in England*, p. 68.
[203] Gibbs, *Ordeal in England*, p. 73.
[204] Gibbs, *Ordeal in England*, p. 74.
[205] Anderson, 'British Rearmament,' p. 31.

by either the testimony of the arms industry's leaders, which if anything tended to confirm many of the 'Merchant of Death' legends, or the great body of public opinion which helped force the Commission's creation. Even the moderate recommendations of the Commission were quietly buried.

At about the same time that he was sitting on the Royal Commission, Gibbs began a 12-year association with the board of the Charing Cross Hospital. At the invitation of Philip Inman, later Baron Inman, Gibbs became vice chairman of the board, a position he only resigned when *The National Health Service Act* (1948) was passed and control of the hospital was ceded to the government. As he had found while working on the Royal Commission there was much to admire in his fellow board members, for the experience was 'a revelation of those qualities of mind and manners which have placed us high among the nations—tolerant of other men's views, in favour of wise compromise, courteous, unexcitable, remarkable in self-control and unstinting in service to some ideal beyond self-interest'.[206] The hospital, which ran on donations, lost something in Gibbs' view when it became a branch of the civil service. He feared the effect of 'the uninspired routine of official status', and though he did not make the connection, a critic of his wartime dispatches might well argue that Gibbs of all men knew how being subsumed into a vast organization could limit initiative and curtail freedoms.[207] Yet typically, it was not merely a question of medical skill for Gibbs, for more important even than that was 'the sympathy, the spirit which seems to inspire them all, and makes this great hospital a friendly place in a rather cruel world. It is truly one of the sanctuaries of our civilisation in which a light is always burning'.[208] In taking this viewpoint, Gibbs was allying himself with the most conservative of all the professions and publically distancing himself from the National Health Service which became one of the most 'stupendous British inventions' and a 'formidably skilful achievement'.[209]

In response to the worsening situation in Europe, Gibbs, due to 'his schematic vision...inclined to appeasement; the new Germany seemed to him cast for the heroic role'.[210] In fact, he did more than incline to

[206] Gibbs, *Crowded Company*, p. 73.
[207] Gibbs, *Crowded Company*, p. 78.
[208] *The British Journal of Nursing*, May 1937, p. 135.
[209] Wilson, *After the Victorians*, pp. 511–12.
[210] Hamilton, *Remembering My Good Friends*, p. 144.

appeasement; he was a passionate advocate of Neville Chamberlain's peace efforts. Yet as one writer noted 'once the battle lines were joined and the political atmosphere was simplified by the easy method of figuring out who was pointing guns at whom, Sir Philip was instantly ready to serve Great Britain'.[211] Though meant kindly, it acknowledged a degree of naivety in Gibbs' political analysis. He was not alone in his views, nor does the death toll in the ensuing conflict suggest that there was anything particularly immoral, or even flawed in his thinking, though in its entirety there is a degree of inconsistency in his analysis which reflected his desperation to avoid war. In 1934, he saw Germany being 'picked upon as the mad dog of Europe' by an England and a France determined to believe that she was 'preparing a war of vengeance and aggression'.[212] The Versailles Treaty, the cause of so much tension, was forced upon Germany 'by defeat, starvation and revolution'.[213] Once he became Chancellor, Hitler acted 'more of a statesmen and less as a barnstormer' and made offers of peace which were 'unequivocal, emotional, and idealistic'.[214] In contrast, three years earlier he had described him as 'a typical fanatic, with the faith of a mystic and a peasant mentality'.[215] The reoccupation of the Rhineland in March 1936, which Gibbs saw as Hitler 'regaining sovereign rights over his own territory', was disingenuously described as an act of technical aggression.[216]

Gibbs believed that much greater weight should have been placed on Hitler's offers of peace which, 'if accepted with instant enthusiasm, would have given peace to Europe for another generation'.[217] In Hitler's speech to the Reichstag on 30 January 1937, Gibbs heard only benevolence in intention and promise.[218] In arguing this case Gibbs was not alone, for as Taylor observed, one of the great errors in the pre-war period was that people listened to what Hitler said rather than what he did.[219] Speaking for the English, Gibbs felt that 'they did not see why these queer races of Czechs, Slovaks, Ruthenians and other oddments of the human tribes with unpronounceable names and unlearnable languages should affect the

---

[211] Obituary, Sir Philip Gibbs, Gibbs Family Papers, details unknown.
[212] Gibbs, *European Journey*, p. 333.
[213] Gibbs, *Ordeal in England*, p. 191.
[214] Gibbs, *Ordeal in England*, p. 187.
[215] Gibbs, *England Speaks*, p. 107.
[216] Gibbs, *Across the Frontiers*, pp. 164–65.
[217] Gibbs, *Across the Frontiers*, pp. 164–65.
[218] P Gibbs (1938) *Ordeal in England* (London: William Heinemann), p. 195.
[219] Taylor, *Origins*, p. 16.

peace in English gardens'.[220] Later, Gibbs would describe Hitler as history's greatest liar, yet even in 1946 he could not rid himself of the conviction that some purpose might still have been served by further negotiation.[221] In 1942, however, Gibbs wrote that had Hitler been allowed to 'get away' with breaking pledges and 'trampling over other people's frontiers', it would be a surrender to the 'powers of darkness'.[222]

Though it is easy in hindsight to view the actions of Germany in the mid- to late 1930s as stepping stones inevitably leading to war, Gibbs was wrong in almost all of the conclusions he drew concerning foreign affairs of this period. The gaps in his war dispatches can be defended on the basis that there were things he could not have known, as well as the limitations imposed by censorship. His failings in this period, written in peacetime and unhampered by censorship, betray a very limited understanding of what was actually happening in Europe. Gibbs' preparedness to take people at face value may well have been a case not merely of excessive credulity, but also an overwhelming desire to believe that it was still within the power of the ordinary people in England and France to avoid the coming catastrophe. He was not alone in that hope. Taylor observed an interesting development, however, that would suggest that England was fortunate that men like Gibbs did not exert a greater influence on the decision to rearm. As fewer people subscribed to the notion of German war guilt and 'since war was always a purposeless evil, the duty of those who wanted peace was to see that their own government behaved peacefully and, in particular, to ensure this by depriving their government of arms'.[223]

In May 1938, Gibbs interviewed Heinrich Himmler. Despite his reputation, Gibbs found him 'strangely attractive, with a charm of manner'.[224] This was in contrast with a later interview with Seyss-Inquart who he found 'sullen, ill-tempered and rude...He was, I thought, the most unpleasant type of man I had ever met, with shifty eyes and a cruel mouth'.[225] In 1946, Gibbs described Himmler as 'Satan's right hand man', one responsible for more 'cruelty, torture, and human agony than any human being in modern times'.[226] By 1957, Gibbs saw him as one of 'the wickedest

[220] Gibbs, *Ordeal in England*, p. 365.
[221] Gibbs, *The Pageant of the Years*, p. 434.
[222] Philip Gibbs (1942) *America Speaks* (London: Heinemann), p. 26.
[223] Taylor, *English History*, p. 362.
[224] Gibbs, *Ordeal in England*, p. 372.
[225] Gibbs, *The Pageant of the Years*, p. 398.
[226] Gibbs, *The Pageant of the Years*, p. 441.

men who ever lived'.[227] In the course of a 35-minute interview, Himmler repeated the assertion that war for Germany would mean ruin and that she was desirous only of 'fair play'. To Gibbs, it seemed that he spoke with sincerity.[228] In one of his autobiographies, Gibbs claimed that Himmler was the only bad man he ever met, and that all others were decent and kindly, 'not angels, but not devils'. With a marked lack of conviction, Gibbs conceded that this may have been the result of deception. Even after two world wars, he could not bring himself to believe ill of his fellow man who had as his chief desire only peace and security.[229] It was a quality recognized by his son Tony, who believed that his father was so 'overflowing with generosity of feeling to all fellow men' that he was 'almost incapable of thinking ill of any person'.[230]

Given his desire to be part of events as well as a chronicler of them, it would have pleased Gibbs enormously to be approached by two Royal Air Force (RAF) officers with 'secret reports' detailing the growing disparity between the relative strengths of the RAF and the Luftwaffe. He agreed to deliver the reports to Winston Churchill, who was then himself engaged in what Gibbs described as 'a constant fire of criticism against the government' over the very same issue.[231] He travelled to Chartwell Manor in Kent, both to deliver the documents and to talk with 'the most brilliant and dynamic figure of our time'.[232] In 1931, he had described Churchill as the 'most wonderful, the most daring, impetuous and unlikely genius in English political life'.[233] Ten years before, he had described him as an 'imperial gambler, the advocate of disastrous adventures, the most reckless spendthrift of public money in profitless campaigns'.[234] In their discussion, Gibbs clung to his mantra that most Germans wished only for friendship with England and of the warm welcome any English traveller received in that country. Churchill, himself part idealist and hard-headed realist, countered that Germany was anxious to be friends on the condition that England refrained from standing between her and her destiny.[235] Though

---

[227] Gibbs, *Life's Adventure*, p. 145.
[228] Gibbs, *Ordeal in England*, p. 378.
[229] Gibbs, *The Pageant of the Years*, p. 524.
[230] A Gibbs, *In My Own Good Time*, p. 50.
[231] Gibbs, *Ordeal in England*, p. 150.
[232] Gibbs, *Ordeal in England*, p. 293.
[233] Gibbs, *Since Then*, p. 37.
[234] Gibbs, *More That Must Be Told*, p. 374.
[235] Gibbs, *Ordeal in England*, p. 296.

Churchill had most of the information Gibbs provided in his possession already, he proved an amiable host. He soured this impression at the end of the meeting by describing Gibbs as a 'goody goody'. Though aware of the inconsistency of carrying these reports when he had actively and publicly opposed the arms race, and perhaps stung by Churchill's half humorous description, Gibbs argued that he would have been more accurately described as a 'stern realist'.[236]

Though Churchill was perhaps more accurate in his assessment of Gibbs in this instance than Gibbs himself, this growing inconsistency in Gibbs' political assessments indicated a growing pragmatism, but one narrowly applied. For though Gibbs could be almost naive in his idealism when dealing with the English, the French, and even the Germans, he had a hard edge of realism when dealing with issues he saw as outside national interests and which could drag Western Europe into another war. Gibbs was not being an idealist when he was tempted during this period to support a policy of allowing Germany and Russia to 'get at one another' and thus save England from another war.[237] He was no idealist with regard to Czechoslovakia when he asked whether millions of Englishmen might die in defence of a country which was 'a hodge-podge of races under the domination of the Czechs'.[238] To Gibbs, the Sudeten crisis was in effect three-and-a half million Germans wishing to 'join their own folk'.[239] Gibbs did recognize the 'tragedy of the Jews' and as an empathetic and sincere man, he rejected the mistreatment of any group by a state with a duty to its citizens. Yet there is an underlying sense that greater than any moral outrage is his fear that it gave support to those who hated Hitler and were advocating that the democracies should oppose Nazism even to the extent of waging war on it. Gibbs acknowledged the mistreatment of the Jews in Vienna after the Anschluss, where they suffered 'many insults, humiliations and brutalities by young Austrian Nazis—mostly boys from 16 to 20—who behaved like hooligans'. He also referred to them as 'ruffians' and 'scallywags', some of whom he was somehow convinced were later 'packed off to concentration camps'.[240] In hindsight, the rather odd choice of language which was more reminiscent of youthful lawbreakers

[236] Gibbs, *Ordeal in England*, p. 299.
[237] Gibbs, *Crowded Company*, p. 128.
[238] Gibbs, *Ordeal in England*, p. 366.
[239] Gibbs, *Ordeal in England*, p. 370.
[240] Gibbs, *Ordeal in England*, pp. 357–8.

in peacetime London rather than the harbingers of a belief system which would end at Auschwitz, was an attempt to trivialize any event which might offer reason to make a stand against Hitler. It is unlikely that they indicate a strain of anti-Semitism, for as early as 1934 he was describing the German treatment of the Jews as a 'hark back to the black days of mediaeval intolerance. It is senseless and mean and cruel'.[241]

In June 1938, just over a month after the Anschluss which had been achieved with the 'enthusiastic consent of the majority', Gibbs wrote to the editor of *The Times* expressing his concern at what he considered to be a 'grotesque paradox'. He could not understand how in the name of collective security, democracy would be defended and dictatorship would be challenged by an alliance between France and Russia 'the most brutal and ferocious dictatorship in the world today'. Portraying himself as one 'who knows the German people and the views of its leaders', he finished with the assertion that there 'is still time to avert a catastrophe'.[242] As early as 1931, Gibbs was certain that Austria could not exist as a separate entity, but was equally certain that Germany would not seek union without the consent of the League of Nations.[243] It was now impossible for him to countenance a war over what he had long seen as inevitable. He saw little wrong with Hitler's aim of rebuilding the Reich, because on that basis there could be discussion and therefore no need for war.[244]

Even in early 1939, Gibbs still believed that by some means or another Germany must, by persuasion and conciliation, be induced to participate in a newly constituted forum of nations. Long after his experience and intellect should have informed him otherwise, Gibbs still hoped that Germany under Hitler might participate in a rebuilding of international law. Even after the annexation of Czechoslovakia in March 1939, a violation which Gibbs felt was inexcusable, based on his conversations with individual Germans he believed 'they want still to be friends with England. They cannot understand why that friendship is thwarted'. Furthermore, he felt that the British Government should direct the full weight of its efforts to persuading the German people 'that we have no quarrel with them...and that if their Leader will listen to reason, and conform to a code of international law, and prove his will to avoid war, we are ready to make a lasting

---

[241] Gibbs, *Ordeal in England*, p. 336.
[242] *The Times*, 3 June 1938.
[243] Gibbs, *Since Then*, p. 172.
[244] P Gibbs (1939) *Across the Frontiers* (London: The Right Book Club), p. 164.

peace by ending the arms race on both sides and by offering Germany full, free and generous opportunities of world trade'.[245] Gibbs believed that no matter how much the English might 'dislike the Nazi creed and methods' and in spite of how 'utterly alien to our ideals of liberty' they were, it was still possible that 'the Nazi regime might be modified and changed in process of time'.[246] This marks a major ideological break in Gibbs' thinking, given that he was once scathing in his criticism of the man for whom 'nothing would justify the unsheathed sword between civilized nations'.[247]

Gibbs continued to draw on the European political situation as inspiration for his literary endeavours. *Broken Pledges* told the story of an American reporter based in London who became a passionate Anglophile in the months prior to the outbreak of war. His reports to the USA are heavily laced with warnings concerning the common danger posed by German militarism. Gibbs appeared in the book as an author whose experiences on the Western Front have led him to dedicate himself to world peace. Being an 'old fashioned liberal, and loyal to all liberties of the mind and soul', for peace, this 'secret and underlying purpose', he risked, like Gibbs himself, being branded a Nazi sympathizer.[248] As war approached, Tony Gibbs noted that his father 'quite deliberately' though 'without deliberate purpose' began to befriend Germans, among them Wolf Dewahl, the London correspondent of the *Frankfurter Zeitung*, Luftwaffe Captain, but later Lieutenant General Ralph Wenninger, the Air Attaché at the German Embassy, and the Ambassador himself, Herbert von Dirksen and his wife.[249] It was a last, futile statement of his faith in the capacity of individuals to shape history and to exert an influence on national policy. It was a faith shortly to be tested by two calamities—the first a world war and the second the death of Agnes from cancer.

[245] Gibbs, *Across the Frontiers*, p. 356.
[246] Gibbs, *Across the Frontiers*, p. 253.
[247] P Gibbs (1913) *The New Man—A Portrait Study of the Latest Type* (London: Sir Isaac Pitman and Sons), p. 58.
[248] P Gibbs (1939) *Broken Pledges* (London: Hutchinson and Company), p. 33.
[249] Gibbs, *In My Own Good Time*, p. 140.

CHAPTER 6

The Pageant of the Years: 1939–1962

The eventual outbreak of war in September 1939 brought with it a double blow for Gibbs. Agnes, who had been ill for some time, died from liver cancer on 4 October and was buried in the Anglican Church at West Clandon where her father and stepmother were buried. In keeping with his intensely private nature with regard to writing about his 'beautiful and beloved Agnes', Gibbs devoted less than two lines in his autobiography to her death.[1] His description of it as his 'private tragedy' indicated the clear demarcation he drew between the public and private domains. Yet he was not a man without passion. Seven years after her death, he looked back over their years of marriage 'as a fairy tale of two babes in the wood, who went hand in hand through the enchantment of life with a hungry wolf around the corner'. Gibbs had begun his literary career writing fairy tales, and it is not surprising that he would return to that imagery late in life. For him, marriage had been a fairy tale, one in which Agnes 'had most of the courage and led the way'.[2] His son Tony displayed the same reticence in discussing something as private as grief in his autobiography. He noted only that he went to France to report on the war 'because my mother died', adding that he would not 'dwell on that because I am not fond of death, and because it is such an intimate thing'. Though Tony was

---

[1] P Gibbs (1946) *The Pageant of the Years* (London: Heinemann), p. 456.

[2] Gibbs, *The Pageant of the Years*, p. 27.

© The Editor(s) (if applicable) and The Author(s) 2016   197
M.C. Kerby, *Sir Philip Gibbs and English Journalism in War and Peace*,
DOI 10.1057/978-1-137-57301-8_6

unwilling to speak of his own grief, he was prepared to describe the effect on his father, who was 'heartbroken'.[3]

Gibbs coped far more easily with the need for an 'about turn' in his ideological convictions. For though he had long argued that there was no need for war with Germany, he was now ready to fully support just such a war. In a complete departure from his pre-war writing, by 1942 Gibbs believed that this war differed from others in that it was a 'straight conflict between good and evil'. A victory for Hitler would mean that 'evil would prevail and the light would go out of life'. Though Gibbs sought to explain the war in moral terms, and one suspects he only just stopped short of seeing it as a crusade, there were also political considerations, though as always his liberalism was more philosophical than pragmatic. Gibbs feared the creation of a world in which 'the human mind itself would be enslaved' and where 'art would die [and] beauty would be killed'. His vision was almost Orwellian in conception, for 'those under the heel of Hitler would not have the right to think freely but would be put in the clamping irons of the Nazi code'. It was the antithesis of the nineteenth-century liberalism, which he had adopted as his own creed, and again, in spite of his revulsion at the thought of another war, he knew that 'it would have to be fought out'.[4]

Owing to his bereavement, his son Tony preceded him to France as a war correspondent for the *Daily Sketch*. Like his father, before him, Tony went dressed for the occasion. He designed his own khaki officer's uniform, a bulletproof vest, and a walking stick containing a rolled umbrella. To finish off an ensemble, which, in the view of at least one officer, 'let the front down', he wore brown suede shoes.[5] Gibbs soon replaced him, perhaps preferring work to inactivity. In his autobiography, he placed his arrival at General Headquarters in Arras by late autumn of 1939. Though now severely hampered by failing eyesight, Gibbs travelled the length of the British line on a number of occasions and was appalled at what he saw. Given his experiences during the First World War, it is not surprising that he felt as though he was a ghost walking among ghosts. For in the passage of 20 years, 'those graves, those dead, the living spirit of those men had never been put out of my mind', and seeing the youth of Britain in

[3] A Gibbs (1970) *In My Own Good Time* (Boston: Gambit Incorporated), p. 159.
[4] P Gibbs (1942) *America Speaks* (London: William Heinemann), p. 26.
[5] M Gibbs (2000) *Seven Generations-Our Gibbs Ancestors* (London: Martin Gibbs), p. 7.

the same towns gave the whole process a surreal experience.[6] This was no doubt heightened by being served in a restaurant by a middle-aged woman who had served him there in 1916.

His sense of gloom, exacerbated by his own grief, found voice in his description of Armistice Day 1939. In a short passage, Gibbs hinted at a crisis of faith far more profound than any experienced during the slaughter of 1916 and 1917. It is perhaps the final and most raw articulation of a philosophical process begun in the immediate aftermath of the First World War:

> We of the older ranks who have dedicated ourselves to the prevention of another war stand amid the ruin of our hopes and false dreams. We failed. The forces of evil have come out against us, so that this young generation may have to pay the price of blood to save all which we believed had been won and secured by the spirit of the dead who are around us today. This evil thing is undefeated, and men with more faith than I have, believe that every sacrifice, however great, must be made by the younger crowd to overcome it lest all in which we hope and believe is utterly destroyed.[7]

This third stint as a war correspondent was barely more successful than his experience in the Balkans in 1912. By now almost blind, he had to be led, often by hand, through the streets of Arras by Geoffrey Harmsworth, nephew of the great man, and is now also a war correspondent. Gibbs' dispatches, which he had to have read over the telephone on his behalf, were cut ruthlessly by the editor of the *Daily Sketch*, leaving Gibbs to observe sadly that the days when he could spread his impressions over five columns were now gone. There were some things, however, which remained unaltered, for even in the relatively short time he spent in France, he found the censorship 'rigid, frustrating and ridiculous'.[8] To show how little the army had actually learnt from the debacles in 1914, even the old rule forbidding any reference to the weather was resurrected. Gibbs was also deeply disturbed by both the paucity of British troops and equipment and the French faith in the Maginot Line. When the phoney war ended in April 1940, Gibbs was in England on leave, and though he managed to return to the Continent, it was not long before he was ordered home.

---

[6] Gibbs, *The Pageant of the Years*, pp. 457–8.
[7] *Daily Sketch*, 13 November 1939.
[8] Gibbs, *The Pageant of the Years*, p. 461.

The summer of 1940, now firmly entrenched in British national mythology, was, as Gibbs noted, an amazing summer. From his garden, he was an avid observer of the dogfights between the Spitfires and Hurricanes of the RAF as they battled Goering's Luftwaffe. At night, he listened with growing apprehension to the BBC nine o'clock news, firm in the belief that he was witnessing a battle for national survival. With echoes of his First World War experience, Gibbs felt that in the event of an invasion, he would be shot with the elders of the village on Shamley Green, though the idea did not frighten him; 'it would be a good death'.[9] With invasion apparently imminent, Arthur Gibbs suggested that Philip's grandchildren Frances and Martin seek refuge with him and his American wife in the still neutral USA. In his autobiography, Tony Gibbs does not mention the offer, choosing instead to portray the move as a means for a decidedly unwarlike 38 year old to contribute to the war effort in the employ of the British Information Services in New York. Philip described it in his autobiography in a slightly different way again. He wrote that his daughter-in-law was 'taking her children to the United States and Tony was going with them to do some newspaper work and lecturing'.[10] It was a perilous journey made in the face of the growing U-Boat scourge, but the family arrived safely, and as was the custom with the Gibbs family, embraced American life, and came to love the country and its people.

As a man fully aware of his own fragility and perhaps one who underestimated his own courage and stoicism, it is possible that Gibbs ascribed to other men a fearlessness he himself desired. It is a quality he shared with his son Tony, who, after observing the quiet courage of Battle of Britain fighter pilots during a visit to Biggin Hill, concluded that 'my trouble was that I knew I could not kill or even maim. Not in any circumstances…I still clung to the conceit, absurdly perhaps, that I was a civilized man. Yet I have no courage, of the ordinary sort. I had not even the courage to become a conscientious objector, which I sometimes think requires the most courage of all'.[11] In 1957, the elder Gibbs remembered the civilian population of 1940 as having displayed 'a supernatural courage…or perhaps some spiritual faith, which annihilated the fear of death'.[12] Every night in Shamley Green, Gibbs heard the German bombers on their way

---

[9] P Gibbs (1949) *Crowded Company* (London: Allan Wingate), pp. 168–9.
[10] Gibbs, *The Pageant of the Years*, p. 496.
[11] Gibbs, *In My Own Good Time*, p. 209.
[12] P Gibbs (1957) *Life's Adventure* (London: Angus & Robertson), pp. 40–1.

to London. He also witnessed, with astonished admiration, the courage and stoicism of the civilians as they endured the blitz. Though a Catholic, Gibbs' faith was always more emotive than intellectual, particularly when witnessing issues touching on national identity. The courage of English civilians under the nightly battering of the Luftwaffe seemed to him supernatural 'in the sense of being beyond ordinary courage and ordinary human endurance'. In the citizens of London, he saw 'the age long tradition of pride and fortitude' shaped by the example of 'their forefathers who had endured and struggled through centuries of war, famine, plague and grim conditions of life'. As a people, Gibbs believed that they had an unspoken faith in English liberty, in London pride, and in an echo of the previous war, they were sustained by humour even in the ruins of their own houses and shops.[13]

In early September 1941, Gibbs travelled to the USA for a lecture tour arranged with the Ministry of Information. Though he does not mention it in any of his autobiographies, part of his motivation was the deteriorating relations between Tony and Arthur Gibbs. The relationship between the two families had reached such an impasse that an ultimatum to vacate the property was averted only by Gibbs' intervention. Having been unable to bring any money from England, and faced with the impossibility of surviving on the limited funds generated by Tony's lecturing and occasional articles for the *Boston Globe*, it was a timely stay of execution for the family. Gibbs gave his son the bulk of the earnings from his lecture tour and shortly after Tony secured employment in Hollywood. In retrospect, the difficulties between the two families were unsurprising, given that Tony and Arthur had never been particularly close. As Martin Gibbs observed, the age difference of 14 years left them relating to each other as rival siblings rather than as nephew and uncle.[14] Perhaps it was equally inevitable that Arthur, the Military Cross winner, would find little in common with his nephew. On Tony's part, he found in Arthur an irrationality and a militant pacifism.[15] Even Gibbs was moved to describe him in a letter to Maisie's mother as 'an ugly tempered man', although with the passage of the years Martin Gibbs came to view his uncle's predicament more sympathetically:[16]

---

[13] Gibbs, *The Pageant of the Years*, p. 488.
[14] Martin Gibbs (2003) *Wartime Convoy to America* (London: Martin Gibbs), p. 6.
[15] Gibbs, *In My Own Time*, p. 216.
[16] Gibbs, *Seven Generations*, p. 9.

It was quite an imposition, suddenly having this strange English family [living with him]. He was very different from my grandfather. He looked rather similar, and was a writer and loved playing the accordion. But he was passionately against the war, against any war, against England. He was so angry about being in the First World War that he decided he couldn't bear living there, which is one of the reasons he went to live in America.[17]

It is interesting to speculate as to whether there were other, deeper forces at work. Though Arthur was a militant pacifist, the outbreak of a second war may have left him a deeply conflicted man, given his own successful participation in combat 20 years before. It is not inconceivable that he experienced guilt at being safe in the USA while his countrymen endured nightly air attacks. Perhaps the sight of a man of military age joining him in exile may have provided a convenient scapegoat for an unresolved love/hate for England and the frustration of late middle age for a man of action.

It took ten weeks of 'desperate endeavour' during which Gibbs pulled 'every wire' to secure permission to travel to the USA.[18] Even then he had to wait in Lisbon for eight days before he found a seat on a pan-American flying boat. His attitude to air travel had matured, for he saw the aircraft as 'a thing of beauty and power, with silver wings and a body like a great lovely bird'.[19] Travelling via the Azores and Bermuda, he arrived in New York 20 hours later, and found it 'a different world...a different planet'.[20] He found in his American audiences a moving respect for the courage of the English people and a desire to provide aid. Nevertheless, he found them equally determined to ensure that this aid stopped short of full American involvement. Gibbs was surprised by the complete lack of interest in Japan and with the benefit of hindsight commented that 'no one heard the hooves of the Four Horsemen riding down Fifth Avenue'.[21]

Conscious that having spent the better part of two decades as a peace advocate he had laid himself open to charges of hypocrisy, Gibbs took pains to argue that this war was different from the previous conflict:

[17] Interview with Martin Gibbs, 7 April 2009.
[18] Gibbs, *America Speaks*, p. 1.
[19] Gibbs, *America Speaks*, p. 3.
[20] Gibbs, *America Speaks*, p. 8.
[21] Gibbs, *America Speaks*, p. 16.

Now I was coming to talk to the American people about another war, worse than the last, more horrible because of its attacks on civilians, not incompatible, as it seemed to me, without inconsistency, with those ideals of peace because the Spirit of Evil had come out of its old lairs and was menacing with frightful power and ruthless cruelty all the decent code of civilised minds, all the liberties for which men have struggled since the beginning of history, and all the spiritual values of life.[22]

The lecture tour did not begin until mid-October, allowing a few weeks with Tony, Maisie, and their children Martin and Frances. During this period he must have dealt with the difficulties between his brother and his son, though in his book *American Speaks*, he was magnanimous enough to credit Arthur with providing Tony and his family with a 'roof over their heads'.[23] Gibbs was always very good with children, and he was delighted to be reunited with his grandchildren, for whom he 'had yearned'.[24] Martin had adapted to American life with 'hilarious delight', while his sister Frances had 'the restlessness and adventurous spirit of Boadicea'.[25] This sojourn in New England exposed Gibbs to small-town America, a world he had probably missed on his previous three speaking tours. He found the people cheerful, friendly, and neighbourly, and their way of life more truly democratic than in England. Their 'magnificent' free education had led to higher standards in intelligence and social behaviour, while the people themselves were cheerful and friendly.[26] In a drive through New England in autumn, he saw a beauty in nature, more 'wonderful than I had ever seen before in any country...Here we drove through peace and loveliness, exquisite beyond words to describe'. Yet like Wordsworth, whose poetry he admired, such beauty always came with some sadness, for a war, which 'may last through many falls', would bring to the American people 'great agony of soul, enormous tragedy, the death of youth, the tears of women, before victory comes'.[27]

The speaking tour required seemingly endless rail journeys, which crisscrossed the country driven by a timetable that was shaped by speaking dates rather than geography. New York, Boston, Ohio, San Francisco,

[22] Gibbs, *America Speaks*, pp. 10–11.
[23] Gibbs, *America Speaks*, p. 17.
[24] Gibbs, *America Speaks*, p. 17.
[25] Gibbs, *America Speaks*, p. 18.
[26] Gibbs, *America Speaks*, pp. 19–20.
[27] Gibbs, *America Speaks*, p. 23.

Omaha, Kentucky, Indiana, Baltimore, Michigan, Chicago, Los Angeles, Texas, and a host of other cities and states whirled by in a tiring journey for a man now in his mid-sixties. Yet he was heartened not just by the welcome, but by the munitions plants he visited, which left him staggered by 'the bigness of this thing being forged in America'.[28] In Detroit, he visited the Ford Works, and described its owner as the 'master blacksmith of the democracies' who was then 'forging the sword to slay the dragon of cruelty devouring women and children and all life's beauty'.[29]

Gibbs was just leaving Baltimore by train when news of Pearl Harbour broke. He was deeply impressed by the manner in which the American people reacted to the news that their country was at war. After the initial shock, 'there was no boasting, no flag waving, no hysteria...They were ready for self-sacrifice'.[30] Yet he saw the significance of American participation, and could not hide his relief that 'civilisation would not go down in darkness after all. The lamps would be lit again one day. Beauty would come back, and decency, and liberty'.[31] It did not diminish the achievement of the British however:

> Nothing will ever rob the British people of the splendour of their spirit in resisting the enemies of freedom and all civilized ideas at a time when they had very little strength beyond their courage, and looked death in the face without flinching, and stood up against heavy bombardment, by day and night, for eleven months of days and nights, amidst their ruins and amidst their dead, unyielding and undaunted.[32]

His lecture tour wound up with a private audience with President Roosevelt. Though he recognized Roosevelt as a shrewd politician with a ruthless streak, he also saw him as a man of faith:

> But personally I remember—and many Americans remember—that it was his clear vibrant voice, his cheerful resolution, which lifted them up, as though by a call of the spirit, when they were sunk deep in despair...His leadership in the war was magnificent in its courage, decision and confidence. I am

[28] Gibbs, *America Speaks*, p. 96.
[29] Gibbs, *America Speaks*, p. 116.
[30] Gibbs, *The Pageant of the Years*, p. 505.
[31] Gibbs, *The Pageant of the Years*, p. 189.
[32] Gibbs, *The Pageant of the Years*, p. 208.

glad to think that one day I sat by his side, and talked with him, and felt the pressure of his hand.[33]

Having ensured that Tony and his family would have somewhere to live, Gibbs returned to England without accommodation himself, as his home, Dibdene at Shamley Green, had been let while he was in America. For a short time, he lived around the corner in a rented cottage in Sweetwater Lane with his nephew Barry Rowland. Before returning home, the cottage was often crowded with relatives and friends seeking relief from the bombing of London. Gibbs recalled restless nights with the cottage shaking from nearby explosions. Even when spared the bombing, he was exposed to the nightly roar of the RAF as Bomber Command returned serve. Remembering his own war 25 years earlier, his 'heart followed them into the fiery furnace in which many of the boys up there would be burnt like moths'.[34] To further complicate Gibbs' domestic arrangements, Cosmo feared that Philip's landlady was 'straining every sinew to become her ladyship No. 2'.[35] His fears proved groundless, and Gibbs returned to Dibdene as soon as he could.

In his dark moods, exacerbated by failing eyesight and being so close to his home, which 'Agnes had made beautiful and where her spirit dwelt', he had the compensation of children.[36] He was adopted by the children of Shamley Green, and with an innocence perhaps sadly lost in a modern setting, these children swarmed about him like 'frisky lambs'.[37] Each year, he gave a Christmas party, intending to limit it to 20 or 30 of the children, but given his popularity and the constant entreaties of 'may I come to your party Philip?' the guest list for the first party eventually grew to 90. The following year it was closer to 120. Gibbs' love of children and his ability to relate to them shows him in all of his humanity and his enormous capacity for human interaction. He had always feared being alone on the battlefield and had always been reassured by the company of others. The children, and the friends who visited him, would have done much to ward off the loneliness of old age.

[33] Gibbs, *The Pageant of the Years*, p. 507.
[34] Gibbs, *The Pageant of the Years*, p. 508.
[35] C Hamilton. Undated letter to his brother Henry in Argentina. Gibbs Family Archives.
[36] C Hamilton. Undated letter to his brother Henry in Argentina. Gibbs Family Archives.
[37] Gibbs, *The Pageant of the Years*, p. 509.

Though his eyesight had been failing for some time, he kept his growing dread to himself, refraining from telling even his son. One December, Tony found him fumbling down the steps with a tight hold of the banister and his eyes shut, practising for blindness. This was the first indication for Tony that his father's eyesight was failing, though he never mentioned the incident until after his father's death a quarter of a century later. Clearly what belonged to the private domain remained there, even between a father and son who shared a relationship closer to friendship than the Victorian ideal may have allowed. Seven years after his father's death, Anthony saw the incident as part of the 'absurd' reserve of the English, and, interestingly, evidence of his belief that the relationship between father and son was fragile.[38] Gibbs was effectively blind for almost two years because of cataracts, and in fact wrote three novels—*The Amazing Summer*, *The Long Alert*, and *The Interpreter* —on his typewriter, hitting keys from memory. An operation, probably in February 1944, restored his vision, but it had been a 'severe deprivation'.[39] Even in hospital, his room became a rendezvous for the nurses and at night it was often filled with laughter and cigarette smoke.

One of the works of fiction Gibbs produced during this period of blindness, *The Amazing Summer*, was an attempt to do for the pilots of the RAF and the infantry who had escaped Dunkirk what he had done for their fathers 25 years before. Drawing on his experience of the Blitz and the evacuation of children from urban centres, it was an overt attempt at national myth-making. Though Gibbs displayed his usual competence, the finished novel is an uneasy mix of philosophy, action, romance, and history. Each of his protagonists becomes an archetype of their class or nationality and a mouthpiece for Gibbs' own philosophy. Furthermore, for a man who had first reported on war in 1912, and who had subsequently witnessed the martyrdom of the Allied Armies on the Western Front, there is little evidence, at least in 1942, of any evolution in his thinking regarding war:

> Those heroic few in Spitfires...who, with a kind of boyish recklessness and exaltation, flew straight into the heart of German air squadrons...with a

[38] Gibbs, *In My Own Good Time*, p. 133.
[39] Gibbs, *The Pageant of the Years*, p. 510.

kind of gay audacity, shooting them down and chasing the remnants of their force back across the sea.[40]

Gibbs received another blow in October 1942 when his brother Cosmo caught pneumonia and died in a Guildford Nursing Home:

> I miss him a lot. He was my staunchest friend, always loyal and overgenerous in his judgement of my work, never quarrelsome though we disagreed about politics and other subjects of discussion, always a good companion.[41]

Cosmo, who was intensely patriotic, ironically worked for a time censoring letters, first in Liverpool and later in London. His department examined thousands of letters from all over the world, which were subsequently summarized into weekly reports, covering issues as disparate as public opinion, morale, and the attitudes of a still neutral America. Gibbs was shocked by the fact 'that all privacy of correspondence had gone' and that 'one's most secret thoughts, the most personal emotions, might be copied and pasted on a slip of paper for the purpose of a report on wartime psychology'.[42]

D-Day came and went leaving Gibbs envious of the modern war correspondents who were 'involved in a glorious and thrilling adventure', one more 'spectacular and exhilarating than anything that had happened in the last war'.[43] His only direct involvement in war reporting after 1940 was some broadcasting to the Dominions with the BBC, a far cry from the maelstrom of the Western Front. Yet in keeping with an established ambiguity in his attitude to war, being at once repelled by it and attracted to the adventure, Gibbs added that the Allied bombing of Germany was a 'war without chivalry, without mercy, without morality'.[44] As he had in 1919, Gibbs saw the guilt of Germany as a major cause of war, for it was she who had 'declared war upon the Christian tradition and creed' and who had 'invoked all the devils of hell'. In a comment, which highlighted Gibbs' anger at the folly of humanity, the waste of war, and perhaps his frustration with the German people whose part he had taken in countless

---

[40] Philip Gibbs (1942) *The Amazing Summer* (London: Hutchinson & Co), p. 236.
[41] Gibbs, *Crowded Company*, p. 95.
[42] Gibbs, *Crowded Company*, p. 94.
[43] Gibbs, *The Pageant of the Years*, p. 517.
[44] Gibbs, *The Pageant of the Years*, p. 517.

arguments in the 1920s and 1930s, he criticized them collectively in a manner he had generally eschewed during the First World War:

> They had derided pity, justice, and all the noble instincts of humanity. They had practised brutality. They had revered torture and all forces of cruelty. Hitler had deliberately sold his soul to Satan, tempted by power over all the world. Now his Master claimed him.[45]

Though he had not left England since returning from America early in 1942, he was still witness to the destructive powers of modern warfare. Having survived the Blitz, and perhaps feeling that the war was winding down, he was startled by an 'apparition' in the sky over Shamley Green, which to his mind looked like it belonged to a Christmas cracker. The arrival of the V-1s over the UK in June 1944, followed by the V-2s in September, heralded another aerial bombardment to be endured by a war-weary England. Gibbs spent much of this period in London sharing a flat with his son Tony near Cadogan Gardens. Again Gibbs was amazed at the 'sang froid, the courage, and the contempt' with which Londoners treated this new threat. Gibbs, being Gibbs, noted that the young female office workers appeared particularly nonplussed by Hitler's last throw of the dice. With what seemed a reasonable fear of flying glass, he relocated his mattress into the bathroom, while another guest in the form of his nephew placed his in the hallway. When the manageress opened the door in the morning, she viewed this arrangement with what Gibbs characterized as 'contempt for the cowardice of men'. The V-2, which arrived soundlessly, outraged Gibbs more than the noisy V-1 or conventional bombing, raging against it as a 'triumph of science' and 'a glorious success for the inventive genius of the scientists'.[46]

In 1945, the Liberal Party, which Gibbs had supported all his life, called on him to make a more direct contribution to the formation of policy. Though his Party was about to be obliterated in the general election, Sir Percy Harris,[47] its Deputy Leader, convened committees to formulate a Liberal response to two of the great issues of the day—how to deal with Germany in the immediate post-war years and the implications of the San Francisco Conference. Strangely in keeping with the fluid

[45] Gibbs, *The Pageant of the Years*, p. 518.
[46] Gibbs, *The Pageant of the Years*, p. 517.
[47] Sir Percy Alfred Harris, 1st Baronet (1876–1952).

nature of Gibbs' own ideology, the committee members espoused general liberal principles rather than membership of the Party, proof enough of the demise of a legitimate third voice in English politics. The Chairman of both committees was Lord Perth,[48] the first Secretary General of the League of Nations, whom Gibbs considered a man of 'experience, judgement and good nature'.[49] In discussing the question of what to do with Germany, they were joined by, among others, Sir Andrew McFadyean,[50] who 'combined severity and fair mindedness', and Dr Gilbert Murray,[51] 'whose mind is steeped in Greek Philosophy who can see further than most men in the realm of civilized ideals because of the learning which does not grow old'.[52] In Gibbs' view, the report was 'thoughtful, practical, just and liberal minded' and allowed the Germans 'a chance at moral and spiritual regeneration'. Sadly, though Gibbs seemed hardly surprised given his experience on the Royal Commission in 1935, like 'so many other reports by men of knowledge and foresight, it dropped with a heavy thud into many waste paper baskets'.[53]

The second committee, also chaired by Lord Perth, included, among others, Sir William Beveridge,[54] Lady Violet Bonham-Carter,[55] and Dr Gilbert Murray. Gibbs was certainly not an uncritical supporter of the United Nations, fearing that the right of veto held by the Great Powers would emasculate the General Assembly. Again Gibbs felt that the committee produced a good document, but fully aware that it had been ineffectual in helping to shape government policy, sought to defend it on abstract grounds. For the document had both defended core liberal principles as well as being an 'interesting experience in the English spirit of finding a common ground of agreement in spite of intellectual differences and free expression of disagreement'.[56] It is interesting that towards the end of a long life, in the shadow of Hiroshima, with his beloved wife dead, and England reeling from another 'victorious war', Gibbs sought to reaffirm his commitment to the liberal values, which had informed all of his

[48] Sir James Eric Drummond, 16th Earl of Perth, KCMG, CB (1876–1951).
[49] Gibbs, *The Pageant of the Years*, p. 519.
[50] Sir Andrew McFadyean (1887–1974).
[51] Dr Gilbert Murray (1866–1957).
[52] Gibbs, *The Pageant of the Years*, p. 519.
[53] Gibbs, *The Pageant of the Years*, p. 519.
[54] William Henry Beveridge, 1st Baron Beveridge (1879–1963).
[55] Helen Violet Bonham Carter, Baroness Asquith of Yarnbury DBE (1887–1969).
[56] Gibbs, *The Pageant of the Years*, p. 520.

work. Yet the war had destroyed Victorianism.[57] As Wilson so aptly put it, the Victorians were dying and so was their England.[58]

If liberalism was dying, its enemies were not. Having earlier referred to communism as 'the red microbe',[59] Gibbs spent considerable time addressing the threat of this 'new philosophy of life', which challenged all ideas, which 'hitherto have been the code of civilisation among the white races'.[60] As the Welfare State took shape around him, Gibbs sensed a danger in the acceptance of a 'loss of liberty by State made regulations and the tyranny of bureaucracy in return for a low level of security'. Though the Welfare State was a strong liberal tradition in the late nineteenth century, Gibbs' fear of state intervention reflected its earlier 'anarchist distrust of government and the belief that a properly educated society would be almost self-directing'.[61] Gibbs' distrust was possibly also a reaction to the peculiar situation which had Labour's welfare policy appearing more liberal and twentieth-century liberalism more socialist than it was prudent for either party to recognize.[62] The socialist overtones in the increasingly interventionist policies of Britain's Labour government in the immediate post-war years could never have been completely acceptable to a man such as Gibbs, regardless of his human compassion for suffering. The challenges facing the Government in these immediate post-war years were nevertheless without precedent. Britain's foreign debt stood at 4198 million pounds, exports had shrunk to 40 % of the 1939 level, and rationing was in force into the 1950s. To make the shortages in fuel, money, and food even more critical, the winter of 1947 was the worst on record. The achievements of the Attlee government in alleviating the distress, particularly by the creation of the National Health System, viewed in the context of the time, were remarkable.

Gibbs believed that the growing government intervention was in fact a 'worship of the State' which threatened English heritage and tradition. His rejection of the Left had its origin not just in his aversion to radicalism, but the very personal memories of the horror of serfdom as he had

---

[57] J Philips and P Phillips (1978) *Victorians at Home and Away* (London: Croom Helm), p. 191.

[58] AN Wilson (2005) *After the Victorians 1901-1953* (London: Hutchinson), p. 500.

[59] P Gibbs (1939) *Across the Frontiers* (London: The Right Book Club), p. 89.

[60] P Gibbs (1931) *Since Then* (London: William Heinemann), p. 329.

[61] B Harrison (1996) *The Transformation of British Politics 1860-1995* (Oxford: Oxford University Press), pp. 137–8.

[62] Harrison, *The Transformation of British Politics*, p. 76.

seen it in Russia. Communism was to Gibbs the 'greatest illusion of all' offering nothing more than 'the ruthless tyranny of a small number of men' over people who have no 'right of free speech, no liberty of the soul, no freedom of individual judgement, no control over their own way of life'. In contrast to the English tradition of personal liberty, Gibbs saw populations 'forced into one mould, obedient to the State under penalty of death of the concentration camp for the slightest deviation'. Worse still was the existence in England of communists and fellow travellers, a small but dangerous minority, who ignored what was commonly known of the excesses of these regimes.[63] Gibbs pictured them 'explaining their creed, while sitting on divans in Chelsea or sipping cocktails in Bloomsbury'.[64]

With the threat of communism in mind, in the autumn of 1949, Gibbs visited Germany and 'wandered among the ruins', a journey which included a visit to the Russian sector of Berlin. Out of this experience he wrote *Thine Enemy*, which one reviewer believed should be read by all who realize that 'if Western Germany were to go the way of Soviet Russia, then Europe will be lost'. Remembering old accusations, the same reviewer assured readers that 'there is no word of propaganda in the book'.[65] Yet in his treatment of the Russian threat to Western Europe, Gibbs, who had spent the interwar years embracing disarmament and appeasement, now felt compelled to warn a seemingly complacent West of the menace from the East. Though an engaging story, to the modern reader it is an uneasy mix of politics and melodrama, struggling under the weight of Gibbs' increasingly overt proselytizing. Again it is a book of archetypes, each character representing a point of view rather than offering a fully rounded characterization. The central protagonist, a German sergeant, having lost all in the War, finds love and redemption as an artist. He articulates Gibbs' hope that Germany will find its 'own soul and own faith'.[66]

In the same year that he visited Germany, Gibbs published *Crowded Company*, a third autobiography, although it was largely an eclectic selection of reminiscences. Unlike the majority of his non-fiction, it was published not by Heinemann, as had been the case for over 30 years, but by Allan Wingate. Having convinced himself that the publisher, not the

[63] P Gibbs (1953) *The New Elizabethans* (London: Hutchinson and Co), p. 133.
[64] Gibbs, *Since Then*, p. 320.
[65] P Gibbs (1950) *Thine Enemy* (London: Hutchinson and Co), Cover.
[66] Gibbs, *Thine Enemy*, p. 301.

author, makes the real money, Gibbs' son Tony had by this time acquired a major shareholding in the company. Three years later, Tony would also publish *A Journalist's London* (1952) which was a much stronger book, marking a return to historical research. His fourth and final autobiography *Life's Adventure* (1957) was published by Angus and Robertson, as were *How Now England?* (1953) and *The Riddle of a Changing World* (1960). As was the case with his shift to Allan Wingate, this was the result of a family connection. Agnes' nephew, Barry Rowland, was the general manager for Angus and Robertson in the UK. Despite the advantages of these connections, most of Gibbs' output in the dozen years until his death was in the form of lightweight fiction, often with a strong historical and autobiographical flavour. From 1950 until 1963 (his final book was published the year after his death), Hutchinson published 14 novels, although his penultimate book *Oil Lamps and Candlelight* (1962) was really a thinly veiled account of his childhood.

Gibbs' growing concerns about post-war taxation are evident in his novel *The Spoils of Time* in which one of his characters argued that the professional and middle classes were 'the victims of a deliberate and well thought out policy'.[67] This policy sought to 'exterminate' them financially in a class war, which would inevitably 'kill the old spirit of adventure which made England great'.[68] Like most of Gibbs' novels, it was also a forum for his political views, in this case a warning about the military threat posed by the Soviet Union. His main protagonist, a widowed author, was, like Gibbs, a frightened old man, but not for himself, but 'for the youth of the world and civilisation'. Gibbs' advocacy of peace in the 1920s and 1930s had fallen on deaf ears, and now it is possible to see his frantic warning of nuclear annihilation, and the Russians, who, if they attacked, 'would be on the coast in a week'.[69] Mirroring Gibbs' own enduring sense of grief, the widower sought solace in youth, who were his 'soul doctors'. Never once though did he tell the children that their play often brought a renewal of grief 'which shook him terribly because it was here that he had first loved [his wife] and every corner brought back her presence'.[70]

---

[67] P Gibbs (1951) *The Spoils of Time* (London: Hutchinson and Co), p. 254.
[68] Gibbs, *The Spoils of Time*, p. 252.
[69] Gibbs, *The Spoils of Time*, p. 254.
[70] Gibbs, *The Spoils of Time*, p. 255.

Finding him seemingly bereft of ideas for another novel, his grandson Martin suggested one about American airmen returning to England and meeting their wartime girlfriends. In due course, *Called Back* was published in 1953. Gibbs' protagonist is the Second World War American fighter ace recalled to active service during the Korean War. Though married, he had fallen in love with an English girl during the War, but at her insistence he had returned to his wife in America. Her subsequent infidelity and his return to England permitted him the opportunity to resume his unconsummated love affair. He is killed on the very day that the reunited 'lovers' are engaged, thus drawing on the familiar themes of veterans struggling with peacetime readjustment and Gibbs' traditional views regarding the sanctity of marriage. Despite a gentle swipe at McCarthyism, it lacked the overt political message of Gibbs' other works of fiction from this period. In the same year, Hutchinson published *The New Elizabethans* based primarily on interviews Gibbs conducted with young Englishmen and women serving in the armed forces, the fire brigade, and the police force, or attending university, or working in factories. The book is pervaded by Gibbs' peculiar mix of pride in social and political advances in England and the simultaneous and often incompatible nostalgia for the past. He saw in the England of Elizabeth I 'brutality, heroism, tavern brawls, bawdy songs, stabbings, coarse laughter, animal love, squalor and splendour, adventure and daring', but just as clearly recognized it as a period in which 'English genius burst forth in glory'.[71] The majority of the book is really a rather pedestrian mix of interviews with the youth of England, and Gibbs' own hopes that the reign of the new Elizabeth might be 'a renaissance of genius, and talent, and high spirit, and high hopes, in this new Elizabethan England'.[72]

Gibbs was on equally familiar ground in *The Cloud above the Green*. His portrayal of pacifists as communist dupes 'susceptible to Peace propaganda' jars with his own flirtation with peace movements in the 1920s and 1930s.[73] The dialogue, which is again a succession of political testaments, is increasingly unrealistic. His use of suicide and chaste love affairs defeated by the indissoluble ties of marriage are again central themes in his brand of tragic melodrama. The extent to which he searched

[71] Gibbs, *The New Elizabethans*, p. 17.
[72] Gibbs, *The New Elizabethans*, p. 216.
[73] P Gibbs (1952) *The Cloud above the Green* (London: The Book Club), p. 243.

for inspiration in his immediate surroundings is evident in the number of identifiable local characters and settings from Shamley Green in the book. Michael Harding, a long-time resident of Shamley Green, remembered him during this period as being an active member of the community, serving as President of the local branch of the British Legion, initiating local play-reading groups, dramatics, Village Institute Educational Improvement lectures on current affairs, and sponsorship of the village cricket club, which had been founded in 1840. He also remembered his character foibles, very middle class in character and perhaps also a very human reaction to his early days in Fleet Street when the social standing of journalists was low. Harding recalled that though Gibbs was:

> In many ways charming, cultured, accessible, open and democratic, he had a reputation for being frightfully snobbish in respect of using every opportunity to include name dropping of well-known or titled people in his conversations. Nevertheless he was well liked and much respected for his kindness and willingness to involve himself in local affairs. As he walked on the Green he was frequently followed like a Pied Piper by a trail of small children with whom he engaged readily in conversation providing them with sweets as he walked to and from the Post Office or shop.[74]

Gibbs' growing conservatism was reflected in *How Now England?* which on its dust jacket trumpets that the author is not an 'angry old man condemning the younger generation' but rather is 'singularly free from the prejudice and intolerance of old age'. Yet when placed in the context of his earlier writing, it is difficult to see this book as anything but a return to the themes of his youth, as anything other than Gibbs' final public testament of his belief in the Victorian values inculcated during his childhood. Though his criticisms were often tempered with some optimism, they now assumed the grimness of a man who had seen too much death and perhaps had lived too long. His fellow correspondents were all dead—Percival Phillips (1937), Herbert Russell (1944), Perry Robinson (1930), Hamilton Fyfe (1951), Beach Thomas (1957), and Tomlinson the following year. His siblings Cosmo (1942), Henry (1948), Frank (1953), and Helen (1956) were also gone. His hopes for peace in the interwar period had been dashed. It appeared as though the Second World War might be a precursor to even greater annihilation. In 1949, in

---

[74] Personal correspondence with Michael Harding, 31 March 2008.

a letter to his nephew Bill Gibbs, he wrote that he feared a nuclear war would come within three to five years. He admitted to selfishness in the expression of a desire to be dead before it happened.[75]

His criticisms in *How Now England?* are far ranging and often eclectic. He moved swiftly from trade unions, who 'have no concern for the opinions or the interests of the nation as a whole', to the increasing level of violent crime to his dislike of being called a Briton for he 'had an old fashioned pride in being English and living in a country called England whose history has not been without greatness'.[76] His sense of being English had a decidedly racial undertone. In one chapter he dealt with immigration, and though a cultured and gentle man, by titling it 'The Invaded Island', he placed himself in clear opposition to any modern conception of multi-culturalism. There was, in Gibbs' view, nothing wrong with migration as it 'makes London a more cosmopolitan city' unless this 'invasion becomes a tidal wave from the countries of the coloured folk...nothing wrong unless we lose gradually our English character and blood by too much mixture of foreign strains'.[77] He was not alone in this concern. Between 1953 and 1959, 134,000 West Indians, mainly Jamaicans, migrated to Britain and inevitably it became an important issue in fringe politics, attracting the attention of men such as Oswald Mosley. It became a mainstream issue in 1958, the year Gibbs published *How now England?*, when throughout late August and early September Notting Hill in London saw some of the worst racial violence in British history. It shows the extent of Gibbs' retreat into conservatism that he would find himself in agreement with a man such as Mosley on so unlikely an issue. Mosley's claim that Britain must live with the 'Negro' as 'friendly neighbours', but that this was not synonymous with 'an admixture of races'[78] is not far removed from Gibbs' belief that 'theoretically one detests racial intolerance' but that 'sympathy and tolerance should not lead us into opening our gates wide to a coloured immigration certain to create this tragic problem of our own'.[79] In contrast, Gibbs had more time for the Poles, betraying either a Catholic or racial bias, perhaps both, for he believed that intermarriage posed no threat as 'the best of them' had brought with them 'a long tradition of

[75] Gibbs, *Seven Generations*, p. 30.
[76] P Gibbs (1958) *How Now England?* (London: Angus and Robertson), pp. 15; 16; 47.
[77] Gibbs, *How Now England?* p. 37.
[78] R Skidelsky (1975) *Oswald Mosley* (London: Macmillan), p. 508.
[79] Gibbs, *How Now England?* p. 44.

culture. They have civilized minds.' But as for the West Indians, Gibbs notes that in cities such as Birmingham, 'these coloured men walk out with white girls, marry them, live with them and have babies by them'.[80]

His view of Empire was also decidedly old fashioned, for he believed that 'time was, not very long ago, when we were admired, if not beloved, by most other countries and especially by most liberal, forward thinking, and peace loving minds'.[81] He added that the English 'have no cause to be ashamed of ourselves as Empire builders in the past, or now as Colonial administrators. We can look back on our record written in the last hundred years, without much apology for what we have done and what we have left behind us'.[82] Of the atomic stockpile, he revealed a surprising strain of pragmatism first evident in the thirties, when he argued that England could not relinquish the bomb unilaterally and must instead strive for general disarmament. He conceded that this was not a spiritual or moral attitude, but one 'dictated by the desperate necessity of safeguarding national survival and perhaps preventing war by the threat of extinction on both sides if such a war should happen'. Yet he reveals the extent to which he believed this almost in spite of himself by adding that the Bishops of the Church of England, who use moral arguments to support the testing and stockpiling of such weapons, are good patriots, but poor Christians.[83] He also made a distinction between conventional and atomic weapons, finding it impossible to reconcile the message of Christ with their use.

Of the Welfare State, he characterized himself as one of the victims of the higher taxation. The world seemed 'topsy-turvy', for though he acknowledged the social advances, 'to an old fashioned man like myself... brain ought to count more than brawn, and that a poet should be more honoured than the plumber'.[84] He questioned whether it was a well-ordered social system that paid a young agricultural worker living with his parents in a subsidized council house the same wage as a bank clerk who had to pay a 'stiff rent for his bed-sitting room, and has to wear a white collar and clean cuffs?'[85] Five years earlier, he had argued that the ruin of the old nobility and landed gentry had almost been accomplished by this social revolution. Though he celebrated the absence of the old

---

[80] Gibbs, *How Now England?* p. 43.
[81] Gibbs, *How Now England?* p. 18.
[82] Gibbs, *How Now England?* p. 25.
[83] Gibbs, *How Now England?* p. 25.
[84] Gibbs, *How Now England?* p. 14.
[85] Gibbs, *How Now England?* p. 51.

grinding poverty, their passing also meant the death of some of the beauty of England:

> The lovely parks on which the new housing estates are springing up, the old mansions turned into flats or bought for government offices or Borstal institutions. With them passes also something that was fine and precious in our character and quality. Snobbishness apart, these old families produced at their best men and women not without a touch of real nobility, in good manners, courage, ideals and gifts of leadership.[86]

Invariably he is unerringly drawn to the themes of his youth. While in London, he observed a 'lack of gaiety...Watch the faces coming up an escalator in one of the tube stations as one goes down...They looked strained, melancholy, dispirited...One does not expect them to be hilarious in such places or to beam upon their fellow travellers, but one might expect a serenity, a hint of some inner light, a little humour in their eyes'.[87] In what were once the poorer districts in London, Gibbs noted that in spite of improved conditions, there was less joy and merriment. He ends the chapter on the Welfare State with the plaintive assertion that 'I am certain we have not lost the old heroic spirit in times of peril and tribulation', but he had lost his old certitude and optimism.[88]

The degree to which Gibbs' political thinking had become moribund was also increasingly evident in his works of fiction. *The Curtains of Yesterday* is not the masterly recreation of the interwar years trumpeted on the book jacket so much as a return to familiar, well-worn themes. His protagonist is Val Tycehurst, a newly demobbed officer married to a German girl. Finding work in journalism, he devotes himself to peace, a development, which permitted Gibbs one final strike at the English press which had failed to support the League. His hero is informed by his editor that he must subordinate his 'beautiful ideals to the level of public opinion, and especially to the personal ambitions and political interests of [his] proprietors'.[89] In contrast to his devotion to peace, Tycehurst's upper-class brother-in-law believed that the war had changed nothing in English society, and sought the illusion of happiness in the fevered gaiety of jazz. For good measure, his long-suffering wife enjoyed a long-standing

[86] Gibbs, *How Now England?* p. 51.
[87] Gibbs, *How Now England?* p. 57.
[88] Gibbs, *How Now England?* p. 60.
[89] P Gibbs (1958) *The Curtains of Yesterday* (London: Hutchinson), p. 87.

chaste friendship with a conscientious objector she had met while serving with an ambulance unit in Belgium. Inevitably the wayward husband is punished for his transgressions and is killed in an air raid with his mistress in 1940. The conscientious objector remained steadfast, as he had done earlier under fire in Dixmude and later in typhus-ravaged Russia. In an echo of *Blood Relations*, a child born of mixed English/German heritage is drawn to Nazism and rejects the England of his father.

Though Mary Agnes Hamilton believed that Gibbs had a genius for titles, *The Riddle of a Changing World* published in 1960 actually communicated more about the author than the book. To Gibbs, the modern world was a riddle. Twenty years before, his agent had described one of Gibbs' critics during the 1941 speaking tour of the USA as a voice crying in the wilderness. It was now Gibbs' voice which called out from the wilderness, struggling for relevance in a world with which he felt little intellectual or spiritual connection. He believed that religion had been abandoned, that science did not promise to make humans more noble and even the prospect of landing on the moon would 'bring us no nearer to God'.[90] Though he meekly suggested that he saw it as an age of adventure and discovery, he no longer could draw comfort from a belief in the intelligence and morality of humankind. Victorian England was gone, Agnes was gone, Cosmo was gone, and all that was left was a world in which he found few of the comforting touchstones of Empire, monarchy, or even any optimism in the boundless potential of people. Gibbs' lifelong fear that he would one day be bereft of inspiration had come to pass. He valiantly tried to remain relevant to the great questions of the age, yet his discussion of space travel, computers, overpopulation, the Commonwealth, and the state of modern art appears increasingly in the form of summations of newspaper articles and books reflecting both his age and his distance from the great adventure of journalism. For example, his interviews of Lord Pethick-Lawrence, the Secretary of State in India 15 years before, and Viscount Samuel, a fellow member of the Reform Club, who were both 87, reflect this separation from contemporary journalism. Interestingly, for the man who had so often failed to provide dates or chronologies, he offers a wealth of detail in these later articles about dates and places and sources.

Gibbs felt that he had to 'guard against gloomy imaginings in trying to read the riddle of a changing world'. He was 'haunted' by the world's

---

[90] P Gibbs (1960) *The Riddle of a Changing World* (London: Angus and Robertson), p. 15.

problems and believed that humanity was at a crossroad, but in reality, it was really the ghost of Victorian England, and of the thousands of dead on the Somme who haunted him. In the face of such anguish, he retreated to a conservatism steeped in nostalgia as a defence against a world he no longer understood.[91]

---

[91] Gibbs, *The Riddle of a Changing World*, p. 9.

CHAPTER 7

Conclusion

Even though his extraordinary capacity to write waned in his final years, and he was still regularly published, Gibbs had little new to say. Nothing, it seemed, was left to say. It was now his own voice which struggled for relevance, crying out at an incomprehensible, foreign world, seemingly driven only by his passion to write and a fear of the taxman. Gibbs' final years were marred by his fear of insolvency, due partly, his grandson Martin believed, to his generous nature and his preparedness to provide financial aid to his family. In addition, Gibbs would receive his tax bill on his book sales some years after that money had been spent, thus necessitating another book, which in turn led to another tax bill. A heavy smoker all his life, he began to cut his cigarettes in half. It is not difficult to see the genesis of his opposition to the level of post-war taxation.

Though his grandson Martin saw him as a mild Catholic, late in life Gibbs regularly received communion from his parish priest Father Gordon Albion. Albion became a friend and regular visitor, and he was convinced that Gibbs was a genuine Catholic, a quality he believed was borne out in his books. In his eyes, Gibbs was 'not a propagandist or polemical Catholic' but one whose faith was noted for its balance and objectivity. Though possibly the view of a zealous parish priest, it is more likely proof of a late-life interest in his Catholicism, an interpretation borne out in his decision to study Greek so that he could read the New Testament in the Greek Text. When he died, a bone relic purported to belong to St Teresa,

© The Editor(s) (if applicable) and The Author(s) 2016   221
M.C. Kerby, *Sir Philip Gibbs and English Journalism in War and Peace*,
DOI 10.1057/978-1-137-57301-8_7

a gift from his sister-in-law, was found in his pyjama pocket. Amusingly, Albion emphasized Gibbs' love of humanity in two quite distinct ways. He described him as a 'war hater who knew how to love an enemy' and an 'old school liberal who understood beatniks'.[1]

In 1923, Gibbs wrote that he hoped to live until 'the pen drops from [my] hand...and [my] head falls over an unfinished sentence'.[2] Though he proved unable to meet death in this preferred manner, he was actually not all that wide of the mark. His 91st book, *The Law Breakers,* was delivered to his publisher on 9 March 1962, the day before he succumbed to pneumonia at the age of 84. After a brief Catholic ceremony at Sutton Place, Surrey, he was buried at the nearby West Clandon Church where Agnes had been buried 23 years before. His tombstone carries the Latin words *tenax propositi* (Steadfast of Purpose), the Gibbs family motto.

That not one of the five correspondents who were knighted at the end of the war have, as yet, attracted the attention of a biographer is surprising. They seem condemned to be remembered as a group, rather than individuals. Their guilt, too, is a collective one. German war guilt is now openly questioned, as it was even in the 1920s, for scholars are more than prepared to recognize systemic faults in European statecraft. Douglas Haig has even shed something of his reputation as a butcher. Yet no such mitigation is found for the correspondents. They alone seem to have operated in a vacuum and can be held completely responsible for what was, in reality, their description of other men's actions. This work will hopefully contribute to historical scholarship by being part of a re-evaluation of the role of the war correspondent between 1914 and 1918, and then by extension, the role of modern correspondents who even as these words are typed, face difficulties in reporting the wars in Afghanistan and Iraq which would be sadly all too familiar to Philip Gibbs. For those who seek, in a modern context, to separate war correspondents into the liars and the truth tellers are just as likely to fall victim to propaganda and myth-making as the most credible newspaper reader in August 1914.

In the shadow of the general election of 1945, Gibbs, then an elderly man, almost 70 years of age, spoke at a political meeting in the new constituency of East Harrow on behalf of his son Tony, the Liberal candidate. Though he had been knighted a quarter of a century before and

---

[1] Obituary, No details, March 1962, Courtesy Gibbs Family Archives.
[2] P Gibbs (1923) *Adventures in Journalism* (London: Harper and Brothers Publishers), p. 1.

had become famous for his work as a war correspondent on the Western Front during the First World War, he was, as always, a reluctant orator. He sought not to denigrate the Conservatives or Labour, but rather to share his own philosophy, deeply rooted in the liberal values of Victorian England and his unshakeable confidence in the decency of the common man and woman. Summarizing his speech a year later, after Labour had swept to a stunning victory, he wrote:

> I tried to show that Liberalism represented more clearly than any other policy the mind and spirit of the English people, hostile to extremes, believing in the liberty of the individual, warm in its humanity, on the side of the little people and little nations, the age long champions of social reform and freedom from tyranny.[3]

Although he spoke these words in support of his son Tony's stillborn political career, Gibbs might just as well have been writing his own epitaph. In a journalistic and literary career spanning almost 70 years during which he published almost one hundred books and wrote thousands of newspaper articles, he was a powerful advocate for international cooperation and an impassioned defender of liberal principles. Knighted in 1920 for his work as a war correspondent, Gibbs witnessed, and reported on, some of the great tragedies of twentieth-century Europe—the Balkan War of 1912, the First World War, the failure of the League of Nations, the rebirth of German militarism, the Second World War, and the advent of the nuclear age. Though he lived with 'the stench of death in [his] nostrils and a horror of war in [his] mind',[4] he wrote 'if I have learned anything it is that pity is more intelligent than hatred, that mercy is better even than justice, that if one walks around the world with friendly eyes one makes good friends'.[5]

When Gibbs' eyesight had been restored in the mid-1940s, he walked out into the streets of London and in his joy felt that 'I could see with the eyes of youth...I could see once again the enchantment and the beauty of the world about me'.[6] Though he had seen as much of war as any man, and at the end of a long life he may well have despaired at the folly of nations, it is unlikely that Philip Armand Thomas Hamilton Gibbs,

---

[3] P Gibbs (1946) *The Pageant of the Years* (London: Heinemann), p. 522.
[4] Gibbs, *The Pageant of the Years*, p. 27.
[5] Gibbs, *The Pageant of the Years*, pp. 529–30.
[6] Gibbs, *The Pageant of the Years*, p. 513.

Knight, war correspondent, author, and liberal, ever really stopped seeing the world with the eyes of youth.

Dean Stanley in his funeral sermon for Charles Dickens in Westminster Abbey spoke of the compassion the writer evoked, and it is just as fitting a tribute to Philip Gibbs who revered this most quintessential Victorian author:

> He laboured to tell us all, in new, very new, words, the old, old story, that there is, even in the worst, a capacity for goodness, a soul worth redeeming, worth reclaiming, worth regenerating.[7]

[7] Philip Collins (1995) *Dickens: The Critical Heritage* (London: Routledge & Kegan Paul), p. 525.

Bibliography

Newspapers/Magazines

Bridgeport Standard Telegram (1919–1923)
British Journal of Nursing (1937)
Capital Times (1919–1923)
Chillicothe Constitution (1919–1923)
Daily Chronicle (1906–1939)
Daily Sketch (1939–1940)
Evening State Journal and Lincoln Daily News (1919–1923)
Fort Wayne Journal Gazette (1919–1923)
Galveston Daily News (1919–1923)
Guardian (1962)
Harpers' Monthly Magazine (1919–1923)
Indianapolis Star (1919–1923)
International Affairs (1935)
Lethbridge Daily Herald (1919–1923)
Muscatine Journal and News Tribune (1919–1923)
Nation (1923–1924)
New York Times (1909–1962)
Oakland Tribune (1919–1923)
Ogden Standard Examiner (1919–1923)
Oxnard Courier (1919–1923)
Salt Lake Tribune (1919–1923)

© The Editor(s) (if applicable) and The Author(s) 2016   225
M.C. Kerby, *Sir Philip Gibbs and English Journalism in War and Peace*,
DOI 10.1057/978-1-137-57301-8

San Antonio Light (1919–1923)
Syracuse Herald (1919–1923)
The Times (1909–1962)
The Ypres Times (1923)
Wichita Daily Times (1919–1923)

MANUSCRIPTS

Blumenfeld Papers, Parliamentary Archives, London
Memorandum on the reconstruction of Russia in relation to world peace and economic recovery. The Lloyd George Papers, Parliamentary Archives, London
Philip Gibbs Letters, Special Collections Research Center, Syracuse University Libraries
Private Papers of Richard Dixon, Imperial War Museum, 2001 92/36/1

INTERVIEWS/CORRESPONDENCE

Martin Gibbs, 7 & 14 April 2009
Michael Harding Letter, 31 March 2008
Richard Rowland, email 10 June 2010

PUBLISHED WORKS

Ackroyd P (2000) London: the biography. Chatto Windus, London
Anderson D (1994) British rearmament and the merchants of death: the 1935–36 Royal Commission on the Manufacture of and Trade in Armaments. J Contemp Hist 29(1):5–37
Badsey S (2005) The missing Western Front: British politics, strategy and propaganda in 1918. In: Connelly M, Welch D (eds) War and the media. IB Tauris, London, pp 47–64
Bailey P (1978) Leisure and class in Victorian England: rational recreation and the contest for control, 1830–1885. Routledge and Kegan Paul, London
Barham P (2007) Forgotten lunatics of the Great War. Yale University Press, London
Barnett C (1970) A military historian's view of the Great War literature. Trans R Soc Lit 36(1970):1–20
Beach Thomas W (1925) A traveller in news. Chapman and Hall, London
Bell M (1995) In harm's way. Penguin, London
Bentley M (1977) The liberal mind 1914–1929. Cambridge University Press, London
Bickersteth B & J (1996) The Bickersteth Diaries. Leo Cooper, London
Bruno G (1977) Site seeing: architecture and the moving image. Wide Angle 19:8–24

Bruntz G (1938) Allied propaganda and the collapse of the German empire in 1918. Stanford University Press, Stanford, CA

Buitenhuis P (1987) The Great War of words: British, American, and Canadian propaganda and fiction 1914–1933. University of British Columbia Press, Vancouver

Campbell I (1974) Thomas Carlyle. Hamish Hamilton, London

Carlyle T (1993) On heroes, hero worship and the heroine in history. University of California Press, Oxford

Carr E (1964) What is history. Penguin, Middlesex

Charteris J (1931) At GHQ. Cassell, London

City of Temptation (n.d.) http://www.allmovie.com/work/city-of-temptation-87356. Accessed 23 June 2009

Collins P (1995) Dickens: the critical heritage. Routledge and Kegan Paul, London

Craig G (1966) Europe since 1815. Holt, Rinehart and Winston, New York

Crary J (1990) Techniques of the observer: on vision and modernity in the nineteenth century. MIT Press, Cambridge, MA

Crawford F (1981) HM Tomlinson. Twayne, Boston, MA

Crick B (1982) George Orwell: a life. Penguin, Harmondsworth

Dangerfield G (1966) The strange death of Liberal England. MacGibbon and Kee, London

Dray W (1964) Philosophy of history. Prentice Hall, Englewood Cliffs, NJ

Edmonds J (1986) The official history of the Great War; military operations, France and Belgium. December 1915-1st July 1916. Shearer, Woking

Fahmy S, Johnson T (2007) Embedded versus unilateral perspectives on Iraq war. Newspaper Res J 28(3):23–39

Farish M (2001) Modern witnesses: foreign correspondents, geopolitical vision, and the First World War. Trans Inst Br Geogr 26(3):273–87

Farrar M (1998) News from the front: war correspondents on the Western Front. Sutton, Phoenix Mill, Gloucestershire

Feinstein A (2006) Journalists under fire: the psychological hazards of covering war. John Hopkins University Press, Baltimore, MD

Fussell P (2000) The Great War and modern memory. Oxford University Press, Oxford

Fyfe H (1935) My seven selves. George Allen and Unwin, London

Gates B (1988) Victorian suicide: mad crimes and sad histories. Princeton University Press, Princeton, NJ

Gibbs P (1900) Founders of the empire. Cassell, London

Gibbs P (1903) India: our Eastern empire. Cassell, Ludgate Hill

Gibbs P (1910a) Intellectual mansions, SW. Hutchinson, London

Gibbs P (1910b) Knowledge is power: a guide to personal culture. Edward Arnold, London

Gibbs P (1912) The deathless story of the Titanic. Lloyd's of London Press, London

Gibbs P (1913) The new man—a portrait study of the latest type. Sir Isaac Pitman, London

Gibbs P (1915) The soul of the war. William Heinemann, London

Gibbs P (1916) The battles of the Somme. William Heinemann, London

Gibbs P (1917) The Germans on the Somme. Darling, London

Gibbs P (1918) From Bapaume to Passchendale. Heinemann, London

Gibbs P (1919) Open warfare: the way to victory. William Heinemann, London

Gibbs P (1921a) More that must be told. Harper, London

Gibbs P (1921b) The hope of Europe. William Heinemann, London

Gibbs P (1923a) Adventures in journalism. Harper, London

Gibbs P (1923b) The cemeteries of the salient. The Ypres Times, April

Gibbs P (1923c) The middle of the road. Hutchinson, London

Gibbs A (1924a) Gun fodder: the diary of four years of war. Little, Brown, Boston, MA

Gibbs P (1924b) Heirs apparent. Hutchinson, London

Gibbs P (1924c) Ten years after. Hutchinson, London

Gibbs P (1931) Since then. William Heinemann, London

Gibbs P (1934) European journey. Literary Guild, New York

Gibbs P (1935a) Blood relations. Hutchinson, London

Gibbs P (1935b) England speaks. William Heinemann, London

Gibbs P (1936) Realities of war. Hutchinson, London

Gibbs P (1938) Ordeal in England. William Heinemann, London

Gibbs P (1939a) Across the frontiers. Right Book Club, London

Gibbs P (1939b) Broken pledges. Hutchinson, London

Gibbs P (1942a) America speaks. William Heinemann, London

Gibbs P (1942b) The amazing summer. Hutchinson, London

Gibbs P (1946) The pageant of the years. Heinemann, London

Gibbs P (1949) Crowded company. Allan Wingate, London

Gibbs P (1950) Thine enemy. Hutchinson, London

Gibbs P (1951) The spoils of time. Hutchinson, London

Gibbs P (1952a) The cloud above the green. Book Club, London

Gibbs P (1952b) The journalist's London. Allan Wingate, London

Gibbs P (1953) Called back. Hutchinson, London

Gibbs P (1957) Life's adventure. Angus and Robertson, London

Gibbs P (1958a) How now England? Angus and Robertson, London

Gibbs P (1958b) The curtains of yesterday. Hutchinson, London

Gibbs P (1960) The riddle of a changing world. Angus and Robertson, London

Gibbs P (1964) The war dispatches. Anthony Gibbs, Phillips and Times Press, Isle of Man

Gibbs A (1970a) In my own good time. Gambit, Boston, MA

Gibbs P (1970b) The street of adventure. Howard Baker, London

Gibbs A (1974) A passion for cars. David and Charles, Newton Abbot

Gibbs P (1979) Oil lamps & candlelight. Remploy, London

Gibbs M (1996) Anecdotal evidence—an autobiography. Martin Gibbs, London

Gibbs M (2000) Seven generations—our Gibbs ancestors. Martin Gibbs, London

Gibbs M (2001) Philip Gibbs: author and journalist. Book Mag Collector 202:72–84

Gibbs M (2003) Wartime convoy to America. Martin Gibbs, London

Gibbs P, Bernard G (1913) The Balkan war adventures of war with cross and crescent. Small Maynard, Boston, MA

Gibson JA (1922) HM Tomlinson. Bookman 62 (April-September)

Gold J (1972) Charles Dickens: radical moralist. University of Minnesota Press, Minneapolis, MN

Goldberg M (1972) Carlyle and Dickens. University of Georgia Press, Athens, GA

Gregory A (2008) The last Great War: British Society and the First World War. Cambridge University Press, Cambridge

Hamilton C (1924) Unwritten history. Hutchinson, London

Hamilton M (1944) Remembering my good friends. Jonathan Cape, London

Harrison B (1996) The transformation of British politics. Oxford University Press, Oxford

Harrison M, Stuart Clark C (1989) Peace and war. Oxford University Press, New York

Hawes D (2007) Charles Dickens. Continuum, London

Hazlehurst C (1971) Politicians at war: July 1914 to May 1915. Jonathan Cape, London

Hoehn M (ed) (1947) 'Sir Philip Gibbs' Catholic authors 1930–1947. St Mary's Abbey, Newark, NJ

Hohenberg J (1964) Foreign correspondence: the great reporters and their times. Columbia University Press, New York

Howells R (1999) The myth of the Titanic. St Martin's, New York

Hudson M, Stainer J (1998) War and the media. New York University Press, New York

Hynes S (1991a) The Edwardian turn of mind. Pimlico, London

Hynes S (1991b) A war imagined: the First World War and English culture. Atheneum, New York

Irwin W (1936) Propaganda and the news. McGraw-Hill, New York

Knightley P (1989) The first casualty. Pan, London

Koss S (1984) The rise and fall of the political press in Britain, Vol. 2: The twentieth century. Hamish Hamilton, London

Kunitz S, Haycraft H (eds) (1942) Twentieth century authors—a biographical dictionary of modern literature. Wilson, New York

Lasswell HD (1927) Propaganda technique in the World War. Kegan Paul, London

Laurence DH (1985) Bernard Shaw collected letters 1911–1925. Max Reinhardt, London

Lee A (1973) Franklin Thomasson and the Tribune: a case study in the history of the liberal press 1906–1908. Hist J 16(2):341–60

Liddell Hart B (1992) History of the First World War. Papermac, London

Lloyd George D (1934) War memoirs of David Lloyd George, vol IV. Ivor Nicholson and Watson, London

Lytton N (1920) The press and the general staff. W Collins, London

Macdonald L (1983) Somme. Michael Joseph, London

Marquis A (1978) Words as weapons: propaganda in Britain and Germany during the First World War. J Contemp Hist 13(3):467–98

Marwick A (1965) The deluge: British Society and the First World War. Bodley Head, London

Messinger G (1992) British propaganda and the state in the First World War. Manchester University Press, Manchester

Mitchell S (ed) (1988) Victorian Britain. Gailand, London

Mitchell S (1996) Daily life in Victorian England. Greenwood, London

Montague CE (1922) Disenchantment. Chatto and Windus, London

Moorcraft P, Taylor P (2008) Shooting the messenger—the political impact of reporting. Potomac, Washington, DC

Morton P (2009) Australia's England, 1880–1950. In: Pierce P (ed) The Cambridge history of Australian literature. Cambridge University Press, Cambridge, pp 255–81

My Seven Selves (n.d.) http://www.greatwardifferent.com/Great_War/Hamilton_Fyfe/Seven_Selves_01.htm. Accessed 23 June 2009

Nicolson J (2009) The great silence: Britain from the shadow of the First World War to the dawn of the Jazz age. Grove, New York

O'Donovan J (1983) Bernard Shaw. Gill and Macmillan, Dublin

Orwell G (1946) Critical essays. Secker and Warburg, London

Overton G (1924) Cargoes for Crusoes. D. Appleton, New York

Phillips J, Phillips P (1978) Victorians at home and away. Croom Helm, London

Playne C (1931) Society at war 1914–1916. George Allen & Unwin, London

Ponsonby A (1928) Falsehood in wartime. George Allen & Unwin, London

Pound R (2004) Gibbs, Sir Philip Armand Hamilton (1877–1962), Oxford dictionary of national biography. Oxford University Press, Oxford

Powell D (2004) British politics, 1910–1935: the crisis of the party system. Routledge, London

Sanders M, Taylor P (1982) British propaganda during the First World War, 1914–1918. Macmillan, London

Schneer J (2001) London 1901: the imperial metropolis. Yale University Press, London

Scott CP (1970) The political diaries of CP Scott, 1911–1928. Collins, London

Seaman L (1973) Victorian England. Methuen, London

Searle GR (1992) The Liberal Party: triumph and disintegration 1886–1929. Macmillan, London

Shirer W (1964) The rise and fall of the Third Reich. Pan, London

Simkin P (1991) World War 1: the Western Front. Bramley, Surrey

Simon B, Bradley I (eds) (1975) The Victorian public school: studies in the development of an educational institution. Gill and Macmillan, Dublin

Skidelsky R (1975) Oswald Mosley. Macmillan, London

Suttie A (2005) Rewriting the First World War: Lloyd George, Politics and Strategy 1914–1918. Palgrave, London

Swinton E (1932) Eyewitness. Hodder & Stoughton, London

Taylor AJP (1964) The origins of the Second World War. Penguin, Middlesex

Taylor AJP (1965) English history 1914–1945. Clarendon, Oxford

Taylor SJ (1996) The great outsiders: Northcliffe, Rothermere and the Daily Mail. Weidenfeld and Nicolson, London

Terraine J (1970) The Western Front 1914–1918. Arrow, London

The Middle of the Road (n.d.) http://greatwarfiction.wordpress.com/2007/11/06/the-middeoftheroad. Accessed 10 Nov 2008

Thomson D (1966) Europe since Napoleon. Penguin, Harmondsworth

Todman D (2005) The Great War: myth and memory. Continuum, London

Tomlinson H (1925) Adelphi Terrace. In: Massingham HJ (ed) HWM: a selection from the writings of HW Massingham. Harcourt Brace, New York

Tosh J (1984) The pursuit of history. Longman, London

Weintraub S (1971) Journey to heartbreak: the crucible years of Bernard Shaw 1914–1918. Weybright and Talby, New York

Wheeler D (1999) Republican Portugal. University of Wisconsin Press, Madison, WI

Willis I (1972) England's holy war: a study of English liberal idealism during the Great War. Garland, London

Wilson T (1966) The downfall of the Liberal Party 1914–1935. Collins, London

Wilson AN (2005) After the Victorians 1901–1953. Hutchinson, London

Wilson AN (2007) The Victorians. Hutchinson, London

http://www.theguardian.com/world/2008/nov/11/ed-morel-anti-war-movement. Accessed 11 December 2015

INDEX

© The Editor(s) (if applicable) and The Author(s) 2016
M.C. Kerby, *Sir Philip Gibbs and English Journalism in War and Peace,*
DOI 10.1057/978-1-137-57301-8

233

Milton Keynes UK
Ingram Content Group UK Ltd.
UKHW020042191223
434617UK00004B/41

9 781137 573001